Counseling Special Populations in Schools

Counseling Special Populations in Schools

EMILY S. FISHER

AND

KELLY S. KENNEDY

OXFORD
UNIVERSITY PRESS

Oxford University Press is a department of the University of Oxford. It furthers the University's objective of excellence in research, scholarship, and education by publishing worldwide. Oxford is a registered trade mark of Oxford University Press in the UK and certain other countries.

Published in the United States of America by Oxford University Press
198 Madison Avenue, New York, NY 10016, United States of America.

© Oxford University Press 2017

All rights reserved. No part of this publication may be reproduced, stored in a retrieval system, or transmitted, in any form or by any means, without the prior permission in writing of Oxford University Press, or as expressly permitted by law, by license, or under terms agreed with the appropriate reproduction rights organization. Inquiries concerning reproduction outside the scope of the above should be sent to the Rights Department, Oxford University Press, at the address above.

You must not circulate this work in any other form
and you must impose this same condition on any acquirer.

CIP data is on file at the Library of Congress
ISBN 978-0-19-935578-5

9 8 7 6 5 4 3 2 1
Printed by Webcom, Inc., Canada

To Raylan Patrick Kennedy, who was born during the writing of this book. May all children know such love, acceptance, and support.

CONTENTS

1. Introduction to Counseling Special Populations in Schools 1

2. Counseling Students Who Are Homeless 7

3. Counseling Students Living in Foster Care 23

4. Counseling Students Involved With the Juvenile Justice System 38

5. Counseling Students Who Are Lesbian, Gay, Bisexual, Transgender, and Questioning 64

6. Counseling Students Who Are Pregnant or Parenting 87
   with Haylea Drysdale

7. Counseling Students Who Are Gifted 103

8. Counseling Students With Incarcerated Parents 118

9. Counseling Students in Military Families 134

10. Counseling Students to Increase Motivation and School Completion 151
    with Brianna Meshke McLay

References 169
About the Authors 205
Index 207

Counseling Special Populations in Schools

1

Introduction to Counseling Special Populations in Schools

The diversity of students being served in schools in the United States is staggering, and no one book could possibly address all these students and their needs. When we were conceptualizing this book, it was important to address student populations whose life circumstances make them more highly vulnerable to poor mental health and academic outcomes and who may be underrepresented in graduate training programs for school mental health professionals. Although some of these students may qualify for special education or meet diagnostic criteria for mental disorders, they all have unique needs that are most often beyond their control. Many of these students demonstrate incredible resilience in spite of their life circumstances, but some need mental health support to manage the impact of victimization, unstable living situations, and social stigma, among other challenges.

Many of the populations discussed in this book intersect and overlap. For example, students who are in foster care are more likely to be involved in the juvenile justice system (Leone & Weinberg, 2012), to experience teen pregnancy (Dworsky & Courtney, 2010), and to be at risk for school dropout (Trout, Hagaman, Casey, Reid, & Epstein, 2008); and students who are lesbian, gay, bisexual, transgender, and questioning (LGBTQ) are overrepresented among students who are homeless (Rosario, Schrimshaw, & Hunter, 2012) and may be at increased risk for teen pregnancy (Saewyc, 2005). This means that for any individual student, the considerations, needs, and counseling approaches discussed in multiple chapters might apply.

SCHOOL-BASED COUNSELING

Because most children and adolescents in the United States attend school, school-based counseling often reaches young people who otherwise would not receive mental health services (Stephan, Weist, Kataoka, Adelsheim, & Mills, 2007; Weist, Myers, Hastings, Ghuman, & Han, 1999) and allows interventions to take place in a more natural environment (Van Acker & Mayer, 2009). This may be particularly true for many of the student populations addressed in this book (Rolfsnes & Idsoe, 2011). Although academic achievement may be the primary goal of schooling, research has consistently found that "students' mental health has a direct impact on academic outcomes" (Suldo, Gormley, DuPaul, & Anderson-Butcher, 2014, p. 90). In addition, factors that place students at risk in one area of development typically place students at risk in other areas (Suldo et al., 2014). Thus, the student populations in this book are not only at risk across different areas of development but may be more likely to consistently attend counseling that is offered at school.

Various mental health professionals in schools may work with the populations of students discussed in this book, including but not limited to counselors, school psychologists, and school social workers. All these professionals may provide counseling for students; therefore, the general term *counselor* will be used throughout this book.

PROMOTING RESILIENCE

In general, this book takes a depathologizing approach, recognizing the unique circumstances under which students live, the many factors that may be beyond their control, and the strength and resilience that many students demonstrate despite the accumulation of risk factors. Masten (2007) defines resilience as "developing well in the context of high cumulative risk, . . . functioning well under currently adverse conditions, and . . . recovery to normal functioning after catastrophic adversity or severe deprivation" (p. 923). Protective factors, or functional strengths, help mitigate some of the cumulative risk experienced by these highly vulnerable students. Some protective factors that are relevant to the school context include positive relationships with adults; healthy peer relationships; high self-efficacy; and effective skills to solve problems, manage stress, regulate emotions, and persist when tasks are difficult (Masten, Herbers, Cutuli, & Lafavor, 2008). Strength-based approaches to working with students are congruent with promoting resilience (Masten et al., 2008).

EVIDENCE-BASED PRACTICE

In general, there is a dearth of counseling interventions that have well-established empirical support for children and adolescents (Ollendick, King, & Chorpita, 2006). This is especially true for the student populations addressed in this book. Counselors should use evidence-based treatments when they are available, but in the absence of counseling approaches with strong empirical support, counselors can use evidence-based practice to determine the appropriate counseling approach and intervention. Spencer, Detrich, and Slocum (2012) outline three components of evidence-based practice. First, counselors should choose interventions that are relevant and based on the best available evidence. Relevant means that the interventions match the student's problem, the desired outcome, and the school context. The best available evidence means that when there is a lack of rigorous research for a particular problem or need, counselors use the best research they can find. That is to say, "Imperfect evidence, used wisely, is better than no evidence at all" (Spencer et al., 2012, p. 133). Next, counselors must use their professional judgment about the best available evidence, in addition to other relevant factors, to select appropriate counseling interventions for individual students. Professional judgment is continually developing through experience and professional development activities, and counselors should conduct ongoing progress monitoring to ensure that counseling is effective. The final component is choosing counseling interventions that are aligned with students' values and the school context. Ethically, counselors are always required to respect the values of students and families when providing services. Further, schools and communities endorse values that must be taken into consideration when planning counseling interventions. Taken altogether, evidence-based practice requires counselors to find the delicate balance among the best available evidence, their professional judgment, and the values endorsed by students and schools.

COUNSELING APPROACHES

This book is intended for counselors who have learned basic counseling skills. Drawing from child, adolescent, and adult literature, it presents important skills for building effective counseling relationships with students, including being warm and open; displaying empathy; respecting students' perspectives and autonomy; and being genuine, predictable, and flexible (Ackerman & Hilsenroth, 2003; Gurland & Grolnick, 2008; Oetzel & Scherer, 2003). Basic counseling techniques that help build rapport and engage students in counseling include listening actively; reflecting content and feelings; reflecting meaning of verbal or play content; and setting appropriate limits and boundaries (Van Velsor, 2004). By employing good basic counseling skills, counselors will set the stage for students to talk about more difficult issues and be open to various counseling interventions.

If counselors have not learned more advanced counseling skills, such as cognitive-behavioral therapy (CBT) and solution-focused brief therapy (SFBT), it is recommended that they seek professional development in these areas. CBT and SFBT are two evidence-based counseling approaches addressed throughout this book, as they are highly relevant for use in the school setting with different populations of students. Although they are outlined briefly here, full reviews of both are beyond the scope of this book; resources for learning more about CBT and SFBT are available at the end of this chapter.

CBT is considered a "probably efficacious" psychosocial treatment for a number of childhood disorders, including anxiety and depression (Ollendick et al., 2006), and evidence is available to support its use with behavior problems (Hofmann, Asnaani, Vonk, Sawyer, & Fang, 2012). The basic principle of CBT is that feelings and behaviors are determined primarily by one's thoughts, that is to say, they are cognitively mediated (Ronen, 2006). In the CBT model, an event occurs that triggers thoughts, feelings, and physical responses, which in turn interact with each other and lead to a behavior that then has some kind of consequence. For example, a student with social anxiety has to give an oral report in front of the class (triggering event), which leads to the student thinking, "Everyone will laugh at me" (thought), feeling incredibly nervous (feeling), and experiencing shallow breathing, sweaty palms, and a rapid heartbeat (physical response). This leads the student to go to the nurse's office (behavior), thereby avoiding the oral report and reducing the student's anxiety (consequence). CBT aims to change this series of reactions by intervening at various points depending on the nature of the problem. In the same example, CBT might begin by teaching the student relaxation skills to help manage the physical response; teaching the student how to identify his or her unhelpful automatic thoughts and counteract them with more helpful ones; and helping the student tolerate graduated exposure to public speaking both to practice these new skills and to change the behavior and consequence. CBT is an active, collaborative approach that incorporates psychoeducation and problem solving (MacLaren & Freeman, 2006). According to Merrell (2008, p. 107), the four general steps of cognitive therapy are

- developing awareness of emotional variability;
- detecting automatic thoughts and identifying beliefs;
- evaluating automatic thoughts and beliefs; and
- changing negative automatic thoughts and maladaptive beliefs.

SFBT is a strength-based counseling approach that focuses on solutions as a way of reconceptualizing and solving students' problems (Sklare, 2014). Although there is less research on SFBT than on CBT, outcome research suggests that SFBT can be used for a wide range of academic and behavioral problems, including externalizing problems and risk for academic failure, and positive change can typically be seen in four to eight sessions (Kim & Franklin, 2009). Cooley (2009, pp. 22–33) outlines the core assumptions that guide SFBT:

- All students have strengths, even if we have not yet recognized them.
- If something is working, do more of it, and if something is not working, try something different.
- Problems are variable, and we want to find times when the problem occurs less or not at all.
- Complex problems do not necessarily need complex solutions.
- Change is inevitable, and change in one area will impact other areas.
- By drawing on students' strengths and resources, we may find that the solution is not directly related to the problem.
- Students are the experts on their problems, even if they need help in recognizing the power they have to make changes.

By adopting an SFBT framework, counselors will conceptualize students' problems differently and ask questions in a way that helps students identify possible solutions (Cooley, 2009; Sklare, 2014). For example, instead of asking a student who was fighting, "What should you have done differently?" an SFBT-based question would be, "Think about a time that you were frustrated in a game and navigated the situation without fighting. How did you manage to make that happen?" SFBT sessions generally follow a structure that includes these elements, as outlined by Sklare (2014, pp. 79–85):

- identifying a positive student-driven goal;
- asking the miracle question, which asks students to talk through what their day would look like if a miracle occurred overnight and their problem was resolved, and then looking for strengths, resources, and solutions in their miracle day;
- asking questions to find out when the miracle has already occurred a little bit by finding out when the problem was less intense or did not exist;
- having students rate the current level of their problem on a scale of 0 to 10, and asking them what it would take to move up one number on the scale; and
- ending the session with a message that compliments students, makes connections to the goals, and provides a task that students have already identified to help with the goal.

SPECIAL POPULATIONS

The student populations covered in this book are by no means the only students in any given school who are at increased risk for poor educational and mental health outcomes; rather, they represent some of the typically underserved groups of students. As mentioned previously, there is a great deal of overlap among these student populations, so several chapters might apply for a student being seen in counseling. Students who are homeless, living in foster care, and involved in the juvenile justice system present with complex and varied needs. They are often mistrustful of adults and the systems with which they are forced to interact. The very fact that these students are coming to school represents a strength that can be drawn on in counseling, and from there, other strengths and resources can be developed. Students who identify as LGBTQ represent a particularly vulnerable group that must contend with systemic and personalized discrimination and victimization. Although LGBTQ students demonstrate great resilience in the face of this oppression, their experiences can put them at risk for negative educational and mental health outcomes. Students who are pregnant or parenting often take on adult responsibilities before they are developmentally ready and without sufficient support at school and home. These demands, along with social stigma and inflexible school policies, place them at great risk for dropping out of school and living in poverty. Students who are gifted have incredible strengths and resources, but they may also struggle to integrate their gifts with other aspects of their development and face social and academic challenges as a result. Although they are at risk in a different way than other groups considered in this book, gifted students are also at risk for underperforming and failing to reach their potential. Anyone working in schools knows the impact that parents have on student outcomes, and students who have incarcerated parents or parents in the military who are deployed face additional challenges at home and in school. These students may need increased support to successfully navigate stresses at home and to be prepared to learn in the classroom. The final chapter of the book addresses increasing motivation and school completion for students who are at risk for dropping out of school, which is highly relevant for many of the students discussed throughout this book. Because school completion is associated with more positive life outcomes, it is something that should be a priority for all students, and those at greatest risk for school dropout will need the greatest support.

RESOURCES

Cognitive-Behavioral Therapy

Creed, T. A., Reisweber, J., & Beck, A. T. (2011). *Cognitive therapy for adolescents in school settings*. New York, NY: Guilford.

Merrell, K. W. (2008). *Helping students overcome depression and anxiety: A practical guide* (2nd ed.). New York, NY: Guilford.

Solution-Focused Brief Therapy

Cooley, L. (2009). *The power of groups: Solution-focused group counseling in schools*. Thousand Oaks, CA: Sage.

Sklare, G. B. (2014). *Brief counseling that works: A solution-focused therapy approach for school counselors and other mental health professionals*. Thousand Oaks, CA: Sage.

2
Counseling Students Who Are Homeless

OVERVIEW

Student homelessness is a growing problem (Sulkowski & Michael, 2014). Each year, the US Department of Education requires Local Education Agencies (LEAs) to report data on the homeless students they enrolled in school. The most recently published report from the National Center for Homeless Education (NCHE, 2014) indicated that in the 2011–2012 school year, there were more than 1 million students who were homeless enrolled in school, and almost 60,000 homeless students who were living without a parent or guardian. Students who were homeless lived in every state, although the highest percentages of homeless youth lived in California (21.3%), New York (8.3%), and Texas (8.1%). As startling as these statistics are, they actually underestimate the magnitude of this social problem, as at least 6% of LEAs did not report data in the 2011–2012 year, not all students who were homeless had been properly identified, and there were homeless youth who were not enrolled in school and thus not counted in this report (NCHE, 2014).

There is considerable overlap among homeless youth and other populations discussed in this book. There is a high prevalence of homeless youth who identify as lesbian, gay, bisexual, transgender, or questioning (LGBTQ; National Coalition for the Homeless, 2009a); up to 20% of homeless young women become pregnant (Thompson, Bender, Lewis, & Watkins, 2008); homeless youth have often been involved in the foster care system (Park, Metraux, Culhane, & Mandell, 2012); and homeless youth are likely to have involvement in the juvenile justice system (United States Interagency Council on Homelessness, 2010). It is therefore necessary to consider how the characteristics of each of these multiple identities are currently impacting any given student, and counselors may need to choose the intervention that best addresses the student's most pressing needs.

There is no question that there are a host of negative outcomes associated with homelessness, and students without a permanent and stable place to live experience high rates of developmental, learning, and emotional problems (Fantuzzo, LeBoeuf, Chen, Rouse, & Culhane, 2012; Tobin & Murphy, 2013). Schools can have a large role in the lives of homeless students, often providing a source of safety and stability that is lacking in their living situations, as well as opportunities to change their life circumstances (Moore & McArthur, 2011). Further, given the barriers these youth face in accessing counseling and other services in the community, counseling services provided in school settings are particularly helpful (Sulkowski & Michael, 2014).

BASIC CONSIDERATIONS

The situations that lead to homelessness are inherently negative, whether youth experience homelessness with their families, to escape their families, or to escape other undesirable living circumstances. Further, once homeless, young people face risks in virtually all aspects of development. Taken together, the instability that leads to homelessness and the experiences youth have once homeless make these students among some of the most vulnerable in our schools.

Becoming Homeless

At a basic level, students who are homeless fall into two categories: *accompanied* and *unaccompanied*. Accompanied homeless students experience homelessness with a parent or guardian and possibly other family members. There are a myriad of reasons that a family experiences homelessness. Family homelessness is linked to poverty, which in turn is closely connected to lack of living wages in many jobs, decreases in public assistance, and lack of affordable housing, including increasing rates of home foreclosures (National Coalition for the Homeless, 2009b). Mothers with children, who represent a large portion of homeless families (National Child Traumatic Stress Network [NCTSN], 2005), often experience homelessness to escape domestic violence (National Coalition for the Homeless, 2009b). Further, accompanied homeless students include more than 11,000 migratory students who do not have a fixed and stable home (NCHE, 2014).

Unaccompanied homeless students are those who are not in the physical custody of a parent or guardian, including those who have run away from home and those who have been kicked out of the home (Aviles de Bradley, 2011). In one study, up to half of youth in shelters reported that a parent or guardian told them to leave home (Walsh & Donaldson, 2010). The National Coalition for the Homeless (2008) describes three interrelated pathways to homelessness for youth. First, many youth become homeless after experiencing physical abuse, sexual abuse, neglect, or highly dysfunctional family relationships. These youth run away to escape abuse or are forced to leave home, often without a parent caring that they are gone. Second, many youth become unaccompanied after a period of accompanied family homelessness. This may be because shelters have restrictions about the age of children able to stay with their mothers or because youth were at some point removed from their families by social services. The third category of unaccompanied homeless youth includes those who have been involved with foster care or other institutions. There is considerable overlap between youth who are homeless and youth involved in the foster care system, with research suggesting that involvement in foster care correlates with becoming homeless at a younger age and staying homeless for longer. Adolescents who are LGBTQ are also more likely to experience abuse, family discord, and homelessness (Keuroghlian, Shtasel, & Bassuk, 2014). It is important to note that these pathways are not distinct; rather, youth experience various conditions that contribute to their homelessness.

Developmental, Academic, and Mental Health Needs

Homelessness might be thought of as the far extreme on the socioeconomic continuum, with homeless youth experiencing greater cumulative risk than their peers living in poverty but in stable and fixed situations (Rafferty, Shinn, & Weitzman, 2004). It is easy to understand that students who are homeless have basic physical and psychological needs that are regularly going unmet, including the need for shelter, food, safety, and security. They experience all the problems of any youngsters living in poverty, but these problems are exacerbated by homelessness (Biggar, 2001). Homeless youth report high rates of exposure to violence, experience significant loss and separation, move frequently from place to place, and are more likely to have mothers with high levels of mental illness and substance abuse, all of which negatively impact development and mental health (Zima et al., 1999).

Biggar (2001) provides a comprehensive review of the literature on development related to children experiencing homelessness, which starts in utero. Pregnant women who are homeless often are undernourished and have higher rates of drug and alcohol abuse, which increases the risk for infection, premature delivery, low birthweight, intellectual disabilities, hearing and visual impairments, and learning and behavior problems. In infancy, homelessness can significantly disrupt bonding and the development of infants' trust in others to meet their needs. In early childhood, homelessness impacts all aspects of development. Homeless children are more likely to be exposed to environmental hazards such as rodents and lead, to experience delays in language and cognition, and to develop undesirable patterns of interaction due to poor parenting practices from highly stressed and unsupported parents.

These early experiences lead to ongoing challenges for school-age children and adolescents, especially in managing the academic and social demands at school. Homeless youth may demonstrate difficulty concentrating in school due to lack of adequate food and sleep, may have compromised health from poor nutrition and exposure to diseases, and may have difficulty establishing friendships (Biggar, 2001). Research has consistently found that academic achievement is negatively impacted by homelessness and high mobility (Cutuli et al., 2013; Obradović et al., 2009; O'Malley, Voight, Renshaw, & Eklund, 2014; Rafferty et al., 2004), and homeless students are twice as likely as their peers to have been retained (Rafferty et al., 2004). Overall, it has been found that students who are or have been homeless have poorer attitudes toward school (Winborne & Murray, 1992). Research has found that up to one third of accompanied homeless youth meet criteria for a psychiatric or behavior disorder, similar to nonhomeless, low-socioeconomic-status youth, but homeless youth are up to four times more likely than their peers to meet criteria for a disruptive behavior disorder (Yu, North, LaVesser, Osborne, & Spitznagel, 2008). These behavior problems extend to school, often co-occurring with academic deficits (Masten et al., 1997).

Unaccompanied youth report that the primary reason they leave home is because of family problems, which includes physical abuse, sexual abuse, domestic violence, and parental discord (NCTSN, 2005; Walsh & Donaldson, 2010). Once homeless, youth experience high rates of physical and sexual victimization (Stewart, Steiman, Cauce, Cochran, & Whitbeck, 2004) and are more likely to engage in risky behaviors, such as trading sex or dealing drugs, which not only increases the likelihood of disease and pregnancy but also puts youth in the company of people who are more likely to exploit and abuse them (Walsh & Donaldson, 2010). Research has found higher rates of psychiatric disorders, such as mood, anxiety, and substance use disorders, among homeless adolescents (e.g., Kamieniecki, 2001), and victimized homeless youth may experience symptoms of post-traumatic stress disorder (PTSD; Stewart et al., 2004). All these factors combine to put homeless youth at greater risk for suicide (Kidd & Carroll, 2007). It should be noted that a disproportionate number of homeless youth are LGBTQ, and these youth experience even higher rates of sexual victimization and mental health problems (Keuroghlian et al., 2014; National Coalition for the Homeless, 2009a).

Homeless Youth and Schools

THE MCKINNEY-VENTO HOMELESS ASSISTANCE ACT

The McKinney-Vento Homeless Assistance Act, Title X, Part C of the No Child Left Behind Act of 2001 (McKinney-Vento Act), was enacted to ensure that homeless students are provided a free and appropriate public education. The McKinney-Vento Act provides a broad definition of homelessness that schools use to identify homeless students, which includes any students who "lack a fixed, regular, and adequate nighttime residence" (www.serve.org/nche). Other key provisions provided by the McKinney-Vento Act include

- allowing homeless students to enroll in school within 48 hours even without required documentation and guardianship;
- allowing homeless students to remain in one school and providing transportation even if they are currently living in another school or district area;
- requiring each LEA to designate a homeless liaison to implement the McKinney-Vento Act and report data from that LEA, conduct outreach

to homeless youth and agencies serving homeless youth, assist with enrollment and attendance efforts, help homeless youth access school and community services, and reduce additional educational barriers; and
- requiring each state to designate a coordinator to ensure compliance with all the provisions of the McKinney-Vento Act.

Educational Barriers and Opportunities

Bowman and Popp (2013) provide an excellent summary of many of the educational barriers experienced by homeless youth, which recaps some important information from earlier in this chapter. First, homeless students arrive at school with their basic needs unmet. They may not have a place to bathe, clean clothes, regular meals, enough sleep, or a place or the materials needed to do homework. Next, homeless students are highly mobile and may temporarily sleep in different peoples' houses, cars, abandoned buildings, motels, or shelters. This does not allow for schedules and structure, impacting students' routines and relationship development. Mobility also increases absences, relates to attending multiple schools, creates academic gaps, disrupts social relationships, and can affect credits toward graduation. Third, homeless students come to school in poor health or may miss school due to health issues. Fourth, homeless students experience high levels of stress and loss, contributing to behavioral and mental health disorders. Further, they often have a history of physical and sexual abuse and assault and symptoms of PTSD. Finally, homeless students encounter invisibility and stigma at school. Many students who are living in unstable situations are not known by those at school to be homeless, and thus school staff may fail to recognize the support needed by these students. Further, the term *homeless* carries significant stigma, which can cause students to hide their circumstances at school.

Fortunately, the news is not all bleak. For homeless students with uncertain and unstable living situations, schools can help support positive development and achievement. Schools can be a place where homeless students feel safe and experience stability, predictability, and normalcy (Moore & McArthur, 2011). In a recent study, O'Malley et al. (2014) found that positive school climate serves as a protective factor for homeless students, increasing their overall academic achievement. Interestingly, it was noted in this study that school climates do not need to be exceedingly positive to have this impact; rather, homeless students benefit from even average levels of positive perceptions of school climate, which for this study included perceptions of relationships with adults at school, opportunities to participate in a meaningful way at school, school safety, and school connectedness. Further, there are homeless students who meet or exceed academic expectations (Cutuli et al., 2013).

Special Education

Students who are homeless are more likely to have developmental, learning, and emotional disabilities requiring special education services, yet there can be significant barriers to assessing and serving homeless students with disabilities (NCHE, 2007; Zima, Bussing, Forness, & Benjamin, 1997). Some of these barriers include determining who can consent to assessment and services for unaccompanied students; how to complete the special education assessment process for students who are highly mobile; and how to take into account high numbers of school transitions, missing records, and excessive absences when looking at eligibility requirements (Bowman & Popp, 2013; NCHE, 2007). These barriers are especially problematic if school personnel are not knowledgeable about the full breadth of students' rights under the Individuals with Disabilities Education Act (IDEA) and the McKinney-Vento Act, which include provisions to ensure that students with disabilities who are homeless receive a free and appropriate education. Examples of such rights include the provision in IDEA for schools to determine a temporary surrogate parent to make educational decisions for youth whose parents cannot be found and the provision in the McKinney-Vento Act that allows for the homeless liaison or an adult from a homeless shelter to act as a temporary surrogate for a homeless student (National Association for the Education of Homeless Children and Youth [NAEHCY], 2009; NCHE, 2007).

COUNSELING APPROACHES

Given the inherent difficulties in conducting research with homeless youth and families due to the highly transient nature of this population, it does not come as a surprise that there is a lack of research on effective counseling approaches. In their systematic review of the intervention literature for homeless and foster youth, Zlotnick, Tam, and Zerger (2012) found that most studies for homeless youth were focused on case management interventions, used devised rather than evidence-based approaches, and did not employ rigorous research designs. Thus, it is necessary to extrapolate from what research is available on working with homeless youth, to consider counseling approaches that take into account the unique features of this population, and to draw from research on counseling approaches that have shown effectiveness with other low-socioeconomic-status individuals.

Consent and Mandated Reporting

Legal and ethical practice is the foundation for counselors, and in working with homeless students, issues can arise around consent for counseling and mandated reporting. For unaccompanied students, the McKinney-Vento Act strives to remove barriers to educational access to provide students an education, but it does not specifically address how counselors should proceed in terms of obtaining parental consent, when necessary, for counseling. Laws differ among states as to age of consent of minors for specific types of counseling, such as seeking counseling for substance abuse, but generally, legal and ethical guidelines require parental consent for ongoing mental health counseling for minors. Legally, counselors must be knowledgeable of and work within their state guidelines. Ethically, however, consent for counseling is more of a gray area. Ethical guidelines typically call for counselors to balance the rights and needs of students with the rights of parents (American School Counselor Association [ASCA], 2010; National Association of School Psychologists [NASP], 2010). Ultimately, counselors must make decisions about seeing unaccompanied homeless students in counseling without parental consent, perhaps consulting with their LEA's homeless liaison and colleagues as part of the decision-making process.

Mandated reporting, although still consisting of gray areas, leaves less to a counselors' discretion but poses potential conflicts when working with homeless students. Many homeless students have had some involvement with the police or child welfare systems and may fear further involvement in the system if they share details about their lives that would fall into one of the categories for which reporting is mandated (NAEHCY, 2009). This is not to suggest that counselors ignore their legal duty to report; rather, counselors should really consider the immediacy and seriousness of the threat to the student's well-being (NAEHCY, 2009). Further, by working with the homeless liaison and the child welfare worker, counselors may be able to help determine what next steps are in the student's best interest. For example, an unaccompanied homeless minor student shares in counseling that his mother physically abused him before the student ran away from home. The student is currently living with a friend from school during the week so he is close to school and living with his aunt just across the state line on the weekend. Although the counselor is mandated to report the physical abuse that was occurring because the student has two younger sisters who live at home, the counselor works with the homeless liaison and the child welfare worker to assign the student's aunt temporary guardianship while they work with the student to determine additional options to provide more housing stability. In this example, the McKinney-Vento Act would require the school to provide transportation from the aunt's house if that is where the student is residing. It should be noted here that the simple act of being an unaccompanied minor does not automatically fall into one of the mandated reporting categories, as the student may be in the care of an adult or otherwise not in immediate danger (NAEHCY, 2009).

Counselor Characteristics

The presence of a caring adult in the lives of homeless students is viewed as a form of help in itself (Aviles de Bradley, 2011; Kurtz, Lindsey, Jarvis, & Nackerud, 2000), and one that might easily be accomplished by counselors. In one study, formerly homeless adolescents identified ways that adults showed caring, including being available, providing individualized attention, being accepting and listening without judgment, and providing emotional support without telling them what to do or trying to solve their problems for them (Kurtz et al., 2000).

Expanding on these, the flexibility of the counselor providing counseling services is critical in working with homeless students. In looking at service use among homeless youth, drop-in services were the most widely used (Kort-Butler &

Tyler, 2012). This means that counselors may need to allow for greater flexibility in seeing students who are homeless rather than relying on seeing them on a certain day and or at the same time each week. This is not to suggest that practitioners should forgo setting boundaries, as this is also an important aspect of helping homeless students (Kurtz et al., 2000); rather, they can be flexible with students within set parameters. For example, if a student drops by the office, the counselor can schedule a time later that day that works to talk with the student rather than dropping everything at that moment unless, of course, it is an immediate crisis situation. Taken another way, the characteristic of flexibility is also important in that counselors working with homeless students need to be creative in finding ways to meet students' immediate needs (Zlotnick et al., 2012). Although it is always helpful to have a plan when going into a counseling session, the lives of homeless students are particularly unpredictable, and counselors need to remain flexible to be responsive to the needs of students in the moment.

Demonstrating sensitivity and building trust are also crucial for effective counseling relationships with homeless students (Kurtz et al., 2000). Many homeless students have had tenuous relationships with caregivers, and they may have had negative experiences with authority figures like police officers and child welfare workers (Kurtz et al., 2000). This means that counselors may need to demonstrate by their actions that they are consistent, accepting, and worthy of students' trust (Kurtz et al., 2000). One aspect of building trust is for professionals to demonstrate sensitivity to students' circumstances. As part of this, counselors should avoid using the word *homeless* with students, as there may be negative stigma associated with this term and this may not be how students view themselves (Bowman & Popp, 2013). Rather, counselors can use students' own language for describing their housing situation, perhaps focusing on the temporary nature of their current living arrangements and their views on this (Bowman & Popp, 2013).

An important aspect of building trust is to ensure that students fully understand the counselor's legal responsibility as a mandated reporter, as nothing violates trust as quickly as breaking confidentiality and involving police or child welfare workers in students' lives. There are several strategies involved in this. At the onset of counseling, the counselor should clearly discuss what it means to be a mandated reporter and the types of situations that would require a report, and should give examples of reportable and nonreportable situations, as well as possible outcomes of reporting. At this time, a counselor can provide students with strategies they can use to find out if something would require a report without actually revealing personal information. One such strategy is to ask about "a friend." For example, the counselor might say to the student, "If you're uncertain about whether or not I would be required to report something, you can always ask me using a friend as the subject. You can say, 'A friend told me about a situation in which her uncle was watching her while she showered and was making comments about her body. Is that something that you would have to report?'" Another similar strategy is to use hypothetical examples. For example, the counselor might say to the student, "You can always use a hypothetical to find out if it's something I'm required to report, such as 'If a student told you that their mother was using drugs, would that be something you would have to report?'" These strategies allow a counselor to ask follow-up questions about the friend or the hypothetical situation, to educate the student about mandated reporting requirements, and to preserve trust. An important note here is that counselors are constantly making decisions about what they believe is in students' best interest. This assumes, to a certain degree, that maintaining a trusting counseling relationship outweighs suspicions of abuse or neglect. There will certainly be situations in which the need to report a suspicion outweighs the possibility of violating the counseling relationship. These ethical gray areas rely heavily on professional judgment.

Finally, as counselors build trust with students, they can begin to challenge them more and hold them accountable for their actions (Kurtz et al., 2000). Formerly homeless adolescents reported that it was helpful to them when caring adults addressed them in a straightforward manner and took the stance that it was their responsibility to make their own lives better (Kurtz et al., 2000). These adolescents did not want pity from adults but did want adults to be supportive and constant in their lives (Kurtz et al., 2000).

Promoting Resilience

In the absence of evidence-based counseling approaches for working with homeless students, there is a growing body of literature focusing on resilience that offers insights as to how counselors may effectively support homeless students' development. Resilience can be thought of as positive adaptation or development in the face of adversity (Masten, 2011). Researchers have identified a number of individual factors that seem to distinguish resilient homeless youth (i.e., those with more positive outcomes) from their less resilient peers. One factor that has been consistently reported in the research involves homeless youths' sense of personal competence to meet their own needs, which has been termed *self-esteem* (Kidd & Shahar, 2008), *inner strength* (Williams, Lindsey, Kurtz, & Jarvis, 2001), and *self-reliance* (Bender, Thompson, McManus, Lantry, & Flynn, 2007). Along with this, more resilient homeless youth were able to learn how to distinguish between trustworthy people and exploitive people, and they were able to accept help from those who were trustworthy (Bender et al., 2007; Williams et al., 2001). Resilient homeless youth demonstrated resourcefulness and good problem-solving abilities (Aviles de Bradley, 2011; Bender et al., 2007; Williams et al., 2001), and they had a sense of hope about their futures (Bender et al., 2007; Williams et al., 2001).

Where to Begin
It seems that the most consistent element in the lives of homeless youth is inconsistency. With uncertainty abounding, it is critical that counselors "make every [session] count" (Bowman & Popp, 2013, p. 79). Ideally, homeless students would be able to work with a counselor over a long period of time to build the kind of

trust necessary to tackle some of the more challenging issues like substance abuse or trauma. However, when a counselor is faced with the reality of this highly mobile population, he or she might consider, "If I only had a child for [a month, a week, a day], what would I want that student to take from [counseling]?" (Bowman & Popp, 2013, p. 79). Although counselors may feel a lot of pressure to make each moment count, at the start of counseling, it is important for them to meet students exactly where they are so as to recognize their unique circumstances, needs, and strengths (Kidd, Miner, Walker, & Davidson, 2007). This means listening and accepting students without judgment, taking the "shoulds" out of the conversation (i.e., what students *should* or *should not* be doing), and approaching counseling without a specific agenda except to better understand the student's individual strengths and needs (Kidd et al., 2007). In these initial conversations, counselors can begin to recognize strengths that may seem to be hidden behind difficult behaviors, and they might even begin to reframe the language that is used in the counseling session. By recognizing students' assets along with their needs, counselors can begin the process of helping to develop strategies and solutions that capitalize on students' strengths to solve problems they are facing (Reed-Victor & Stronge, 2002).

A Resilience Framework

In an excellent summary of the risk and resilience research, particularly as related to youth experiencing extreme adversity including homelessness, Masten (2011) draws together research and practice to provide a general framework for resilience-promoting interventions that can be applied to counseling homeless students. The guiding principle of this framework is to develop positive goals that focus on what progress will look like rather than on what behaviors or symptoms will be abated. Next, by adopting a broader perspective on change that includes positive outcomes along with abatement of risks, counselors can consider a wider range of intervention strategies that aim to prevent further problems, promote competence, and help students get back on track developmentally. The idea here is that positive outcomes build upon each other, and that as students achieve growth in one area of development, this growth will transfer to other areas. Along with this, interventions to promote resilience may integrate multiple approaches that aim to reduce or eliminate risks and to increase assets and resources to compensate for or moderate risks. Another aspect of this framework is measuring outcomes. This can be more straightforward when considering outcomes that are specifically targeted by goals, but it can be more challenging for outcomes that occur as students' development in the targeted areas positively impacts other, non–specifically targeted areas. Along the way, it should be noted that students' development might need to inform the timing of interventions to boost effectiveness. Counselors will need to consider the different needs of younger homeless students and older homeless students, the experiences that have shaped students' development, and how to maximize the impact of interventions by capitalizing on times when students may be more responsive to change.

Resilience in Action: Strength-Based, Solution-Focused Brief Therapy

In the literature focusing on resilience among homeless youth, there has often been a recommendation for strength-based interventions (e.g., Bender et al., 2007; Thompson, McManus, & Voss, 2006), yet there is a lack of specific strategies for what these might look like in practice. In addition to the resilience framework, other research has described important aspects of strength-based approaches. For example, Garrett et al. (2008) conclude that homeless youth need to be able to imagine a different life in order to find the motivation to make changes, and once they have the motivation, they need support in identifying and developing the skills needed to take the next steps. Similarly, Aviles and Helfrich (2004) state that homeless youth "need assistance in prioritizing their responsibilities to identify small steps to facilitate goal attainment" (p. 337), which can lead to increased self-confidence. From their study, Bender et al. (2007) conclude that "emphasis should be placed on fostering a sense of control, autonomy, and self-efficacy by way of collaboration and allowing the client to establish the direction of the interaction and target for change" (p. 39). Finally, Bowman and Popp (2013) advocate for problem-solving approaches to working with homeless students in schools. Taken together, a solution-focused counseling approach ties together the resilience framework and recommendations from the literature, is highly appropriate for short- or longer-term counseling, and employs more of a collaborative relationship between counselor and student rather than an authoritative one.

A growing body of research on solution-focused brief therapy (SFBT) suggests that it can be an effective approach for students experiencing academic and behavior problems (Kim & Franklin, 2009). This approach may lend itself particularly well to students who are homeless because counselors may be able to have an impact in a few sessions (typically four to eight), which addresses the issue of high mobility. SFBT also focuses on the student as the expert, which allows him or her to maintain autonomy and a feeling of control.

There are several important considerations when using SFBT with students who are homeless. Goal setting and the miracle question are strategies that may require particular attention, especially during early stages of counseling. When working with students to set goals, it is critical to guide the process so that they set realistic goals that are achievable and in which they are the focus, rather than goals focusing on other people or situations that are completely out of students' control. For example, a homeless 10th-grade student may have the goal of graduating from high school. With that goal in mind, the counselor can use a series of questions to help reframe and shape this overarching goal into more immediate and concrete goals that the student can tackle. In this scenario, the counselor might say, "Let's break that goal down into some smaller pieces. Right now in 10th grade, what are some things that need to happen for you to be on track to graduate from high school?" With the student's responses, the counselor can continue to hone the goal into objective ideas that focus on the student with questions like, "If you were on track right now, what are some things I would see you doing? How would you be feeling about school? What would I notice if I saw you in the hallway?" Ideally, these will suggest concrete actions that can help reframe and focus on the larger goal of graduating from high school and will provide a clear, objective, concrete picture of the goal so that these elements can be infused into the miracle question.

When considering the miracle question under these circumstances, it is recommended that counselors adapt the question to be more structured and less open-ended, which again helps keep the focus on things on which the student might be able to have an impact. Using the same example, the miracle question might start as follows: "Imagine you went to sleep tonight and a miracle occurred and you are on track to graduate from high school. You are focused on the things you need to do in 10th grade, such as [insert student's own suggested behaviors, actions, feelings here]." Note that in this example, the student's larger goal is still being used, and the primary focus is on what the student is doing, saying, or feeling during the miracle day. This can continue to be prompted as the counselor walks the student through the miracle day, using the student's own words from the goal-setting process to build the miracle day, thereby providing the student with ideas about specific actions (i.e., solutions), in her own words, to take in order to begin addressing her goal.

As the student and counselor proceed through the rest of the SFBT steps, the counselor may use reframing to help the student recognize strengths and solutions. When looking for instances and exceptions, the counselor can ask questions about this year in 10th grade but also about previous years in school in which the student experienced some success. It is also important to provide encouragement and help the student recognize small successes he or she is already having. For example, in this same scenario, the student might give a 2 on the scaling question asking about how much progress has been made toward meeting a goal. The counselor can respond with a compliment, something like: "Even though things feel really low right now, it's really admirable that you are so invested in graduating from high school. You've already taken a lot of the first steps by identifying that goal and coming to talk with me today. I wonder what it would take to move from a 2 to a 3."

Cognitive-Behavioral Therapy

Among the limited research on effective counseling approaches for homeless youth, there is some support that counseling that incorporates elements of cognitive-behavioral therapy (CBT) may help reduce psychological distress and substance use (Altena, Brilleslijper-Kater, & Wolf, 2010). Further, Sulkowski and Michael (2014) suggest that trauma-focused CBT (TF-CBT) may be appropriate to use in schools for those homeless students who have experienced trauma. One CBT-based program that may be appropriate for homeless students is Structured Psychotherapy for Adolescents Responding to Chronic Stress (SPARCS). This is a group counseling intervention for adolescents who have been exposed to chronic and traumatic life events and those living with ongoing stress, such as interpersonal and community violence (Cohen & Mannarino, 2010; Weiner, Schneider, & Lyons, 2009). SPARCS incorporates mindfulness, coping skills, and interpersonal skills to help students with emotional regulation and impulse control; enhance students' self-perception and relationships; and help students understand their purpose and meaning in life (Cohen & Mannarino, 2010; Weiner et al., 2009). SPARCS has been found to effectively address symptoms of PTSD and related domains of functioning (Cohen & Mannarino, 2010), and research suggests that it is appropriate to use with culturally diverse students, showing the strongest effects for African American adolescents (Weiner et al., 2009). Two additional trauma-focused counseling approaches, TF-CBT and Cognitive Behavior Intervention for Trauma in Schools (CBITS), are reviewed in Chapter 3 of this volume.

Family Involvement in Counseling

It is widely accepted that family involvement in schooling has positive benefits for students, and generally, this holds true for homeless students as well. For unaccompanied students who are open to family involvement and for accompanied students who are experiencing family homelessness, involving families in some aspects of counseling can help strengthen family relationships and capitalize on the support families can provide for students (Reed-Victor & Strong, 2002).

UNACCOMPANIED STUDENTS

For unaccompanied homeless youth, family members have likely contributed to their leaving home, with up to half of homeless youth living in shelters reporting that they were asked to leave home by a parent or guardian (Walsh & Donaldson, 2010). Family reconciliation is not an appropriate goal for all unaccompanied homeless youth (Karabanow & Clement, 2004), but some youth report that they want to reconnect with parents and caregivers (Aviles de Bradley, 2011), and some families want to reconnect with their children (Nebbitt, House, Thompson, & Pollio, 2007). For those youth who want reunification, adults at school may help facilitate productive conversations with family members (Aviles de Bradley, 2011).

In cases where students have been abused at home, counselors will want to proceed cautiously in discussions of reunification (Karabanow & Clement, 2004). This may be a situation in which counselors want to consult with social service personnel who can offer supports and services for youth and families to ensure students will not be in danger during interactions with parents or caregivers. In situations not involving abuse, counselors can help students improve their communication skills and articulate what they would like to see happen with their family to make things better at home.

Successful reunification requires that both students and families want to reconnect and are willing to make changes (Nebbitt et al., 2007), and it is important for counselors to assess each party's willingness to engage in the process (Karabanow & Clement, 2004). With the student's permission, counselors can reach out to parents to communicate that the student is interested in meeting together to talk (Slesnick, Meyers, Meade, & Segelken, 2000). During this initial contact with parents, Slesnick et al. (2000) suggest that counselors listen empathically to parents and offer support and help for parents if they want to participate in counseling. If parents want to participate, counselors might ask a question like, "What would you like to see happen with your child?" (Slesnick et al., 2000, p. 220) to inform and guide counseling.

Thompson and Sanchez (2012) suggest a solution-focused approach to family counseling for homeless youth who have run away. The first step in counseling is to help everyone involved clearly articulate and envision what it would look like if all of the difficulties were resolved. Next, counseling interventions should assist all family members to set concrete and specific goals that will be evaluated in each meeting. Ongoing discussions may focus on areas of need (e.g., managing conflicts or school problems), and during discussions, counselors help "the family construct and identify the part each member [plays] in the sequence of behaviors leading up to an identified problem" (pp. 218–219). Exception questions may be used to help the family identify solutions rather than focus on problems. Throughout sessions, the focus should be on small changes, exceptions to problems, strengths, and resources.

Accompanied Students

For homeless students accompanied by a parent, the research is pretty clear: Effective parenting practices during or following a period of homelessness positively impact students' development and school success (Herbers et al., 2011). That is to say, when parents display "warmth, structure, consistent discipline, and positive expectations" (Herbers et al., 2011, p. 96), children are better able to "pay attention, control impulses, follow directions, think flexibly, and cooperate" (p. 96), all of which are associated with success in the classroom. Two key mechanisms for this appear to be emotional regulation and executive functioning, which, taken together, can be thought of simply as students' ability to appropriately manage thoughts, behaviors, and emotions. Although emotional regulation and executive functioning are complicated constructs that involve interactions between children and their environments, both can be impacted by parenting practices (Bernier, Carlson, & Whipple, 2010; Southam-Gerow & Kendall, 2002).

When providing counseling services in school settings, there may be an opportunity to support parenting practices that help foster students' development and resilience and mitigate some of the risks associated with homelessness. First, counselors must recognize the high levels of stress, uncertainty, and instability experienced by homeless families and show empathy and understanding for the challenges of parenting under these circumstances (Swick & Bailey, 2004). Next, counselors can work to build relationships with parents by recognizing their assets and resources (Swick & Bailey, 2004), perhaps taking a strength-based approach by first asking parents about the positive things they are doing with their children and what they are finding is working for them as parents. To build on this, counselors might then ask about what parents would like to work on to make interactions with their children more enjoyable. The focus here is to find out what small parts are working and to set short-term goals as a foundation for improving parenting practices that will ultimately support students' development.

Research offers several specific ideas of parenting practices that counselors can promote to support the development of emotional regulation and executive functioning. It is important to help parents understand how to scaffold experiences to allow children to experience and master appropriately challenging tasks and feel a sense of autonomy (Bernier et al., 2010; Southam-Gerow & Kendall, 2002). In looking at maternal scaffolding to support children's autonomy, Bernier et al. (2010) identified key elements, which counselors might use as a guide when working with parents. First, parents recognize the child's needs and adapt the task to make it challenging but achievable. Next, parents encourage the child to persist at the task, offering suggestions or hints and being available to help without taking over and doing the task for the child. Through this, parents try to see things from the child's perspective and take flexible approaches to keep the child on task. Finally, parents follow the child's pace, accept the child's choices, and allow the child to complete the task to whatever degree he or she is able. Further, parents can support children's development by narrating what the child is doing or feeling during the task. For example, parents might say something like, "You want to put your shoes on yourself" or "You feel frustrated when you can't get the laces tied." This not only shows that the parent is tuned in to the child's wants and emotions but also can help the child begin to label and talk about emotions (Bernier et al., 2010; Southam-Gerow & Kendall, 2002).

BEYOND THE COUNSELING OFFICE: COLLABORATION

Collaboration is the final component of the resilience framework previously described, as working with a multidisciplinary team across systems allows for the development and implementation of the most innovative and effective interventions (Masten, 2011). As a first step to collaboration, counselors should ensure that they actually know the district's homeless liaison. Once this relationship is established, counselors working with homeless students can collaborate with the homeless liaison to help address students' basic needs, implement school-wide policies and procedures to promote a positive school climate for all students, and build links with community agencies to support homeless students and families (Sulkowski & Michael, 2014). Counselors can also work with the homeless liaison to implement professional development programming for teachers to provide information about homelessness and the McKinney-Vento Act; combat misperceptions; help create safe and supportive classroom environments; recognize and support academic gaps; and promote positive peer relationships (Moore, 2013).

RESOURCES

NATIONAL ASSOCIATION FOR THE EDUCATION OF HOMELESS CHILDREN AND YOUTH

http://www.naehcy.org/

The National Association for the Education of Homeless Children and Youth is an advocacy organization focused on the educational needs of homeless children. It provides training and professional development for those involved in educating homeless children. The website includes several resources encompassing K–12 education, early childhood education, higher education, food and nutrition, and unaccompanied youth. Educational videos and podcasts are also available.

NATIONAL CENTER FOR CHILDREN IN POVERTY

http://www.nccp.org/

The National Center for Children in Poverty is a public policy center that advocates for low-income families at the state and federal levels. The website details projects related to education, mental health, and housing and provides publications on child poverty, healthy development, immigrant families, early care and learning, and mental health.

NATIONAL COALITION FOR THE HOMELESS

http://nationalhomeless.org/

The National Coalition for the Homeless is an organization that provides information on employment, health, youth, families, LGBT individuals, and crime as it pertains to homelessness. Resources include teaching supports such as lesson plans for grades 3 through 5 and online coursework.

3

Counseling Students Living in Foster Care

OVERVIEW

In the United States, approximately 400,000 youth are in foster care (U.S. Department of Health and Human Services [DHHS], 2014). This represents a significant decline over the last decade (DHHS, 2013b). Children of color, specifically Black/African American and Native American children, are overrepresented in the child welfare system, while Latino children are overrepresented in some states and underrepresented in others (McRoy, 2014). The majority of research on overrepresentation of children of color in the child welfare system has focused on Black/African American youth, with findings that indicate that overrepresentation is likely due to a complex interplay of risk factors that contribute to and stem from low socioeconomic status, such as "young maternal age, absent fathers, and poor child health" (Putnam-Hornstein, Needell, King, & Johnson-Motoyama, 2013, p. 42). As of 2012, 42% of youth in foster care were White, 26% were Black or African American, 21% were Hispanic, and 2% were American Indian or Alaskan Native (DHHS, 2013a).

Understanding the impact of being in foster care is complicated. A counselor working with these youth must consider both the series of events that led to placement in the system and the experiences a youth has during his or her time in this system (Zlotnick, Tam, & Soman, 2012). That is, youth enter the foster care system after some kind of significant negative life experience, such as abuse or neglect, and once in the system, many youth continue to have experiences that place them at greater risk for negative outcomes (Harden, 2004). What is clear, however, is that youth involved in the foster care system, "face multiple threats to their healthy development, including poor physical health, attachment disorders, compromised brain functioning, inadequate social skills, and mental health difficulties" resulting from risk factors and conditions such as maltreatment and poverty (Harden, 2004, p. 31).

One theme that emerges for students in foster care is the critical importance of social support. Although it is important for counselors to understand issues facing students in foster care and counseling approaches that may benefit these students, simply being present and consistent in the lives of students in foster care can provide some much-needed support and help students feel more open to seeking and accepting help.

BASIC CONSIDERATIONS

The research on youth in foster care is fairly grim, with a host of well-documented negative outcomes extending into adulthood. There is no way to deny the multiple sources of risk for these young people, but as with any highly vulnerable group of children, there are those who demonstrate extraordinary resilience in the face of adversity. There is a small but growing body of literature on factors that promote resilience among foster youth, which provides hope for and insight into how counselors may be able to help foster youth build the internal capacity to overcome obstacles and reach their potential.

Development and Mental Health

Some youth enter the foster care system due to the inability of a parent to provide adequate care (e.g., parental incarceration, death, abandonment, substance abuse, or mental illness); most youth enter the foster care system after experiencing multiple forms of significant and substantiated maltreatment, including physical and emotional neglect and emotional, physical, and sexual abuse (Bruskas, 2008; Chipungu & Bent-Goodley, 2004; Harden, 2004; Oswald, Heil, & Goldbeck, 2010). Child maltreatment is associated with a host of negative outcomes, and research has found that up to 80% of children entering foster care have significant mental health problems (Kerker & Dore, 2006), up to 60% have health problems (Oswald et al., 2010), and up to 60% have developmental delays (Leslie et al., 2005). Youth in foster care experience both externalizing and internalizing disorders, with up to 40% to 50% of youth meeting diagnostic criteria for disruptive behavior disorders and 30% to 40% meeting criteria for mood disorders (Oswald et al., 2010). Foster youth also experience high rates of post-traumatic stress disorder (PTSD), with those who experienced sexual or physical abuse impacted the most (Oswald et al., 2010). Trauma and PTSD are associated with a host of other psychological sequelae such as depression, anxiety, and behavior disorders (Dorsey, Briggs, & Woods, 2011). Adolescents in foster care have high rates of alcohol and marijuana use (Thompson & Auslander, 2007), and research has found that up to 35% of adolescents in foster care have a substance use disorder (Vaughn, Ollie, McMillen, Scott, & Munson, 2007). Adolescents with PTSD or conduct disorder may be at greatest risk for substance abuse (Vaughn et al., 2007). Foster youth are at much greater risk for suicide than their peers, with 15% of adolescents in foster care reporting suicide attempts (Pilowsky & Wu, 2006).

Raviv, Taussig, Culhane, and Garrido (2010) report that common events experienced by foster youth, such as physical and sexual abuse, school and caregiver transitions, and exposure to community violence, are cumulative in terms of their negative impact on their development and mental health. Thus, each additional type of negative life experience places foster youth at higher risk for significant mental health problems (Raviv et al., 2010).

Mental health services may be available to foster youth through child welfare systems, ranging from outpatient therapy to residential treatment to inpatient psychiatric care. At least half of youth in foster care receive mental health treatment (Leslie, Hurlburt, Landsverk, Barth, & Slymen, 2004), and because the likelihood of having received treatment increases with age, approximately three quarters of adolescents in foster care report having received outpatient therapy at some point in their lives (McMillen et al., 2004). Foster youth who have been sexually abused and those who have been physically abused who also exhibit significant behavior problems are the most likely to have received mental health services (Garland, Landsverk, Hough, & Ellis-MacLeod, 1996). Foster youth who experienced neglect or parental abandonment are less likely to receive services, despite the impact these events have on development (Garland et al., 1996). Research consistently finds that many foster youth who need mental health services do not get them (Petrenko, Culhane, Garrido, & Taussig, 2011; Shin, 2005). This may be particularly true for foster youth of color, with research finding that African American, Latino, and Asian foster youth receive fewer mental health services than their White peers, despite high levels of need (Dettlaff & Cardoso, 2010; dosReis, Zito, Safer, & Soeken, 2001; Kerker & Dore, 2006; Leslie et al., 2000, 2004; McMillen et al., 2004).

Attachment and Relationship Development

Secure attachment is the emotional bond between a child and a caregiver (Harden, 2004); the foundation of trust and the capacity to build relationships throughout life (Thompson & Auslander, 2007); and the way in which children come to see the world as reliable and understand that they are lovable (Gilligan, 2000b). Secure attachment allows children to seek comfort from caregivers and to feel safe exploring different environments (Gilligan, 2000b; Harden, 2004). Children in foster care who experience family instability and maltreatment are more likely to experience insecure or disorganized attachment (Harden, 2004). Along with the unstable, unreliable, and traumatic family experiences leading to placement in foster care, children in foster care may experience continued attachment disruption and trauma by being removed from their families, being maltreated in foster care, and being in multiple foster care placements (Bruskas, 2008; Kerker & Dore, 2006; Thompson & Auslander, 2007). These experiences can also impact foster youths' peer relationship development, with research finding that childhood maltreatment is associated with fewer prosocial skills and more difficulties in peer relationships, and foster youth may experience further difficulties due to school transitions as they change placements (Price & Brew, 1998).

Contemporary perspectives offer a more fluid understanding of how early attachment impacts later development, recognizing that early attachment experiences are extremely important, but also that later experiences can shape developmental trajectories (Dore, 2014). This means that although children in foster care frequently have disrupted attachment with their parents, they can form healthy attachments with other people, such as peers, relatives, foster parents, mentors, or teachers (Gilligan, 2000b). These relationships may take on greater meaning for children in foster care (Gilligan, 2000b), and social support is frequently cited as an important factor to promote resilience, including educational attainment, for current and former foster youth (Collins, Paris, & Ward, 2008; Courtney & Dworsky, 2006; Day, Riebschleger, Dworsky, Damashek, & Fogarty, 2012). For example, research suggests that social support from classmates, such as being liked by classmates and not being teased by peers, has been found to predict engagement in fewer risk behaviors (Taussig, 2002). Further, Gilligan (2000b) explains that parental relationships remain salient for many children in foster care, and children benefit when these relationships with important others can be nurtured in a way that allows children to stay connected with their parents in some manner rather than forcing children to choose between caregivers.

School and Educational Attainment

Students in foster care often have poorer school outcomes and can struggle to meet the academic, social, emotional, and behavioral demands of school. They experience greater absenteeism (National Working Group on Foster Care and Education, 2014) and higher rates of grade retention (Burley & Halpern, 2001; Stone, 2007). Students in foster care experience greater school mobility due to entering foster care and changes in placements (Burley & Halpern, 2001; Stone, 2007); their school records may become lost, and school credits may not always transfer between schools (Bruskas, 2008). Older students are twice as likely to be suspended and three times as likely to be expelled from school (National Working Group on Foster Care and Education, 2014). All of these are risk factors for poor school functioning and dropping out (Stone, 2007; Trout, Hagaman, Casey, Reid, & Epstein, 2008). The National Working Group on Foster Care and Education (2014) reports that only 50% of foster youth complete high school by the age of 18.

Students in foster care are significantly more likely to receive special education services (National Working Group on Foster Care and Education 2014; Stone, 2007), with as many as 44% of foster youth receiving special education services (Geenen & Powers, 2006). Research consistently reports that foster youth are often classified as emotionally disturbed (Stone, 2007), likely due, in part, to the impact that trauma has on foster youths' ability to regulate emotions and to "focus, remember, learn, and engage in self-control" (Harden, 2004, p. 36).

Research has also found that foster youth classified as emotionally disturbed are at much greater risk for school problems than foster youth in general and nonfoster youth classified as emotionally disturbed (Smucker, Kauffman, & Ball, 1996).

Although positive school climate has not been found to serve as a protective factor for students in foster care (O'Malley, Voight, Renshaw, & Eklund, 2014), school stability appears to be an important factor in promoting educational attainment. In a study of former foster youth attending a four-year university, researchers found that more than 80% had completed high school or some amount of college prior to leaving foster care, with just over half having attended only one high school and almost another quarter having attended only two high schools (Merdinger, Hines, Osterling, & Wyatt, 2005).

Foster Care Placement

There are three types of general placements in the foster system, with approximately half of youth placed in nonrelative family care, a quarter in kinship care, and 16% in group homes or residential institutions (Annie E. Casey Foundation, 2011). Although most states have laws that give preference to placing children in kinship care when possible, the number of children served in this manner decreases as children age, such that adolescents are more likely to be placed in group homes or residential facilities (Annie E. Casey Foundation, 2011). These nonkinship placements also typically serve children and adolescents who have more serious health or mental health needs (Harden, 2004). A subset of nonrelative family care is therapeutic or treatment foster care, which requires foster parents to have specialized training to better meet the needs of children who have more intense social, emotional, and behavioral issues and who often have been unsuccessful in other placements (Hussey & Guo, 2005; Thompson & Auslander, 2007).

Foster care placements range from supportive and nurturing to neglectful and abusive, and everything in between. Negative experiences while in foster care, most often taking the form of poor parenting practices, put children at further risk for negative outcomes, and research has found that placement instability, that is changing foster placements, increases childrens' risk for negative outcomes (Harden, 2004). Although it can be difficult to tease apart the contribution that pre-foster and in-foster care experiences have on placement instability and children's outcomes, it has been found that even when children entering foster care did not exhibit behavior problems, having an increased number of placements was predictive of having more internalizing and externalizing problems (Newton, Litrownik, & Landsverk, 2000; Rubin, O'Reilly, Luan, & Localio, 2007). In fact, each additional foster care placement predicts an increase in academic skill delays (Zima et al., 2000) and internalizing and externalizing disorders (Hussey & Guo, 2005). Foster youth in group homes, often placed there because of difficulty in other placements, are at the highest risk for behavior and achievement problems (Gramkowski et al., 2009).

Transition to Adulthood

The difficulties faced by youth in foster care continue as adolescents transition to adulthood and are no longer eligible for services, which is often referred to as *aging out* of the child welfare system. In fact, "the majority of youth who age out of foster care face enormous challenges" (Avery & Freundlich, 2009, p. 248), with research suggesting that these young adults are at even higher risk for emotional and behavioral disorders and substance abuse once they age out because they have access to fewer supports and resources than they did while in foster care (Pecora, White, Jackson, & Wiggins, 2009). Further, young adults leaving foster care are at increased risk for housing instability and homelessness (Dworsky, Napolitano, & Courtney, 2013), which in turn is associated with greater victimization, more emotional and behavioral problems, and more criminal involvement than those with more stable living situations (Fowler, Toro, & Miles, 2009). These young adults also have more health problems, leading to an inability to work and dependence on government financial support services (Zlotnick et al., 2012). These risks are even greater for young adults who experienced placement instability while in foster care, with a history of placement instability being associated with higher rates of teenage pregnancy and repeat pregnancy among young women who have aged out (Dworsky & Courtney, 2010), increases the likelihood of substance abuse (Stott, 2012), and higher rates of homelessness among young adults who have aged out of the system (Dworsky et al., 2013).

Fostering Connections Act

Research on risk and resilience of foster youth is leading to ongoing policy changes aimed at providing greater protections and rights for these young people. The Fostering Connections to Success and Increasing Adoptions Act of 2008 (P.L. 110-351; Fostering Connections Act) was enacted to promote greater well-being among foster youth, to promote greater stability for youth in home and school placements, and to provide funding for states to extend services for youth through 21 years of age if they are engaged in work or school-related activities (Leone & Weinberg, 2012; Schelbe, 2011; Stoltzfus, 2008). Provisions of the Fostering Connections Act related to school are aimed at increasing school stability by taking into account the educational appropriateness of the school when foster placements are made, such as considering the proximity of the new placement in relation to the child's current school, and by providing funding for education-related transportation costs to reasonably allow the child to stay at his or her current school (Leone & Weinberg, 2012). The Foster Connections Act also requires that, if it is not in the child's best interest to stay at the current school, the child must be immediately enrolled in the new school, and all of his or her educational records must be provided to the new school (Leone & Weinberg, 2012). Although the intentions and spirit of the Foster Connections

Act are noble, it is difficult to measure if all states and counties have met its requirements and have been provided adequate funding to support them.

COUNSELING APPROACHES

When starting counseling with students in foster care, counselors may feel unprepared to address the intensive needs of this group. Instead of thinking of school-based counseling as a "fix," with counselors somehow trying to undo the impact of students' experiences, counselors can consider it as one additional area of support for students in foster care. With this mindset, they can approach counseling in a way that helps build students' resourcefulness and coping strategies, providing building blocks to help students become better self-advocates and to be more open to accessing counseling and other support services throughout their lives. With some additional training, counselors may be able to help students in foster care address traumas that are impacting their healthy development and ability to access curriculum and social support at school. Further, counselors can help to coordinate school services with any outside mental health services students are receiving.

Empowerment and Self-Determination

Being placed in foster care impacts almost every aspect of students' lives (Lawrence, Carlson, & Egeland, 2006). Students often have no control over the changes in family, school, community, and peer group, and they must endure great ambiguity once they are in a system with no clear outcomes or endpoints (Lawrence et al., 2006). A first step in helping students feel more empowered is to ensure that they understand why they are in foster care (Gilligan, 2000b). Counselors can use open-ended questions to find out what students know about the situations leading to foster care and make sure that students have accurate information appropriate to their developmental level. A next step in this process is to ensure that students understand their rights and whom they can talk to if they feel they are being treated poorly (Gilligan, 2000b). It might be necessary to provide students with guidance about how to communicate effectively if they believe their rights are being violated, such as using scripts or role plays. Another important step, especially for older students, is to engage students in discussions about planning for the future and the ways that students can impact their own outcomes (Gilligan, 2000b). Foster youth may need guidance and support to learn how to make decisions, especially difficult decisions that have long-reaching consequences (Quest, Fullerton, Geenen, Powers, & the Research Consortium to Increase the Success of Youth in Foster Care, 2012). These are critical skills for foster youth to have to help them be successful when they age out of the system (Geenen & Powers, 2007), and whenever possible, counselors can collaborate with and include students' social workers in these discussions as a way to empower students to understand and communicate their experiences and desires.

Solution-Focused Brief Therapy

In promoting self-determination, it is helpful for counselors to view students in foster care as "resources in the process of seeking solutions in their lives" (Gilligan, 2000b, p. 119) and to recognize that self-efficacy, an important aspect of resilience, can be developed when students believe they can overcome obstacles and master situations (Drapeau, Saint-Jacques, Lépine, Bégin, & Bernard, 2007). Using a strength-based, problem-solving counseling approach, such as solution-focused brief therapy (SFBT), is ideal to help empower foster youth. A good deal of research supports the use of SFBT (Kim & Franklin, 2009), which has been applied to youth in foster care in individual and family therapy. For example, Koob and Love (2010) found that SFBT with foster youth and families increased placement stability; Cepukiene and Pakrosnis (2011) found that foster youth who participated in individual SFBT made significant behavioral improvements. Based on the research on SFBT, Pakrosnis and Cepukiene (2012) concluded that it "can be considered not only an effective but also an appropriate method for treating adolescents . . . and can be recommended as one of the first choices when working with adolescents from foster care" (p. 314). Chapter 2 of this volume provides more in-depth information about using SFBT, including examples of how to structure goal setting and the miracle question.

Social Support

Research has found that foster youth have better psychological adjustment when they experience more positive social support (Legault, Anawati, & Flynn, 2006), but students in foster care often have multiple disruptions in their relationships that impact social support. In counseling, they may need targeted interventions to develop appropriate social and communication skills, with the overarching goal of increasing social support. One important source of social support comes from peers, as these relationships help meet students' needs for acceptance and companionship and can serve as models for developing other relationships (Haskett, Nears, Ward, & McPherson, 2006; Price & Brew, 1998). In fact, Price and Brew (1998) posit that for foster students, "peer relationships are essential for the normal progression of development by providing [them] with a unique socialization context in which to learn and develop cognitive, social, and emotional competencies" (p. 201). Counselors can help students in foster care by assessing the quality of their social skills and peer relationships and providing interventions for areas of deficit. For example, students may need to learn how to enter a new group, how to stay engaged in social activities rather than withdrawing, and how to manage their anger and aggression in a prosocial manner

(Price & Brew, 1998). Further, students in foster care benefit from engaging in recreational activities with peers, which serves multiple purposes, including helping them develop peer relationships and feeling a sense of purpose and mastery (Clausen, Landsverk, Ganger, Chadwick, & Litrownik, 1998; Gilligan, 2000b). Counselors can help students develop skills to successfully navigate the social demands of these activities and skills for social problem solving and conflict resolution.

Relationships with foster families and families of origin are another source of social support. As Gilligan (2000a) states, "Children in [foster] care are not easily parted emotionally from their family of origin" (p. 43). In counseling, it is important to help students process their feelings about being removed from home and being placed in foster care separate from their feelings about their foster family. For example, Kerker and Dore (2006) report that younger foster students may blame themselves for family dysfunction and older foster students may project anger about their situations onto their foster families, both of which can disrupt bonding with foster families. Counselors can help students in foster care recognize that building relationships with their foster families does not make them disloyal to their families of origin. Counselors may want to emphasize that families of origin can *care about* their children even if they cannot *care for* them (Gilligan, 2000b). Research has found that adolescents, including those who have aged out of the system, report having ongoing contact with their biological families, especially their mothers and siblings, and this can serve as an important source of social support (Collins, Spencer, & Ward, 2010; Courtney & Dworsky, 2006). Counselors can work with older students in foster care to help them develop appropriate expectations about interactions with their families, set boundaries in a way that feels comfortable, and cope with changes that have occurred in the family since their removal (Collins et al., 2008).

Cognitive-Behavioral Therapy for Trauma

Cognitive-behavioral therapy (CBT) is widely recognized as an effective approach for addressing a range of psychological issues experienced by children and adolescents, such as depression, anxiety, anger, and PTSD, all of which can impact students in foster care. In recent years, CBT protocols have been developed specifically to address trauma and the associated trauma-related sequelae in children and adolescents (Dorsey et al., 2011), and CBT has been successfully adapted to be relevant and sensitive across cultures (Kar, 2011). In reviewing CBT for PTSD and related disorders, Dorsey and colleagues (2011) found that effective treatments generally include the following common elements: psychoeducation about trauma and its impact on children; affect regulation and relaxation training to help manage the psychological and physiological responses to trauma; gradual exposure and desensitization related to memories of the trauma or other triggering stimuli; and cognitive restructuring to provide more realistic and helpful ways to process the trauma. Research suggests that schools can be an ideal place to use

CBT to address trauma because many barriers to treatment, such as attending counseling sessions, are reduced in the school setting (Rolfsnes & Idsoe, 2011; Wong et al., 2007). Two CBT-based interventions are reviewed here, trauma-focused CBT (TF-CBT) and Cognitive Behavioral Intervention for Trauma in Schools (CBITS), both of which have evidence of effectiveness and are appropriate to use with diverse student populations. A third intervention, Structured Psychotherapy for Adolescents Responding to Chronic Stress (SPARCS), which incorporates CBT and is appropriate for students in foster care who have experienced chronic trauma and life stress is reviewed in Chapter 2 of this volume. With some research and training, counselors can use these programs to help address the needs of students in foster care.

Trauma-Focused Cognitive-Behavioral Therapy

For students who have experienced significant trauma, either as a single event or as a series of events, TF-CBT can help them work through trauma and develop strategies to manage psychological and physiological responses (Mannarino, Cohen, & Deblinger, 2014; Weiner, Schneider, & Lyons, 2009). TF-CBT typically consists of 8 to 16 sessions and can be used with both children and adolescents (Mannarino et al., 2014). TF-CBT involves a significant parent component, and in the case of students in foster care, this purpose can be served by substituting a trusted caregiver, such as a foster parent, in place of a parent (Mannarino et al., 2014; Weiner et al., 2009). If it is not possible to engage a caregiver in the treatment, counselors can still use TF-CBT and provide periodic updates to caregivers via phone or email (Mannarino et al., 2014). There is strong evidence to support the use of TF-CBT with diverse students, including students in foster care, who have experienced different types of trauma (Cary & McMillen, 2012; Dorsey et al., 2014; Mannarino et al., 2014; Weiner et al., 2009). In reviewing the research, Mannarino and colleagues (2014) found that TF-CBT has shown efficacy for addressing trauma-related symptoms for students who have experienced sexual abuse, domestic violence, traumatic loss of a parent, and multiple traumas. For diverse youth in foster care, it was effective in reducing symptoms of traumatic stress and increasing youths' strengths (Weiner et al., 2009). Further, there is a growing body of literature about implementation of TF-CBT in school settings (Fitzgerald & Cohen, 2012).

Mannarino and colleagues (2014), who have widely researched TF-CBT, provide a review of the process of treatment, which occurs primarily in parallel individual counseling sessions with the student and caregiver, with some conjoint sessions. The first phase, *stabilization and skill building*, helps students regulate emotions and behaviors. In this phase, psychoeducation is used to help students and caregivers understand the psychological and physiological responses to trauma, the efficacy of TF-CBT, and, for caregivers, how the trauma is related to students' behavioral issues and how to manage these behaviors more effectively. Skills training, which provides students with foundational regulation and coping strategies, includes relaxation training, such as guided imagery, deep breathing, and progressive muscle relaxation; affective regulation, such as identifying and expressing feelings and developing a picture of a "safe place" to go to calm down if the feelings become too strong; and cognitive coping, which teaches students how thoughts, feelings, and behaviors are connected. These skills are practiced in session and at home as students gradually talk more about the trauma.

The second phase, *trauma narrative and processing*, helps students gain mastery over their trauma-related memories. In this phase, the student and the counselor collaborate to identify what specific trauma or traumas will be the focus of the narrative. Students can develop their trauma narrative in many different forms, such as writing a story or poetry, creating a book, drawing pictures, or using play materials. As students develop their narratives, the counselor encourages them to add more details, including their thoughts and feelings, to help the process of desensitization. As cognitive distortions or maladaptive thoughts arise, counselors can use cognitive processing techniques, such as Socratic questioning or reframing, to help students develop new ways to process the trauma. At this point in treatment, counselors help students put their trauma in context by focusing on what they have learned, how they have grown and gotten stronger, and how they would help others who have had similar experiences.

When students have completed their trauma narratives, they are ready to move into the final phase, *consolidation and closure*, which is typically done through conjoint sessions with caregivers. In this phase, students share their trauma narratives with their caregiver, which empowers students to face their trauma, process it in this new context, and build communication with the caregiver. During this phase, counselors can help students and caregivers plan for the future by engaging them in conversations about how they will manage future reminders of the trauma and practicing safety and assertiveness skills, as appropriate. Throughout the three phases, in vivo exposure techniques can be used to address specific and generalized fears.

There are some important considerations for counselors before they use TF-CBT with students in foster care. First, it is critical to ensure that there is some degree of placement stability so that treatment is not interrupted, which can be particularly damaging if it occurs during the second phase of treatment when desensitization is occurring as students create their narratives (Mannarino et al., 2014). Second, this is not an appropriate treatment to use if students are suicidal, and treatment should be suspended if students become suicidal (Mannarino et al., 2014). In this case, counselors should focus on emotional regulation and other coping skills rather than directly addressing the trauma. Third, TF-CBT should not be the first treatment for students with serious behavior problems or psychotic disorders; rather, these issues need to be addressed first with other evidence-based interventions before considering using TF-CBT to address trauma (Mannarino et al., 2014). Finally, counselors should be thoughtful about ensuring that students feel calm and safe and ready to return to class at the end of sessions (Mannarino et al., 2014).

Cognitive Behavioral Intervention for Trauma in School

CBITS is a group counseling intervention for students in 4th through 12th grade who have symptoms of PTSD, anxiety, and depression related to exposure to violence and other trauma (Jaycox, Kataoka, Stein, Langley, & Wong, 2012; Stein et al., 2003). It was originally developed for schools serving primarily low-socioeconomic-status, urban, middle school students (Stein et al., 2003), but it has been expanded for use with older teens. Research has shown a significant decrease in self-reported PTSD and depression symptoms and parent-reported psychosocial dysfunction for students receiving the CBITS intervention (Stein et al., 2003). Research has also found that CBITS may have a small but positive impact on academic achievement (Kataoka et al., 2011). Because CBITS was originally developed for recent immigrant students, counselors are encouraged to incorporate student examples and adapt activities to make it meaningful for students whenever possible. For example, when cultural adaptations were made to the program to be relevant for rural American Indian students, such as modifying case examples, adding native linguistic concepts, and embedding allegories in the lessons, similar results were found for decreased symptoms of PTSD and depression (Morsette et al., 2009). Although the program contains a parent component, this is not a requirement, and students can benefit without parent participation (Jaycox et al., 2012), which makes this program a good fit for students in foster care.

The full CBITS program includes 10 group counseling sessions, 1 to 3 individual counseling sessions, 2 to 4 parent education sessions, and 1 teacher education session (Jaycox et al., 2012). The 10 group sessions are conducted using a combination of psychoeducation, examples and games, worksheets, and homework, and students are encouraged to apply what they are learning to their individual situations and problems (Stein et al., 2003). Jaycox and colleagues (2012) outline the content of the program, which includes

- psychoeducation for students, parents, and teachers about common reactions to trauma and stress to help everyone understand the connection between past traumatic experiences and current symptoms and behaviors;
- relaxation training for students and parents through guided imagery, progressive muscle relaxation, and breathing;
- helping students understand how thoughts, feelings, and behaviors interact;
- teaching students how to challenge dysfunctional thoughts;
- teaching students how to use a feeling thermometer to monitor their emotional responses and progress;
- working with students individually and in groups to recognize triggers and avoidance behaviors related to the trauma;
- creating a fear hierarchy and making a plan to systematically approach fears;

- using talking, writing, and drawing to gradually expose students to their traumatic memories and help them process the memories using the new skills they are learning; and
- improving students' social problem–solving skills by teaching them new ways to cope with problems occurring in their lives.

BEYOND THE COUNSELING OFFICE: TRANSITION PLANNING

The transition from adolescence to adulthood often looks very different for youth in foster care. For many youth not in foster care, the transition to adult independence happens gradually, often with ongoing financial and emotional support from their families as they pursue higher education or seek employment. In contrast, many foster youth age out of the foster care system, usually at age 18 years, which forces them to "attain independence prior to achieving stability in housing, education, and employment" (Collins, 2014, p. 468). One requirement of the Fostering Connections Act is that caseworkers help youth in foster care develop a personalized transition plan 90 days prior to aging out of the foster care system (Collins, 2014), but this three month plan is clearly insufficient because foster youth who age out of care are highly vulnerable for a host of negative outcomes as described earlier in this chapter. Developing effective transition plans is well within the scope of practice for some counselors working in schools, and as is done with students receiving special education services, it is suggested that transition planning be initiated early for all foster youth, long before they age out of the system (Daining & DePanfilis, 2007).

Integrating the research on transition planning in special education with the research on transition planning in foster care, a clearer picture emerges about what best practices might look like for all students in foster care. At a very basic level, transition planning works most effectively when interagency collaboration is highly valued and families are actively involved (Geenen & Powers, 2007; Morningstar, Kleinhammer-Tramill, & Lattin, 1999). The student should always be at the center of any transition planning meeting (Kohler & Field, 2003), and there is no limit to who else can be included, such as school personnel, caseworkers, foster parents, and other interested and invested adults, which could possibly include biological parents or relatives as appropriate. Self-determination is often cited as a critical component of students' transition to more independent living; if all meetings and discussions are focused in a way that promotes students' self-determination, students will feel more empowered to identify and communicate their goals and dreams; advocate for themselves; actively participate in creating and evaluating the steps through which they will reach their goals; and feel more comfortable asking for help when they need it (Kohler & Field, 2003; Morningstar et al., 1999; Mueller, Bassett, & Brewer, 2012). It is important to note that the skills for self-determination can be taught to students, perhaps through counseling, as described earlier in this chapter. Research has also found several specific practices that lead to better outcomes for students in special education, which seem highly applicable for students in foster care regardless of their educational status, including participation in employment preparation programs, paid and unpaid work experience during high school, and training in social skills and daily living skills (Landmark, Ju, & Zhang, 2010).

In considering the specific needs of students in foster care, a major component of transition planning must include identifying specific supportive individuals and developing social support networks that will help youth prior to and after they age out of foster care (Collins, 2014; Merdinger et al., 2005; Pecora, 2012). This ongoing relationship with caring and supportive adults is consistently cited in the literature as one of the best predictors of a successful transition into adulthood for foster youth (Geenen & Powers, 2007; Pecora, 2012). Many adults could serve in this role, such as mentors, counselors, caseworkers, foster parents, or biological family members. Given that many youth transitioning out of foster care reconnect with parents and other family members, sometimes even living with them as young adults (Collins, 2014; Collins et al., 2010), part of the transition plan may need to include family counseling to help students develop more functional relationships with family members. Educational attainment and postsecondary education are two other key areas to consider in transition planning with students in foster care. This might include identifying needs and resources to support high school graduation, as this increases the likelihood of postsecondary education and employment (Pecora, 2012). Similarly, students in foster care need concrete advisement and guidance about college, financial aid, and college preparation classes (Merdinger et al., 2005).

Related to transition planning, programs that teach independent living skills are commonly available for youth in foster care, although there is little standardization across organizations and states (Collins, 2014; H.R. Rep. No. HEHS-00-13, 1999). These programs often include services to assist youth in completing high school, finding employment, and learning independent living skills such as money management, hygiene, and nutrition (H.R. Rep. No. HEHS-00-13, 1999). Although research suggests that these programs can be beneficial, they have not been found to "alter the course of the transition trajectory in a positive direction that impacts outcomes at a substantial level" (Collins, 2014, p. 473) for foster youth. One finding that stands out related to these programs is that foster youth who participated in independent living programs were more likely to stay in contact with former caseworkers and counselors, increasing social support networks for these young adults (Lemon, Hines, & Merdinger, 2005). These ongoing, stable relationships with adults can help former foster youth better navigate the transition to adulthood and learn strategies to meet the demands of independent living (Collins, 2014), highlighting once again how critical social support is for ongoing success.

Although effective transition plans cannot address all of the ongoing challenges of young adults with this level of heightened vulnerability, they can help ease the transition to adulthood. Similarly, school-based counseling services are not likely to be the only supports that youth in foster care need or are provided with, but they represent an important resource in the lives of these youth.

RESOURCES

Casey Family Programs

www.casey.org

Casey Family Programs is a foundation that aims to improve the lives of children and adolescents in the foster care system. The website includes unique resources such as current research, case studies, data overviews, and policy and practice toolkits.

Cognitive Behavioral Intervention for Trauma in Schools

http://cbitsprogram.org/

This website provides information about the CBITS program and online and in-person trainings.

Foster Care to Success

http://www.fc2success.org/our-programs/information-for-students/

Foster Care to Success is a website aimed at students in foster care who want to attend college. This website provides college funds, scholarships, mentorship programs, and a comprehensive knowledge center with valuable resources for students and for professionals involved in helping students transition out of high school.

National Resource Center for Permanency and Family Connections

http://www.nrcpfc.org/is/education-and-child-welfare.html

The National Resource Center for Permanency and Family Connections is a comprehensive website that provides foster youth, foster parents, and social service–based professionals with various types of resources. Online toolkits are available for training on working with youth, foster siblings, guardianship, family engagement, and placement stability. Handbooks and podcasts are also available that provide valuable insight on the intricacies of foster parents, foster youth, emancipation, and legislation.

Trauma- Focused Cognitive-Behavioral Therapy

http://depts.washington.edu/hcsats/PDF/TF-%20CBT/pages/traumafocused_cbt.html

This website provides information, resources, and printable handouts and worksheets related to TF-CBT.

4

Counseling Students Involved With the Juvenile Justice System

OVERVIEW

Juvenile offenders can be a challenging group to work with for most mental health professionals. They often have complex needs and are served within overburdened systems, in which interprofessional collaboration is critical but often very difficult to achieve. Additionally, many counselors were not trained to work with this population in their graduate programs and therefore must seek additional knowledge and training before commencing any counseling work within juvenile justice settings. In spite of all these challenges, working with juvenile offenders can be highly rewarding.

Young people commit crimes. These offenses vary from serious crimes (e.g., assault, robbery, rape) to status offenses, which are illegal only for minors (e.g., truancy, curfew violations, running away; Granello & Hanna, 2003). The term *adjudicated* refers to youth under age 18 (or other age of adulthood, depending on the state) who have committed a status offense or violated the law and are involved in the juvenile justice system (Scott, Nelson, & Liaupsin, 2002). When discussing juvenile offenders, it is important to note that only a small portion of youth who commit offenses fall into this category; many never get arrested or never formally reach the juvenile justice system (Himelstein, 2011; Scott et al., 2002; Sickmund & Puzzanchera, 2014).

Sickmund and Puzzanchera (2014) edited the most recent national report on juvenile crime published by the National Center for Juvenile Justice. This report contains data regarding juvenile crime and arrest rates, adjudications, and confinements, as well as information about juvenile offenders, including demographics and victimization rates. In 2010, the juvenile justice system processed 1.4 million court cases. Although this is not a perfect estimate for the entire population of juvenile offenders, it provides some context for the number of youth that fall into this category. After an arrest and if an offender is adjudicated, only a small portion of youth, about 20%, are incarcerated. In 2010, about 70,000 juvenile offenders were in residential placements as a result of their involvement with the juvenile justice system. Although this number may appear high to some, the current detention rates are significantly down from those in the late 1990s and early 2000s. The most frequent (37%) of offenses committed by adjudicated juveniles were property offenses (e.g., burglary, vandalism, trespassing); the next highest category was public order offenses (e.g., disorderly conduct, weapons offense, liquor law violations); about a quarter of arrests were for person offenses (e.g., assault, robbery, sex offenses, homicide); and the remaining offenses (12%) were drug law violations.

BASIC CONSIDERATIONS

Demographics

Juvenile offenders are disproportionately males and youth of color (Atkins et al., 1999; Granello & Hanna, 2003; Sander & Fisher, 2014). About 60% of incarcerated juvenile offenders are of color, the majority of whom are African American (Sickmund & Puzzanchera, 2014). Compared with White youth, African American youth are twice as likely to be arrested and seven times more likely to be incarcerated (Underwood, Phillips, von Dresner, & Knight, 2006). Arrest rates for minority youth are particularly disproportionate for violent crimes (Sander & Fisher, 2014). Although the causes for this disproportionality are not known, it is hypothesized that disproportionate levels of risk factors such as poverty and systemic bias may play a role (Jonson-Reid, Williams, & Webster, 2001).

Female juvenile offenders are a minority within this population and have largely been overlooked (Underwood et al., 2006). Females made up 29% of the total juvenile arrests in 2010, and although overall arrests have been on a downward trend over the last decade, arrests of female juvenile offenders increased for most offenses (e.g., assault, vandalism, driving under the influence; Sickmund & Puzzanchera, 2014). Unfortunately, female offenders are also more likely to have been victimized and have higher rates of internalizing disorders than male offenders (Arnold et al., 2003; Kinscherff, 2012; Underwood et al., 2006).

Overview of the Juvenile Justice System

It is important for counselors working with this population to have a basic understanding of the juvenile justice system, which is a "decentralized system of services intended to rehabilitate and reduce juvenile crime" (Sander & Fisher, 2014, p. 227). The broad goal of rehabilitation requires a multifaceted approach because the causes of juvenile offending are so complex. Besides addressing mental health needs, rehabilitation, as defined within the juvenile justice system, may require additional services such as traditional and vocational education, substance abuse treatment, and the involvement of social services (Kinscherff, 2012). Other missions of the juvenile justice system include accountability, deterrence of crime, and punishment, many of which would lead to opposing or contradictory service approaches when contrasted with the goal of rehabilitation (Trupin, Stewart, Beach, & Boesky, 2002).

Youth enter the juvenile justice system via an arrest, which can be for either an illegal offense or a status offense, although not all arrests lead to involvement in the juvenile justice system. More than 30% of juveniles who are arrested are not referred to juvenile court but instead are handled within the police department, with nearly half of those cases ending in an informal probation arrangement (e.g., consent decree or written agreement to participate in conditions such as counseling or substance abuse treatment; maintain school attendance; provide victim restitution; or abide by a curfew; Sickmund & Puzzanchera, 2014). Youth are adjudicated when they have been referred to juvenile court and given a formal or informal sanction as a result of their actions (Scott et al., 2002). Thus, an adjudicated youth, or juvenile offender, is one who not only has violated a law or committed a status offense but also is involved in the juvenile justice system. This is an important distinction, as broader terms such as *delinquent* refer to youth who have committed a crime but who either have not been caught or are not formally involved in the juvenile justice system.

Placements

Once youth are adjudicated, placements range from secure facilities to participation in community-based programs and may include involvement in public or community services, educational or vocational programs, psychotherapy, or family services (Sander & Fisher, 2014). Although the majority of adjudicated youth receive formal or informal probation and related services, about 25% are sent into restrictive residential placements, such as juvenile hall or specialized group homes (Sickmund & Puzzanchera, 2014). These are typically youth who are considered to be serious offenders or those with more complex behavioral or psychological needs (Sander & Fisher, 2014). Youth may also be housed in residential facilities while they are awaiting court appearances or placement changes (Sickmund & Puzzanchera, 2014).

Not surprisingly, research that differentiates between juvenile offenders as a whole and those who are detainees has found that youth in residential facilities have very high behavioral and mental health care needs (Underwood et al., 2006). Unfortunately, it is also clear that many of these facilities are not adequately equipped to meet these needs (Kinscherff, 2012). Additionally, because these facilities focus on discipline and punishment, youth with emotional and behavioral problems may paradoxically be removed from services (e.g., placed in segregation or isolation, not attending school) as a result of behavior infractions (Trupin et al., 2002). Some detention facilities are run by counties; others are state-based and serve serious offenders or those with more comprehensive psychological and behavioral needs (Sander & Fisher, 2014).

Trends in Juvenile Justice

Although the juvenile justice system has a relatively short history, it has gone through several distinct phases. This system began in the early half of the 20th century to ensure that youth were not processed through the adult criminal system because that system's focus was strictly punitive, and it was believed that juvenile offenders would be better serviced in a system that focused on rehabilitation and the prevention of future criminal activity (Granello & Hanna, 2003). The juvenile justice system officially separated from the adult criminal system in the 1970s following passage of the Juvenile Justice and Delinquency Prevention Act of 1974 (Sickmund & Puzzanchera, 2014). In the 1990s, juvenile arrests were on the rise, bringing public and media attention to the juvenile justice system and "epidemic" levels of juvenile crime (Sickmund & Puzzanchera, 2014, p. 83). As a result, 47 states adopted new legislation that broadened transfer laws and expanded sentencing options, making it possible for increasing numbers of juvenile offenders to be prosecuted through adult criminal court systems (Granello & Hanna, 2003; Koocher & Kinscherff, 2016; Sickmund & Puzzanchera, 2014). Since 2010, this trend toward increased focus on punitive approaches has reversed, with arrests, incarceration, and transfers to adult court systems significantly down from the late 1990s (Sickmund & Puzzanchera, 2014).

Recidivism

Progress toward the juvenile justice system's goal of rehabilitation is often measured via recidivism rates. Unfortunately, these are extremely problematic to capture for a variety of reasons. First, decisions must be made regarding the length of post-arrest time included in these statistics, because some methods follow youth only until age 18 and others following them for a certain number of years, regardless of age (Sickmund & Puzzanchera, 2014). Additionally, decisions are made regarding which types of violations count toward recidivism rates (Sickmund & Puzzanchera, 2014). For example, status offenses are often not counted, given that these violations are much more likely to come to the attention of the system once a youth is already involved (e.g., has an assigned probation officer). Although no national recidivism rates are available for juvenile offenders (Sickmund & Puzzanchera, 2014), some researchers report rates for their samples or the facilities in which they collected data. For example, Stein and colleagues (2011) reported a recidivism rate of about 35%. Regardless of the exact rate, it is well established that a high proportion of adult offenders were juvenile offenders, highlighting the pressing need to support rehabilitation in the juvenile justice system to reduce adult crime rates (Himelstein, 2011).

Educational Settings

Like all students, juvenile offenders have a right to an education. How they receive this education can vary tremendously, with some youth who are on probation continuing to attend their home comprehensive middle or high schools, and others attending schools within detention centers. It is helpful for counselors to be familiar with the array of educational placements for this population, as well as the advantages and challenges associated with each.

Because juvenile detainees are legally required to receive an education, many state- and county-run detention centers house their own schools. These schools receive public funding and are subject to all the applicable laws and regulations of any other public school (Sander & Fisher, 2014). Unfortunately, these schools are notorious for having insufficient funds, inadequate facilities, and a focus on behavioral compliance rather than learning (Gagnon & Barber, 2010). Some may provide no instruction related to job, life, or independent living skills (Clark & Unruh, 2010). Like all schools, these schools may have teachers with varying levels of ability and enthusiasm, with some teachers having a genuine passion for working with juvenile offenders (see Wilder, 2004), and others working there as a result of poor performance or limited options (Sander & Fisher, 2014). In addition, these schools are challenged with educating youth of all ages and educational attainment levels, including large percentages of students with both identified and unidentified special education needs, who may enter or exit at any point during the school year, and who attend their schools for variable lengths of time (Sander & Fisher, 2014). It is incomprehensible that these schools do not receive more funding, more resources, and more qualified teachers than traditional schools, given the magnitude of the challenges they face.

Youth who are not detained in residential facilities or who are detained at facilities that do not have schools (e.g., private facilities, group homes) may attend their original comprehensive schools or alternative schools. The term *alternative education* can refer to a variety of programs, including "special schools, evening programs, independent study programs, community-based instructional programs, school-based programs for chronically disruptive students, alternative learning centers, multi-agency instructional arrangements, functional vocational programs with integrated instruction, project-based instruction, and day treatment programs" (Scott et al., 2002, p. 544). What this vast spectrum of schools shares is the provision of educational services in a manner that provides an alternative to traditional schools (Granello & Hanna, 2003). Many of these programs focus on individualized instruction and goal-oriented work (e.g., packets designed to cover discrete learning outcomes, typically directly linked to earning credits toward a diploma; Scott et al., 2002). Unfortunately, the majority of these programs do not offer the extracurricular opportunities, such as clubs and sports, that most comprehensive schools have. This is unfortunate because these additional programs often serve as important protective factors that increase school engagement, provide meaningful participation, connect youth with prosocial peers, provide supervision outside of school hours, and connect youth with caring adults (Masten et al., 1997).

Delinquency

Juvenile offending is complex, both to understand and to treat. A developmental perspective allows counselors to view delinquent behavior in the contexts of young people's histories to see that there may be many different routes that bring youth to the same outcome. Many different developmental trajectories may be at work in bringing children and adolescents into the juvenile justice system for the same offenses (Kinscherff, 2012). Research on juvenile delinquency has highlighted a few trends that are helpful for better understanding the developmental trajectories of this population. First, delinquency in juveniles follows a relatively predictable course, with the most offenses occurring around age 17, then dropping off sharply as early adulthood approaches (Borum, 2006). Additionally, there are several subtypes of youth who commit crimes, with the majority being adolescent-limited offenders, sometimes referred to as *desisters*, and a smaller proportion (around 10%) being chronic offenders, or *persisters*, who may continue committing crimes into adulthood (Borum, 2006; Sickmund & Puzzanchera, 2014). Interestingly, original crimes are not accurate predictors of which juvenile offenders will desist or persist, and neither are placements, services, or sentences (Sickmund & Puzzanchera, 2014). One characteristic that is noted in those who are most at risk for continued involvement in criminal activity is that they tend to have the most severe mental health problems, including clinical and personality disorders (Borum, 2006).

Juvenile offenders are heterogeneous in terms of life histories, symptomologies, learning abilities, mental health needs, and family dynamics, yet they are often labeled and viewed in light of the only things they have in common, which are their offenses and their involvement in the juvenile justice system (Kinscherff, 2012; Underwood et al., 2006). For this reason, identifying youth by offense or status as an offender is not remotely useful for treatment purposes (Kinscherff, 2012; Scott et al., 2002). Instead, counselors should focus on underlying risk conditions and the presence of mental health, learning, and other needs that are related to young people's engagement in whatever activities brought them into the justice system.

As a whole, juvenile offenders are disproportionately likely to be impacted by negative life events and other risk factors that put them at greater risk for internalizing and externalizing behavior problems (Jonson-Reid et al., 2001; Kinscherff, 2012). These risks may be viewed from an ecological framework as psychosocial (e.g., school problems, abuse, neglect, exposure to violence, traumatic events); individual (e.g., negative attitudes and attributions, substance abuse, impulsivity); familial (e.g., familial involvement in criminal justice system, familial mental health or substance abuse problems); and social/contextual (e.g., lack of personal/social support, lack of supervision, delinquent peer group, gang involvement; Borum, 2006; Granello & Hanna, 2003; Sander & Fisher, 2014; Sickmund & Puzzanchera, 2014; Underwood et al., 2006; Wood, Wood, & Mullins, 2008). Although it may be viewed both as a risk factor for engagement in delinquent activity and as an outcome based on the risks discussed earlier, the most commonly discussed area of need for juvenile offenders is mental health (Atkins et al., 1999; Granello & Hanna, 2003; Kinscherff, 2012; Trupin et al., 2002; Underwood et al., 2006).

Externalizing Disorders

Externalizing disorders are what most people, especially those outside of the mental health profession, most associate with juvenile offenders. Although rates for these disorders, specifically oppositional defiant disorder (ODD), conduct disorder (CD), and attention deficit hyperactivity disorder (ADHD), are very high within this population, as are externalizing symptoms such as irritability, impulsivity, and aggressive behavior (e.g., Borum, 2006; Gagnon & Barber, 2010; Jonson-Reid et al., 2001), it is important to keep in mind that very few juvenile offenders have externalizing behavior problems in isolation (Atkins et al., 1999). Because externalizing behaviors are easily noticed and are most likely to have gotten an offender into the juvenile justice system in the first place, these behaviors often take a place of prominence and allow internalizing and other problems to go overlooked (Kinscherff, 2012).

INTERNALIZING DISORDERS

The rates of internalizing disorders in juvenile offenders are surprisingly high (e.g., Arnold et al., 2003; Gagnon & Barber, 2010; Kinscherff, 2012; Veysey, 2008). Although rates vary by sample and methodology, they are higher than those found in the general population (Atkins et al., 1999). For example, Kinscherff (2012) reported that approximately 26% of male and 56% of female juvenile offenders had anxiety, and 14% of male and 30% of female offenders had mood disorders. Similarly, in a review of extant literature, Veysey (2008) found that rates for depressive disorder ranged from 15% to 73% for females and from 13% to 26% for males. Unfortunately, internalizing problems, with symptoms such as inattention, fatigue, and withdrawal from peers, can manifest in ways that get juvenile offenders mislabeled as oppositional (Wood et al., 2008), which can prevent youth from getting much-needed services. Similarly, in youth with abuse histories, reactions such as anger and aggression are often misinterpreted as oppositional behaviors (Arnold et al., 2003). Worse yet, these misunderstood symptoms can result in further disciplinary actions for disruptive behavior or nonparticipation in mandatory activities (Kinscherff, 2012).

TRAUMA

The rates of exposure to violence, abuse, and neglect for youth involved in the juvenile justice system are very high (Gagnon & Barber, 2010; Jonson-Reid et al., 2001; Koocher & Kinscherff, 2016; Sander & Fisher, 2014; Veysey, 2008). Rates vary across populations and methodologies (e.g., self-report, history of involvement with child welfare or child protective services) but generally are well above 50% for this population, with approximately 16% to 57% meeting the criteria for post-traumatic stress disorder (Kinscherff, 2012; Ovaert, Cashel, & Sewell, 2003; Veysey, 2008). Past experiences with abuse make it more likely for youth to have engaged in violent offenses (Jonson-Reid et al., 2001), and to have more overall impairments in functioning, including higher rates of suicidal thoughts (Arnold et al., 2003) than offenders without these histories. Abuse and neglect are also linked with a variety of negative outcomes, including earlier involvement with delinquent activities and higher rates of offending, detention, and recidivism (Sickmund & Puzzanchera, 2014). Within the juvenile justice population, female offenders and those of color are most likely to have histories of maltreatment or neglect (Underwood et al., 2006). The rates of victimization experienced by Black youth in the juvenile justice system are nearly two times those experienced by White youth (Sander & Fisher, 2014; Sickmund & Puzzanchera, 2014). Symptoms of trauma exposure and trauma reactions are easily overlooked or mislabeled within the juvenile justice system. Symptoms and reactions such as violence, anger, and impaired empathy for others may not be easily recognizable, making it likely that treatment needs go unmet (Kinscherff, 2012), and may be mislabeled as oppositional or defiant behavior (Arnold et al., 2003). Given the prevalence of trauma within this population, it is critical that all juvenile offenders are screened for traumatic histories.

Psychotic Symptoms

Juvenile offenders, particularly violent offenders, are also known to experience higher levels of psychotic symptoms (e.g., delusions or hallucinations) than their peers (Atkins et al., 1999; Borum, 2006; Veysey, 2008). For example, in a study that compared a sample of incarcerated youth with a sample from a community-based mental health clinic and a sample from a psychiatric care hospital, incarcerated youth had higher levels of a variety of symptoms, including psychotic symptoms, than the community mental health clinic sample, but fewer symptoms than hospitalized youth (Atkins et al., 1999). In a review of the extant research, Veysey (2008) found that 0% to 12% of female juvenile offenders and 1% to 16% of male juvenile offenders met criteria for psychotic disorders. Unfortunately, the behaviors that are often associated with these symptoms, such as impulsivity, a perceived lack of self-control, or behavioral outbursts, may be misinterpreted in juvenile justice facilities by both staff and peers, and untreated youth with psychiatric symptoms may become violent (Underwood et al., 2006). It is particularly important that counselors help to identify and advocate for the needs of youth experiencing these symptoms, as they require specialized care. Youth with psychotic symptoms should be moved from juvenile justice placements and into psychiatric care as soon as needs are identified (Underwood et al., 2006).

Substance Abuse

Youth involved in the juvenile justice system use drugs and alcohol at higher rates than their peers (Gagnon & Barber, 2010; Kinscherff, 2012; Stein et al., 2011; Underwood et al., 2006). These youth self-report high levels of alcohol and drug usage prior to arrest, and estimates of substance abuse disorders among these youth range from 39% to 100% (Kinscherff, 2012; Stein et al., 2011; Veysey, 2008). Many youth are involved in the juvenile justice system for alcohol- or drug-related violations, although some authors have found that juvenile offenders with those violations do not always report high levels of use or abuse (Atkins et al., 1999). As a counselor, it is helpful to remember that substance use and abuse problems are very likely to be comorbid with other internalizing or externalizing problems and should therefore be treated within the overall context of a youth's needs (Kinscherff, 2012; Stein et al., 2011).

Learning Disabilities and Low Achievement

A large portion of students involved in the juvenile justice system struggle academically. When compared with peers who are not involved in this system, these students are more likely to perform far below grade level in reading and math, have identified or unidentified learning disabilities, have emotional disturbances that adversely impact their ability to learn, have acquired (e.g., fetal alcohol syndrome) or congenital (e.g., autism spectrum disorder) developmental and cognitive delays (Gagnon & Barber, 2010; Kinscherff, 2012; Koocher & Kinscherff, 2016; Sander & Fisher, 2014). As a result of many years of academic struggles, many juvenile offenders have developed behavior patterns such as aggression, defiance, or apathy in order to escape academic demands (Wood et al., 2008). Unfortunately, as described earlier in this chapter, they also may be served in educational settings that are not equipped to meet the needs of such challenging students.

In a study examining youth in the California Youth Authority (CYA), a series of facilities that work with California's serious and chronic juvenile offenders, Jonson-Reid et al. (2001) found that incarcerated youth qualified for special education services under the category of emotional disturbance (ED) at about seven times the rate of their nonincarcerated peers. These students were also twice as likely as their fellow detainees to come from single-parent homes and have a history of involvement with child welfare agencies. Interestingly, the average amount of time students had been identified as having special education needs prior to incarceration at CYA was about six months, which means that their ED was identified at the same time as or after they engaged in the behavior that brought them into contact with the juvenile justice system, accounting for the time it takes to process and adjudicate a case prior to detention. These authors speculate that the emotional needs of many of these youth likely went unidentified for some time, coming to the attention of the educational system only when their behavior became problematic.

As highlighted in studies by Jonson-Reid et al. (2001) and others, high proportions of students in the juvenile justice system are eligible for special education services, under the eligibilities of ED and specific learning disability (SLD) (Koocher & Kinscherff, 2016; Underwood et al., 2006; Wood et al., 2008). Experts posit that many juvenile offenders also have unidentified needs that would qualify them for special education if they were adequately assessed (e.g., Gagnon & Barber, 2010; Koocher & Kinscherff, 2016; Sander & Fisher, 2014). As a federal mandate, special education is required to be provided for any qualified student, regardless of his or her placement. Unfortunately, for a variety of reasons, including delays in paperwork transfers and lack of resources, special education services are not always consistently provided to students in juvenile justice settings (Scott et al., 2002). Counselors working with this population are urged to verify that their students' educational rights and needs are being met, as well as to consider how these learning needs may impact students' ability to benefit from counseling services. For example, it would be important for a counselor to understand a student's reading level, comprehension level, and writing abilities before providing information or engaging in activities that involve handouts, worksheets, or journaling.

Comorbidity

One of the most common terms used to describe juvenile offenders in the counseling literature is *complex*. Youth in the juvenile justice system are highly likely to present with multiple comorbid diagnoses and conditions, with comorbidity being the most common presenting condition (e.g., Atkins et al., 1999; Kinscherff, 2012; Sander & Fisher, 2014; Townsend, 2007; Underwood et al., 2006; Veysey, 2008). Although rates vary with samples and methodologies, it is expected that in this population, more than half of youth will have at least two diagnosable conditions. Given that some studies examine only mental health diagnoses, these cases may be even more complex when identified and unidentified cognitive and learning needs are simultaneously considered (Gagnon & Barber, 2010; Wood et al., 2008).

COUNSELING APPROACHES

The counseling strategies presented in this chapter represent the scant literature on evidence-based strategies for working with juvenile offenders. Many different techniques described here can be modified for use in individual or group approaches (Granello & Hanna, 2003), although information on groups is presented in a separate section of this chapter. The application of experience and professional judgment is crucial in the selection of strategies for any given student, especially for this heterogeneous and complex population. One thing that the counseling techniques presented here have in common is that the majority focus on skill building and skill development. In order to help counselors understand the types of skills that may be relevant for working with juvenile offenders, Houchins (2001) compiled a list of skill deficits that are commonly cited in research on this population, including

- being unreflective and unaware of wants and needs;
- being overly reactive and lacking self-control;
- creating problems and solving problems using physicality rather than cognitive strategies;
- discounting their intellectual abilities and lacking effective communication skills;
- being controlled by their environments;
- being self-destructive; and
- and working against their own best interest.

This list of potential skill deficits highlights the need for skill-building approaches in counseling. However, given the complex nature and likelihood of comorbid concerns and conditions within the juvenile offender population, the needs of students must be carefully prioritized when selecting treatments. Further, counselors should be prepared to engage in crisis counseling for immediate or pressing needs (Underwood et al., 2006).

Counseling is not effective in isolation; the multifaceted needs of juvenile offenders require multifaceted and comprehensive treatment plans. In a review of efficacy research for this population, Guerra, Kim, and Boxer (2008) noted four qualities of treatment programs that are effective in helping juvenile offenders, which include treatments that

- are highly structured;
- involve a cognitive-based component and target specific skills;
- involve families, particularly when families were a risk factor for delinquent behavior; and
- are comprehensive (i.e., address risks across multiple contexts).

Counselors can work within their capacities to play an important role in a youth's overall treatment plan, but counseling services per se should be only a portion of a multifaceted intervention for juvenile offenders.

Ensuring Competence

The histories and presenting concerns of juvenile offenders are complex, and most graduate training programs do not adequately prepare counselors to work successfully with this population (Kinscherff, 2012). The literature related to counseling these youth is replete with cautions and reminders regarding experience, expertise, and the importance of seeking training or professional consultation (e.g., Gagnon & Barber, 2010; Kinscherff, 2012; Underwood et al., 2006). Many authors recommend that counselors who want to work with juvenile offenders should take steps to educate themselves about the juvenile justice system as a whole, including keeping abreast of state and federal laws that relate to juvenile offending and familiarizing themselves with the array of services and placements involved for youth in their area (Granello & Hanna, 2003; Kinscherff, 2012; Koocher & Kinscherff, 2016). Counselors should seek additional expertise in developmental perspectives on delinquency and violent behavior/patterns of delinquent behavior (i.e., desisters and persisters); and knowledge regarding specialty populations, such as LGBT offenders, offenders with psychotic disorders, gang-involved youth, fire starters, and sexual offenders (Koocher & Kinscherff, 2016). It is also important for counselors to engage in professional development regarding therapeutic approaches for juvenile offenders. Several of the counseling approaches that will be discussed in this chapter require specialty training and ongoing clinical consultation and supervision (e.g., DBT, MST; Trupin et al., 2002); others (e.g., SFBT, CBT) will need to be implemented with integrity to maximize their efficacy with this challenging group (Sander & Fisher, 2014). Finally, counselors should engage in self-reflection to ensure that they are not harboring any biases or judgments that may impair their ability to work with juvenile offenders (Himelstein, 2011). Some juvenile offenders may have committed crimes that will carry social stigma, and many adults likely have judged them for their crimes rather than for who they are as individuals. In order to have compassion for this population and form authentic working relationships, counselors will need to reflect on their own views and beliefs and to view these students with the full picture of their case histories, experiences, and needs in mind (Himelstein, 2011).

Ethical Considerations

One aspect that distinguishes juvenile offenders from other populations discussed in this book is the fact that they may participate in treatment under court orders. In all counseling relationships with minors, it is important to establish assent, in spite of the legal authority for consent coming from a parent or guardian. When youth are participating in counseling without the right to decline, this matter becomes more delicate. It is recommended that counselors attempt to establish assent, even when counseling is mandatory (Koocher & Kinscherff, 2016). When counseling is mandated, counselors may also be placed in the challenging position of needing to report progress in counseling to an outside party. Judges, probation officers, and case managers may all ask for and expect progress updates regarding a youth's treatment. When counseling is court ordered, counselors need to be explicit regarding the limits to confidentiality in the counseling relationship and to be cognizant of providing information only about a youth's specific progress as it relates to counseling goals or symptoms. Unless they are specifically trained to do so, counselors should avoid providing forensic opinions regarding recidivism risk (Koocher & Kinscherff, 2016).

Case Formulation and Diagnosis

Given the complex histories and needs of juvenile offenders, extra time and attention need to be paid to case formulation and diagnosis. The types of risks and symptoms experienced by juvenile offenders make diagnosis particularly challenging, and counselors should consider diagnoses to be hypotheses that are subject to change and require periodic review and modification (Kinscherff, 2012). As reviewed earlier in this chapter, juvenile offenders come into the juvenile justice system labeled by the crimes they committed. Unfortunately, these labels rarely tell the whole story of a child or adolescent given that different youth will commit the same offenses for very different reasons. For example, two offenders may be in counseling, with each having been arrested for assault. One adolescent may be experiencing trauma reactions and having difficulty controlling emotional flooding, especially while using substances, while the other may have developed angry and aggressive behavior as a compensatory strategy to avoid work that he is not capable of completing due to learning challenges. In these cases, the diagnoses and case formulations should lead to very different treatment courses (Sander & Fisher, 2014).

Aside from the fact that the majority of juvenile offenders will qualify for at least two diagnoses, their clinical pictures are also complicated by the fact that symptoms they are experiencing could be criteria for multiple diagnoses (Kinscherff,

2012). For example, both irritability and inattention can be symptoms of major depressive disorder, bipolar disorder, or post-traumatic stress disorder. For this reason, anyone involved in making diagnoses for juvenile offenders needs to complete thorough assessments across developmental domains of functioning, including emotional, cognitive, and social, which can be difficult due to these young people's complex histories (Kinscherff, 2012).

Treatment Planning and Tailoring Interventions

Once diagnoses have been made or clarified, counseling should begin only after careful treatment planning has occurred. Optimally, treatment plans are made as a collaborative effort involving all parties invested in the youth's care (e.g., parents or guardians, probation officers, residential facility staff), are multifaceted, have clear and measurable goals and objectives, and are consistently reviewed and updated based on student progress (Underwood et al., 2006; for more on professional collaboration and team-based supports for juvenile offenders, see the "Beyond the Counseling Office" section later in this chapter). In the absence of comprehensive treatment plans, counselors still need to consider all aspects of a youth's needs when selecting and tailoring interventions (Borum, 2006; Sander & Fisher, 2014).

Given the complexity of the case formulations found within this population, it is rare to work with a student who is not receiving multiple interventions to address various domains of need. For example, many incarcerated youth are receiving individual and group-based counseling or psychoeducation regarding substance abuse, in addition to individual counseling for trauma exposure or internalizing symptoms. If providers of different services are not communicating effectively about youth's needs, interventions may prove ineffective. For example, Stein et al. (2011) examined the impact of a group-based motivational interviewing treatment on juvenile offenders' substance abuse. They found that the group was effective, except for youth experiencing high levels of depression symptoms. As Stein et al. (2011) note, interventionists need to consider all aspects of a youth's needs to ensure that he or she is ready and able to benefit from planned services.

Selecting the appropriate behaviors or symptoms to focus on in counseling is an important aspect in treatment planning. Counselors should start by focusing on eliminating risk factors for recidivism that they are able to change (Underwood et al., 2006). In other words, factors such as an offender's history of abuse and neglect are not changeable, whereas helping that offender to control his or her behavior during trauma reactions is a behavior that is within reach. Borum (2006) suggests that counseling focus on behaviors that are most likely to reduce future contact with the juvenile justice system, such as barriers to treatment (e.g., negative thoughts about counseling, defiant behavior toward facility staff), building vocational skills or assisting with job placement, and self-control. Interventions should be tailored to meet the needs of each individual juvenile offender. Although a few specific interventions and broad counseling approaches have demonstrated efficacy for this population, it is understandably difficult to find empirically validated interventions that are designed for each offender's unique cluster of experiences and needs. Therefore, counselors may need to make selections based on empirical support but also consider the individual strengths and needs of each youth while making decisions about how to tailor interventions to maximize efficacy (Gagnon & Barber, 2010), a need that is consistently stressed throughout the literature on counseling this population (e.g., Borum, 2006; Gagnon & Barber, 2010; Kinscherff, 2012; Sander & Fisher, 2014; Trupin et al., 2002). It also is important to consider students' cognitive and learning abilities and needs. Given the high rates of underachievement and identified and unidentified learning disabilities found in juvenile offenders, many approaches may not be appropriate. For example, CBT should not be used with a student with very low cognitive abilities (Borum, 2006); a student with auditory processing deficits may not benefit from a psychoeducational group with only orally presented information; and journaling should not be assigned as a homework task for a student with minimal writing skills (Kinscherff, 2012).

Relationship Building

The establishment of rapport is crucial in all counseling scenarios, and particularly so when working with juvenile offenders. Aside from the fact that many will be participating in counseling without a right to decline, juvenile offenders are likely to come to the counseling relationship with a history of strained and negative relationships with adults and before being ready to accept and change any problems they may be experiencing (Himelstein, 2011; Wilder, 2004). There are many suggestions in the literature for establishing successful counseling relationships with juvenile offenders. One approach is to avoid opening discussions by reviewing a juvenile's crimes (Sander & Fisher, 2014). Although this may be counterintuitive given the nature of court-mandated treatment, if counselors take the perspective that delinquent activity was a symptom of more important underlying conditions (e.g., trauma reactions, depression), it is easier to see why a discussion of offenses is not necessary. Many of the relationship-building strategies (i.e., joining) utilized in SFBT may also be useful, such as being patient with silences, using scaling questions, and avoiding closed-ended questions and problem talk (Corcoran, 1997). It may also help counselors to adopt an overall tone of positivity and hopefulness when building relationships with students and families, as this will run counter to any stigma or punitive messages they may receive from others who are part of the juvenile justice system (Sander & Fisher, 2014).

Himelstein (2011) discusses the value of appropriate self-disclosure in relationship building with juvenile offenders, that is, self-disclosures that are done in the interest of the student. From a humanistic-existential perspective, appropriate self-disclosure may help establish the counselor as an authentic person and assist in breaking down relationship barriers caused by power differentials.

Additionally, Himelstein notes that it is common for youth in this population to respond poorly to the use of deflection techniques when they ask counselors personal questions. As these techniques can create power struggles within the counseling relationship, it is better for a counselor to carefully and authentically respond to a personal question rather than deflect it.

Cognitive-Behavioral Therapy

Cognitive-behavioral therapy (CBT) is the most consistently recommended counseling orientation for working with juvenile offenders (Borum, 2006; Gagnon & Barber, 2010; Guerra et al., 2008; Himelstein, 2011; Sander & Fisher, 2014). Interventions based on CBT have been demonstrated to be effective in reducing symptoms of PTSD, depression, suicidal behaviors, self-destructive behavior, and comorbid depression and conduct disorder in this population (Townsend, 2007). From a CBT orientation, delinquent behavior is viewed as a result of maladaptive thoughts, including overgeneralizations such as "they all hate me" or attribution errors such as "that wasn't an accident, he did that on purpose to bother me," and skill deficits. Using CBT, counselors help students to identify and challenge maladaptive thoughts and to learn prosocial life and problem-solving skills that will enhance their ability to be successful in the future (Guerra et al., 2008; Hollin, 2003; Houchins, 2001; Townsend, 2007). Skills are taught in individual or group settings and are reinforced via handouts, role plays, modeling, feedback, and homework assignments (Hollin, 2003; Townsend, 2007). As with all approaches, it is important that counselors implement any CBT-based strategies or curricula with integrity (Sander & Fisher, 2014).

Townsend (2007) provides a review of the strengths of CBT approaches for this population. First, CBT approaches are relatively brief and are focused on current problems, which is important given the limited time often available due to the transience of this population. Next, CBT approaches have detailed training and implementation manuals, making them accessible to counselors from a variety of training backgrounds, and also making them easier to implement with fidelity. Finally, CBT approaches have been found to be effective for juvenile offenders in both residential and community-based settings. Interestingly, results tend to be stronger for programs delivered to incarcerated youth, which is attributed to higher attendance and compliance rates.

Solution-Focused Brief Therapy

Solution-focused brief therapy (SFBT) is also recommended for use with juvenile offenders, although there is only minimal research to support its efficacy. Specific strategies used in SFBT are particularly helpful when working with this population. Juvenile offenders, particularly those in residential facilities, may be temporary clients because they may change placements quickly or be mandated to attend only a small number of counseling sessions, for which SFBT is ideal (Corcoran, 1997). Also, many juvenile offenders will be nonvoluntary participants; for them, a helpful SFBT approach would be to ask them what change the mandating party (e.g., judge, probation officer) would need to see in order to decide that counseling is no longer needed, which can then become the goals for counseling (De Jong & Berg, 2008). Exception questions (e.g., "What was different about the time when you were teased and you responded without violence?") and scaling questions (e.g., "On a scale where 1 is the action that got you arrested and 10 is what you should be doing in order to exit the system, where are you now?") are also useful SFBT strategies to try (Corcoran, 1997). Another recommended SFBT approach is to maintain a positive stance by utilizing definitive phrasing, for example, "What *will* be different *when you are coming* to school every day?" instead of "What *would* be different *if you were coming* to school every day?" (Corcoran, 1997). A final SFBT strategy to use with juvenile offenders is to focus on strengths. Corcoran (1997) provides an example of a youth who had been dealing drugs, with whom the counselor asked what types of skills this involved, then praised the youth for those skills (e.g., personal discipline, math, and financial skills), and discussed how these attributes could be applied in other ways.

Dialectical Behavior Therapy

Dialectical behavior therapy (DBT; Linehan, 1993) has been demonstrated to be successful in working with juvenile offenders (Trupin et al., 2002; Underwood et al., 2006). This approach was developed for work with individuals with borderline personality disorder and requires training, expertise, and support for implementation with integrity (Trupin et al., 2002). DBT, which consists of weekly individual psychotherapy and group therapy skill training, focuses on emotional regulation, successful use of interpersonal skills, and learning to accept or tolerate the experience of distress (Linehan, 1993). It is described as an "application of a wide assortment of cognitive-behavior[al] strategies combined with a philosophical emphasis on dialectics, the aim being to find the synthesis between two seemingly opposite positions" (Trupin et al., 2002, p. 122). In DBT, youth are taught to view maladaptive behaviors as unsuccessful, in that they often do not lead to desired outcomes, and are encouraged to utilize skills learned in treatment to enhance their interpersonal effectiveness (Trupin et al., 2002).

Although only a small portion of juvenile offenders likely have borderline personality disorder, DBT can be adapted for work with this population given its focus on highly relevant behaviors such as self-injury, behaviors that interfere with counseling, and responses to post-traumatic stress symptoms (Underwood et al., 2006). In a study by Trupin et al. (2002), DBT was used with female juvenile offenders in the most restrictive placements within an incarceration facility. Results indicated that participation in DBT allowed youth greater access to general programming (i.e., employment opportunities, GED completion, drug and alcohol programming). These researchers hypothesized that DBT helped these offenders by reducing behaviors that were interfering with rehabilitation, such as defiance toward the unit or correctional staff, violence, self-harm, and noncompliance with treatment protocols.

As mentioned earlier in this chapter, DBT is a specialized treatment approach that requires specific training. Unless a counselor was specifically taught DBT during his or her professional coursework or supervised field experiences, additional training is required before this approach is implemented with clients. More information on professional development training and resources for DBT is provided in the resources section at the end of this chapter.

Motivational Interviewing

Motivational interviewing (MI; Miller & Rollnick, 2013) is a promising approach for working with juvenile offenders. There are a number of MI-based interventions in the counseling literature for this population, the majority of which are focused on substance abuse treatment, and because MI is a relatively brief approach, it is particularly appropriate for use in juvenile justice settings (Stein et al., 2006a). The four basic principles of MI are a focus on empathy, enhancing self-efficacy, respecting personal choice, and developing discrepancy between where youth are and where they would like to be (Stein et al., 2011). Motivational interviewing is covered in greater depth in Chapter 10 of this book.

MI focuses on reducing ambivalence toward change by identifying and enhancing *change talk* (i.e., statements that indicate a positive stance toward change), while highlighting and reducing *sustain talk* (i.e., statements that support making no changes; Miller & Rollnick, 2013). From an MI perspective, change talk enhances a youth's ability to change undesirable behaviors (D'Amico et al., 2015). Counselors can use reflection statements to help direct a youth's statements toward change talk. D'Amico et al. (2015) give the example of a client saying, "I like smoking pot but it keeps getting me into trouble" (p. 75), to which a counselor could reflect, "Even through you like getting high, you recognize that if you keep doing it, it's going to keep getting you into trouble" (p. 75), which could lead to change talk, rather than "You like getting high" (p. 76), which would lead to sustain talk.

Stein and colleagues (2006a, 2006b, 2011) explored the efficacy of MI-based substance abuse group treatments for incarcerated juvenile offenders. Results were positive, finding both reduced rates of alcohol and marijuana use after release (Stein et al., 2011) and reduced rates of driving under the influence or being a passenger with a driver under the influence after release (Stein et al., 2006a). The efficacy of participation in the MI group was impacted by depressive symptoms, such that the intervention was not effective for youth with high levels of depressive symptoms (Stein et al., 2006a, 2011), which reinforces the concept that each offender's treatment needs must be considered and prioritized in treatment planning. D'Amico et al. (2015) also examined MI-based group counseling for juvenile offenders but focused their study on the amounts of change talk and sustain talk occurring during group sessions. They found that greater amounts of change talk were significantly correlated with lower rates of alcohol use and abuse after youth were released from their residential facility. D'Amico et al. (2015) noted that in the group setting, group sessions tended to trend toward either more sustain talk or more change talk, with change talk leading to further change talk, and sustain talk leading to further sustain talk. They also noted that the overall amount of change talk in group sessions was correlated with lower substance use and abuse levels even for youth who were not directly participating in the conversations, suggesting that even passive experiencing of change talk can be beneficial.

Addressing Trauma

There are very few trauma-specific interventions discussed in the literature for juvenile offenders, although several authors make recommendations that can provide guidance for working with youth impacted by trauma. Veysey (2008) notes that counselors working with youth who have experienced trauma need to consider how trauma reactions, other internalizing or externalizing disorders, and substance abuse are interacting and impacting functioning. Granello and Hanna (2003) recommend that counseling start by acknowledging hurt and emotional pain, noting that juvenile offenders are often more comfortable displaying anger than other emotions and may need assistance in recognizing and accepting that they have a right to be hurt about trauma they have experienced. Once pain is acknowledged, youth can benefit from being taught how to manage their responses to trauma triggers (Granello & Hanna, 2003). Noting that trauma can cause or trigger maladaptive perceptions, attitudes, beliefs, and strong emotional reactions, Kinscherff (2012) suggests helping youth identify these reactions and work to manage or replace them with more productive responses.

Ovaert et al. (2003) evaluated the impact of an MI-based group intervention on offenders with PTSD. They reported that the intervention did significantly reduce symptoms of PTSD, particularly arousal and intrusive symptoms, but did not impact symptoms of depression or generalized anxiety, which the authors suggested may need to be addressed separately. This intervention was most effective for participants who had experienced gang-related trauma, and it was recommended that future interventions may consider separating out participants by type of trauma (e.g., forming separate interventions for those with gang-related trauma and those who had experienced sexual assault or physical abuse). These authors also recommended carefully screening participants for group-based trauma interventions because some participants may not be ready to address their trauma in this setting.

Specific trauma-based counseling interventions are discussed in Chapters 2 and 3 of this volume, but they are not specific for youth involved with the juvenile justice system.

Multisystemic Therapy

Multisystemic therapy (MST) is often presented as an effective treatment for juvenile offenders (e.g., Granello & Hanna, 2003; Guerra et al., 2008; Sander & Fisher, 2014), but as a specialty therapy requiring intensive training, supervision, and funding, MST is not a strategy that can be employed by individual counselors. However, it is included here as an effective treatment so that counselors can find out if such a program is available for students in their area, and so that they can serve as school-based collaborators if the program is being implemented. Henggeler, Schoenwald, Borduin, Rowland, and Cunningham (2009) wrote the primary handbook for MST, *Multisystemic Therapy for Antisocial Behavior in Children and Adolescents*, which is currently in its second edition. According to these authors, MST is based on reciprocal ecological theory, recognizing the multidetermined nature of behavior, as well as the reciprocal interactions of a youth with his or her environment. The goal of MST is to modify all environmental contexts surrounding a youth (e.g., home, school, peers) to support prosocial behaviors. A fundamental task of MST is to gain a deep understanding of the family and its worldview, and MST counselors assist families in utilizing their strengths and resources to decrease any barriers to effective parenting (e.g., parental substance abuse, hopelessness).

Group Counseling

Groups are commonly used with juvenile offenders to address a wide range of counseling topics, including skill building, substance use and abuse, and trauma reactions. Although most strategies used with this population can be adapted for either individual or group use (Granello & Hanna, 2003), there are many factors to consider when preparing to work with groups of juvenile offenders. First, counselors should be wary of the potential unintended negative impact of group participation for this population (e.g., D'Amico et al., 2015; Stein et al., 2006a). Because counseling is likely to be mandated, in groups that are composed of youth who are not ready to change, counselors may find conversations quickly spiraling off topic or toward the opposite direction than what was intended (e.g., substance abuse group topic drifts into why adolescents enjoy drinking and how fun it is to get high; D'Amico et al., 2015; Stein et al., 2006b). As with many counseling groups, counselors should enlist a qualified co-facilitator for groups with this population when at all possible (Underwood et al., 2006). It is also recommended that counselors carefully screen students prior to group sessions to ensure that their needs can be met within the group setting, especially if group counseling was mandated by a person without a background in mental health (e.g., judge, probation officer). Counselors should also meet with students individually to review rules and expectations for group participation in advance.

Elliot (2002) provides a review of strategies for group counseling with juvenile offenders, noting that difficulties are often experienced in the areas of resistance and power struggles. Elliot presents three methods to work with these challenges: (a) redirection (i.e., ignore off-topic comments and firmly and swiftly change back to the original topic; shift conversations away from past behavior and toward current and future behaviors); (b) reframing (i.e., use semantics to reframe comments without being confrontational, such as when a student denies participation in a certain action, and the group leader replies that the student is not ready to discuss that action); and (c) reversal of responsibility (i.e., point out flaws in logic when students place responsibility for their actions solely on others). These strategies should be applied with clinical judgment and within the context of other group leadership techniques.

Aggression Replacement Training

Aggression Replacement Training (ART; Glick & Gibbs, 2015) is a CBT-based group intervention that is commonly cited as an effective intervention for juvenile offenders (Guerra et al., 2008; Himelstein, 2011; Hollin, 2003; Holmqvist, Hill, & Lang, 2009; Underwood et al., 2006). The three main components of this 30-session multimodal program are social skill training, anger control training, and moral reasoning (Glick & Gibbs, 2015). ART is designed to help youth recognize their anger triggers and reactions and learn ways to respond more appropriately through psychoeducation, feedback, role plays, and coaching (Hollin, 2003). The moral reasoning component of ART aims to increase participants' concerns for the rights and needs of others, as well as their sense of fairness and justice (Glick & Gibbs, 2015).

BEYOND THE COUNSELING OFFICE: COLLABORATION AND ADVOCACY

The needs of juvenile offenders are vast and complex. Their needs cannot be met within the confines of a counseling office, and counseling itself shows little efficacy unless it is a part of a comprehensive treatment plan (Guerra et al., 2008). Counselors working with juvenile offenders should expect to spend a large portion of their time preparing youth for transitions, collaborating with other providers and agencies, and advocating for their rights and needs.

Transition and Re-entry

For those juvenile offenders who are placed in any type of residential facility, the transition back to home and school can be very challenging and requires a great deal of support (Atkins et al., 1999; Clark & Unruh, 2010). Unfortunately, youth are often released into the same contexts that may have contributed to their delinquent behavior (e.g., parental substance abuse, delinquent peer group, lack of supervision; Granello & Hanna, 2003), and they need to be prepared to maintain progress and prosocial trajectories in spite of the renewed presence of these risks. Although life in incarceration is hardly ideal, many aspects of life are taken care of for youth while they are in these settings that will need to be worked on when they are transitioning. For example, while youth are in residential facilities, they do not need to take responsibility for most aspects of their daily lives (e.g., preparing meals, doing laundry, taking medication, getting to or from school) that they may need to take care of when they are released (Houchins, 2001). Because smoother transitions are linked to lower recidivism rates (Sander & Fisher, 2014), counselors should make it a priority to help ensure that students are well prepared for release and re-entry into the family, school, and community.

Fortunately, most youth do not completely exit the juvenile justice system upon release from a residential facility, which means they should have continued access to a variety of services, including social services, counseling, and other aspects of rehabilitative care. However, the transition from residential to home settings may mean that youth are transferred to new service providers, in which case communication and collaboration across treatment teams is essential to ensure continuity of care. A number of suggestions for supporting youth as they transition from residential care are provided in the literature. Because the re-entry into school settings represents the re-entry into a different system, suggestions focus on communication and collaboration between juvenile justice and school systems, although most of the principles covered can be applied to any service or agency that may be interacting with juvenile offenders upon release.

GIVE ADVANCE NOTICE OF RELEASE

Releases from residential facilities can happen at any point during the year. Unfortunately, schools are often unprepared to accept new or returning students at all times, and they may suggest that juvenile offenders wait until a natural starting point to re-enter school (e.g., start of school year, return from winter break). To prevent this gap in services and to create smooth transitions without missed school, counselors can communicate with residential facilities serving their students and request to be notified of upcoming releases well in advance (Hogan, Bullock, & Fritsch, 2010).

TRANSITION RECORDS IN ADVANCE

Educational files are notoriously delayed when students transfer schools. This can cause a disruption in educational services, particularly for students in special education. To prevent such disruptions, it is strongly recommended that records be transferred in advance of youth being released (Clark & Unruh, 2010; Hogan et al., 2010). Counselors may have to work collaboratively with probation staff to help with the transfer of records and follow up to ensure that all parties have the needed documentation (Sander & Fisher, 2014).

Hold Transition Meetings in Advance

It is strongly recommended that treatment teams of incarcerated youth meet with community-based teams, including school teams, in advance of a student's release (Clark & Unruh, 2010; Hogan et al., 2010; Scott et al., 2002). Teams can discuss students' needs and ensure that all necessary services are available for youth when they return home. For students in special education, these meetings should include a discussion of special education goals and services, as well as any existing behavior plans, which may need to be updated or amended to fit the new school setting (Scott et al., 2002). Clark and Unruh (2010) suggest that treatment teams in residential facilities should prepare what they call a "student education passport" (p. 46), which is a file that includes records such as assessments, transcripts, individualized education plans (IEPs), and student work samples. School psychologists who provide counseling to students in the juvenile justice system may be familiar with these transition plans and special education documents, whereas counselors from other professional backgrounds may not be. Regardless of counselors' backgrounds, it is important that they be aware of what should be happening and advocate on their students' behalf.

Plan for Continuity of Medication

Another important consideration regarding the transition from a residential facility to home is medication (Underwood et al., 2006; Wood et al., 2008). If youth were prescribed and taking medication while incarcerated, they were doing so in a highly structured setting. Outside of that setting, students and families may need help in establishing medication management routines at home and school (Wood et al., 2008), as well as in getting access to psychiatric care (Underwood et al., 2006). As with working with IEP documents and transition plan meetings, these tasks may be more familiar to some counselors than to others, depending on one's professional background. For example, a social worker may be very comfortable in assisting a family in obtaining insurance or accessing community-based medical facilities, whereas a school psychologist may need to consult with other professionals to provide this type of support.

Meeting Needs at School

When youth are released from incarceration, they will need to return to school. Counselors should be cognizant of the fact that the schools students may be returning to, especially comprehensive middle or high schools, may not be welcoming to these students (Clark & Unruh, 2010). Students' educational placement options will range from no services (e.g., back at comprehensive high school in the general population), to alternative or continuation schools, or restrictive special education placements such as a class for students with emotional disturbances (Scott et al., 2002). Counselors can help ensure appropriate placements by working with students and their families to discuss options and by advocating for students when necessary.

OTHER TRANSITION STRATEGIES

Counselors can play a large role in supporting youth released from residential facilities. Spending time discussing fears or concerns regarding the transition can be helpful, as can teaching and role-playing skills that will be useful for a successful transition, such as social skills needed for a work setting, decision-making, and self-regulation skills (Clark & Unruh, 2010). For students in special education, for whom a formal transition plan is required, it may be beneficial to use a self-determination curriculum that can help teach self-awareness, goal setting, and decision-making skills to help meet transition needs (Hogan et al., 2010). Other approaches that counseling providers may utilize include helping students prepare for the school setting by familiarizing them with school rules and policies, working with the school team to select a schedule for students, and arranging tours of the new campus if possible (Hogan et al., 2010). Finally, counselors can support transitions by helping to establish connections with prosocial peers, such as helping to support students in enrolling or engaging in other activities based on availability or interest, or helping students secure employment (Clark & Unruh, 2010). Clubs, sports, and other group-based structured activities will be more accessible to youth transitioning back to comprehensive schools, but counselors can help those preparing to attend alternative program by finding community-based programs and activities (Clark & Unruh, 2010).

Collaboration

Counselors who work with youth involved in the juvenile justice system need to be prepared to dedicate time and attention to interagency collaboration (Kinscherff, 2012). At a foundational level, collaboration should occur with juvenile justice employees (e.g., judges, probation officers, case managers) to help facilitate positive changes and provide services that meet the expectations of those recommending or mandating treatment (Granello & Hanna, 2003). Additionally, given the complexity of these clients' needs, it is likely that treatment will involve team-based wraparound services, and potentially involve other mental health professionals, behavioral interventionists, state and local education agencies, alcohol or drug treatment services, vocational rehabilitation or workforce investment agencies, and housing services (Clark & Unruh, 2010; Sander & Fisher, 2014; Scott et al., 2002; Wood et al., 2008).

Effective collaboration requires careful and detailed communication. To facilitate timely and consistent communication, counselors need to identify contact persons at each agency (Wood et al., 2008). Ideally, collaboration should involve multiagency treatment planning, where all involved parties work together to review relevant data, establish goals, and plan services (Scott et al., 2002). A treatment plan could help eliminate redundant services and carefully time other services to ensure that the student receives them when ready (e.g., holding off on substance abuse treatment until depression symptoms are managed); regular meetings and updates would allow various professionals to share progress and other important treatment information.

Advocacy

Counselors working with juvenile offenders quickly become aware of the need to advocate for these youth. Sadly, given that public perception of this population is often colored by reports of a few high-profile, typically violent acts, the needs of this population are often overlooked by the general public. As professionals who are well educated in the needs of juvenile offenders, counselors may elect to become advocates for change. The complexities and flaws of the juvenile justice system are so vast that this could become an overwhelming prospect, but several areas of need that are highlighted in the literature represent good starting points.

A Response to Intervention Approach

A broad shift that counselors may elect to advocate for is the application of a response to intervention approach to the juvenile justice system (Gagnon & Barber, 2010). This model, originally a public health framework that has been extensively used in school settings, focuses on universal screening (more on this topic in the next section), early intervention, and the use of systematically collected data to make decisions about the types of treatment needs of a given student. Perhaps the greatest change here would be a shift toward prevention and early intervention, which would be difficult given the reactionary nature of the juvenile justice system.

Screening

As established earlier in this chapter, youth in the juvenile justice system likely face a number of serious challenges, including a history of abuse, neglect, or exposure to violence; mental health disorders; and learning problems. Counselors who are advocating for these youth can help by asking for universal screening for these issues. In their report on the juvenile justice system, Sickmund and Puzzanchera (2014) provide statistics regarding screening procedures for the minority of juvenile offenders (approximately 25%) who were in residential facilities. For 2010, they reported that 86% of placements screened all youth for educational needs, 70% screened for substance abuse, 93% screened for suicidal ideation, and 60% completed mental health evaluations on all residents. Similar statistics were not available for youth who were receiving home-based services, although it is presumed that rates would be lower. Although some of these rates are promising (e.g., 93% screening for suicidal ideation), they are still not acceptable. Given the high rates of risks found in this population, as well as the potential to provide more appropriate, need-based services to youth and therefore facilitate more effective rehabilitation, the juvenile justice system should implement universal screening procedures for all involved youth (Gagnon & Barber, 2010; Sander & Fisher, 2014; Underwood et al., 2006).

Education

Counselors may need to advocate for their students to ensure that they are receiving their right to an education. In the same report on the juvenile justice system, Sickmund and Puzzanchera (2014) provide statistics regarding the education of juvenile offenders. They reported that in 2010, 92% of youth in residential facilities were attending school on- or off-site. Counselors should advocate for students' rights because this number needs to be 100%. Additionally, Sickmund and Puzzanchera reported that 71% of residential facilities offered GED preparation, and only 38% offered vocational education. If the juvenile justice system is going to meet its goal of rehabilitation, these numbers need to be much higher. Finally, only 82% of facilities offered special education services. This is unacceptable when such a high portion of juvenile offenders have identified (i.e., they are qualified for special education services) and unidentified special education needs. Under federal law, all youth have the right to an education, and all youth with identified disabilities have a right to special education. Overall, these youth need counselors who understand their unique and complex profiles and who are willing to support them in any way possible.

RESOURCES

Center for Youth Law and Policy

http://www.cclp.org/JJDPA_resources.php

The Center for Youth Law and Policy is a public interest group that works to protect the rights of youth involved in the juvenile justice system. It also aims to reform juvenile justice via advocacy, litigation, public education, training, and research. Priority issues for this organization include racial disparities in juvenile justice, sexual victimization of incarcerated youth, and identifying alternatives to juvenile incarceration. Its website hosts reports and fact sheets on a variety of related topics, including *Working With Families of Children in the Juvenile Justice and Corrections Systems: A Guide for Education Program Leaders, Principals, and Building Administrators*, *Addressing the Unmet Educational Needs of Children and Youth in the Juvenile Justice and Child Welfare Systems*, and *America's Invisible Children: Latino Youth and the Failure of Justice*.

Linehan Institute

http://www.linehaninstitute.org/index.php

The Linehan Institute is a private organization that focuses on increasing access to quality and effective mental and behavioral health treatment by providing trainings for counselors and psychotherapists, as well as conducting research regarding the efficacy of treatments for specific populations. Primarily, the institute serves as a host for introductory and advanced training in dialectical behavior therapy. Current training offerings are posted in the "Events" section of the institute's website.

NATIONAL TECHNICAL ASSISTANCE CENTER FOR THE EDUCATION OF NEGLECTED OR DELINQUENT CHILDREN OR YOUTH

http://www.neglected-delinquent.org/

The National Technical Assistance Center for the Education of Neglected or Delinquent Children or Youth aims to support the education of youth involved with the juvenile justice system. This organization provides resources and supports to parents, schools, and states regarding information, program planning, and technical assistance on topics such as coordination and collaboration, family engagement, and safe and supportive learning environments. Its website hosts data, reports, and informational videos, as well as contact information for liaisons for each state. Additionally, the organization holds an annual conference that brings together various stakeholders to discuss research and policy related to juvenile justice.

5

Counseling Students Who Are Lesbian, Gay, Bisexual, Transgender, and Questioning

OVERVIEW

Lesbian, gay, bisexual, transgender, and questioning (LGBTQ) students are at increased risk for victimization and discrimination at school, at home, and in the community, and these ongoing experiences can lead to negative educational outcomes and mental health problems (Kosciw, Greytak, Palmer, & Boesen, 2014; Toomey, Ryan, Diaz, Card, & Russell, 2013). Being LGBTQ does not in itself place students at significantly greater risk; rather, being LGBTQ in heterosexist and homophobic environments impacts students' educational attainment, mental health, and overall well-being (Kosciw et al., 2014; Russell, Ryan, Toomey, Diaz, & Sanchez, 2011). As the sociopolitical landscape for LGBTQ individuals is slowly beginning to change in the United States, LGBTQ students are reporting less victimization and greater support at school overall (Becker, 2014; Kosciw et al., 2014), but LGBTQ students still experience significantly high levels of LGBTQ-related victimization, demonstrating that there is still a long way to go to ensure that all students feel safe and supported at school (Kosciw et al., 2014).

Sexual orientation and gender identity are separate but overlapping constructs, and to this end, both groups of students are included in this chapter. Whenever possible, efforts have been made to distinguish research that specifically addresses sexual orientation (LGB) and research that specifically addresses gender diversity (T). However, counseling approaches for both groups are generally similar in that both groups of students can experience distress due to victimization that occurs in homophobic and transphobic environments, and that both groups can benefit from affirmative counseling approaches that support healthy sexual and gender identity development.

BASIC CONSIDERATIONS

Terminology

Sexual orientation refers to the gender to which one feels an emotional and sexual attraction. It is commonly accepted that *gay* (G) refers to boys or men who have attractions to other boys or men; that *lesbian* (L) refers to girls or women who have attractions to other girls or women; that *bisexual* (B) refers to individuals who have attractions to both girls/women and boys/men; and that *heterosexual* or *straight* refers to girls/women who are attracted to boys/men and vice versa. *Gay* is also used as an umbrella term that encompasses any nonheterosexual individual. *Sexual identity* is one's internal sense of his or her sexuality and is usually congruent with sexual orientation. *Gender identity* refers to one's internal sense of maleness or femaleness, with current conceptualization focusing on a spectrum of maleness and femaleness rather than a binary, and *gender expression* refers to how individuals choose to express their identity in external ways (e.g., clothing, behavior). *Transgender* (T) is an umbrella term that encompasses individuals whose gender identity does not correspond to their anatomical sex, while the term *cisgender* describes individuals whose gender identity is congruent with their anatomical sex. The terms *gender queer, gender diverse,* and *gender variant* are used to describe the spectrum of gender identities and gender expressions. *Questioning* (Q) most often refers to individuals who are exploring their sexual orientation but have not identified as LGB, but questioning can also refer to individuals who are exploring their gender identity and expression. The Q can also refer to *queer*, which can encompass both sexual orientation and gender identity in a myriad of forms, but it should be used cautiously by those who identify as heterosexual and cisgender. Sexual orientation and gender identity are separate constructs with different developmental pathways, but the two do overlap in that individuals who identify as transgender or somewhere along the gender continuum can also identify with any sexual orientation or sexual identity. Two terms that should be avoided are *sexual preference*, which implies that sexual orientation is a choice, and *gay lifestyle*, which implies that all LGBTQ individuals live in the same way and enjoy the same activities and hobbies. Although it is important for counselors to understand and be comfortable using this basic terminology, youth themselves may use a variety of different terms to self-identify and may resist society's labels of their sexuality and gender identity (Higa et al., 2012).

Sexual and Gender Identity Development

Sexual orientation and sexual identity are often thought of as existing on a continuum, with research supporting a conceptualization of sexuality that allows for typical exploration, fluctuations, and flexibility (Glover, Galliher, & Lamere, 2009). Children usually experience their first sexual attractions in preadolescence and have their first sexual experiences in adolescence, which help them learn how to manage physical and emotional intimacy (DeLamater & Friedrich, 2002). Research has found that sexual identity development and sexual identity integration follow multiple paths (Rosario, Schrimshaw, & Hunter, 2008), and that adolescents are labeling their sexual orientation and identity at younger ages than in the past (Glover et al., 2009). These self-labels are generally consistent into adulthood (Glover et al., 2009), although some youth who label themselves as bisexual in earlier adolescence may later identify as gay or lesbian (Rosario, Schrimshaw, Hunter, & Braun, 2006). This is to say, bisexuality is a stable sexual identity for some youth, but for others, it represents their best understanding of their sexuality during a natural phase of exploration (Kennedy & Fisher, 2010; Rosario et al., 2006).

There is much that researchers do not know about the complexities of gender identity development. Some researchers believe that gender identity is a fixed and stable internal construct, while others believe that gender identity undergoes subtle changes as individuals interact with their environment and redefine themselves in different life contexts (Fausto-Sterling, 2012). Gender identity likely develops as a result of an interplay among biological, psychological, and social factors that influence and are influenced by the environment (Adelson, 2012). Aspects of gender identity are visible in early toddlerhood, with children labeling themselves as boys or girls and engaging in gender-typed play around 18 months, and gender identity becomes more developed and stabilized over the first 5 years of life (Fausto-Sterling, 2012). It is typical for children to engage in cross-gender behaviors and play (Moller, Schreier, Li, & Romer, 2009), and it is important that parents and professionals do not jump to the conclusion that this is an indicator of transgender development. Rather, transgender gender identity involves strong feelings of incongruence between one's biological sex and internal gender identity. In a study of transgender youth, Grossman and D'Augelli (2006) found that youth varied widely in the timing of their awareness of this incongruence, with reports of this awareness occurring between 6 and 15 years of age. In this same study, youth identified with the label of transgender between 7 and 18 years of age. Further, these transgender youth expressed initial confusion about the interplay of their sexual attractions and their gender identity, but they eventually came to understand these as separate aspects of their identity (Grossman & D'Augelli, 2006).

Many models of sexual and gender identity development have been proposed and modified over the past 25 years, and with changes in the larger sociopolitical context and LGBTQ youth becoming aware of and disclosing their identities at earlier ages and in multiple ways, strict linear models may not capture the full range of LGBTQ identity development experiences (Russell, Toomey, Ryan, & Diaz, 2014). Rather, what is important to understand is that, unlike heterosexual and cisgender youth who develop their sexual and gender identities without much thought, LGBTQ identity development is often characterized by various stages that might include confusion, struggle, integration, and synthesis (Russell et al., 2014).

Sociopolitical Context

There is still a long way to go for LGBT individuals to be afforded the same rights, benefits, and protections as heterosexual and cisgender individuals, but over the past few decades, general public attitudes toward LGBT civil rights have slowly shifted as reflected by public policy and law (Becker, 2014). For example, the U.S. military no longer bans LGB individuals from serving, although the policy has yet to extend to openly transgender individuals (http://www.hrc.org/resources/transgender-military-service), and in June 2015, the U.S. Supreme Court ruled that bans on same-sex marriage were unconstitutional (http://www.hrc.org/campaigns/marriage-center), a decision that made same-sex marriages legal in all 50 states.

In spite of, and perhaps in reaction to, these changes, some members of our society remain opposed to the progression of LGBT civil rights. Individuals with more conservative religious and political values are less likely to support LGBT rights (Becker, 2014), and LGBT students living in more conservative areas, such as in the southern and midwestern United States, experience more victimization at school (Kosciw et al., 2014). As the sociopolitical landscape continues to change, so will the experiences of LGBTQ students.

The larger sociopolitical context also impacts how sexual and gender identity are viewed by medical and mental health professionals. Since the American Psychiatric Association published the first edition of the *Diagnostic and Statistical Manual of Mental Disorders* (*DSM*) in 1952, there has been controversy about viewing homosexuality and related "disorders" as pathological (Drescher, 2010). It took almost 30 years and several editions before all forms of homosexuality were removed from the *DSM*, reflecting shifting social, political, and professional ideology about LGB individuals (Drescher, 2010). Similarly, the most recent edition of the *DSM*, published in 2012, removed gender identity disorder as a diagnosis, representing a shift in thinking about transgender and gender-diverse individuals (Drescher, 2010; Zucker et al., 2013). Instead, the *DSM*-5 includes gender dysphoria as a diagnosis, which centers on feelings of significant distress and impairment in life functioning that individuals may experience when their internal gender identity is incongruent with their assigned gender (American Psychiatric Association, 2013). Essentially, this recognizes that it is the affective and cognitive distress that is problematic for the individual, not the experience of one's gender identity (Zucker et al., 2013). However, unlike other disorders listed in the *DSM*, individuals with gender dysphoria can, and often do, make lifestyle changes (e.g., making a social transition to living as their desired gender, undergoing sex/gender reassignment) that reduce or alleviate their distress, calling into question the classification of this as a disorder (Zucker et al., 2013). Over time, as society at large comes to better understand gender variance as a natural part of the human condition, it is likely that there will be further changes to the *DSM*. Perhaps it will even be recognized that the distress that these individuals experience most often comes from social stigma (Zucker et al., 2013) rather than a psychiatric disorder, and like homosexuality, gender variance will no longer be pathologized.

Experiences at School

LGBT students experience greater victimization at school than their heterosexual peers (Toomey & Russell, 2013), and this victimization leads to poorer educational and life outcomes (Kosciw et al., 2014; Toomey et al., 2013). Every two years, the Gay, Lesbian and Straight Education Network (GLSEN) surveys LGBT students across the United States to learn about their experiences in school and factors that impact school climate and students' well-being. Findings from the 2013 survey, reported by Kosciw et al. (2014), revealed that the majority of LGBT students heard derogatory remarks about sexuality and gender expression from their peers, teachers, and other school staff. LGBT students also reported high rates of verbal harassment (e.g., being called names or threatened), physical harassment (e.g., being pushed or shoved), and physical assault (e.g., being punched or injured with a weapon) at school due to their sexual orientation or gender expression (Kosciw et al., 2014). Given these findings, it is not surprising that LGBT students felt unsafe at school, which caused them to miss school, avoid gender-segregated spaces like bathrooms and locker rooms, and avoid school functions and extracurricular activities (Kosciw et al., 2014). Higher levels of LGBT victimization are associated with lower academic achievement and lower educational attainment, including fewer plans for postsecondary education (Aragon, Poteat, Espelage, & Koenig, 2014; Kosciw et al., 2014). Kosciw et al. (2014) also found that LGBT students experienced discriminatory treatment at school that included

- being disciplined for displays of affection for which heterosexual students were not disciplined;
- not being allowed to attend school functions with someone of the same gender;
- being restricted from forming a gay-straight alliance (GSA) or similar club at school; and
- being prevented from writing about LGBT topics and wearing pro-LGBT clothing.

Survey results also indicated that transgender students reported high levels of systemic discrimination at school, with 42.4% of transgender students not being allowed to use their preferred name; 59.2% being required to use the bathroom or locker room of their legal sex; and 31.6% not allowed to wear clothing that was considered inappropriate based on their legal sex (Kosciw et al., 2014).

However, because schools are a microcosm of society, LGBTQ students' experiences at school can vary greatly and are often reflective of the social and political values and the availability of resources where they live. Research has found that LGBT students living in the northeastern and western United States experience less victimization and have more school resources than students living in the South and Midwest (Kosciw et al., 2014). Similarly, LGBT students living in communities with a higher proportion of college graduates experience less victimization (Kosciw, Greytak, & Diaz, 2009). In contrast, LGBT students living in areas with high poverty rates, in rural areas, and in small towns report higher rates of victimization and fewer school supports and resources (Kosciw et al., 2009; Kosciw et al., 2014). Similarly, LGBT students attending schools in communities in which football and religion play a prominent role experience a decreased sense of well-being, which may be more pronounced in nonurban settings (Wilkinson & Pearson, 2009).

Although LGBTQ students continue to experience significantly high levels of victimization and discrimination at school, things are slowly changing for the better. School climate for LGBT students is improving, the number of LGBT students reporting victimization is slowly declining, and more LGBT students are reporting positive supports at school that impact them and their educational experiences (Kosciw et al., 2014). There are more GSAs on campuses (Kosciw et al., 2014), which are associated with less victimization (Goodenow, Szalacha, & Westheimer, 2006; Kosciw, Palmer, Kull, & Greytak, 2013). More schools are creating and promoting inclusive antibullying policies that specifically protect students based on sexual orientation and gender expression and multicultural curriculum that is inclusive of LGBT students, and more LGBT students report feeling supported by teachers and other school personnel (Kosciw et al., 2014). This support by adults at school is "one of the strongest predictors of a less hostile school climate and of greater self-esteem for LGBT students" and is associated with better school attendance and a higher grade point average (Kosciw et al., 2013, p. 58). Transgender students benefit from all these school supports, and the positive effects (e.g., better school attendance) of having comprehensive antibullying policies and GSAs on campus are even stronger for transgender students (Greytak, Kosciw, & Boesen, 2013).

Coming Out and Being Out

As students begin to self-identify as LGBTQ, they may decide to disclose their sexual orientation or gender identity to others, termed *coming out*. Coming out is a process that happens over time as students decide when, where, and to whom to disclose. Students are coming out at younger ages than in the past (Grov, Bimbi, Nanin, & Parsons, 2006; Russell et al., 2014), and although coming out certainly has risks for LGBTQ students, it can also have benefits (Harper, Brodsky, & Bruce, 2012).

IMPACT AT SCHOOL

In a recent study involving a large sample of LGBT middle and high school students, Kosciw, Palmer, and Kull (2015) found that almost two thirds were out to most or all of their peers while just over one third were out to most or all of their teachers. Being out at school is associated both with increased victimization and with higher self-esteem and decreased depression, and the balance of how these impact students seems to depend in part on the community context and students' internal and external resources and supports (Kosciw et al., 2015). For example, in rural areas, increased victimization may have impacted students more and was not counterbalanced by the positive benefits of being out (Kosciw et al., 2015), while being out at school in a more supportive community (i.e., San Francisco Bay Area) was associated with more positive adjustment, less depression, and higher self-esteem (Russell et al., 2014). According to Kosciw et al. (2015), "The decision to disclose may reflect an already present resilience, or individual quality or personal characteristic" (p. 168).

Impact at Home

Parental reactions to youths' disclosure of LGBT identity run the gamut from accepting and supportive to rejecting and abusive (Ryan, 2010). In general, family functioning prior to disclosure predicts family functioning after disclosure (Goodrich & Gilbride, 2010). Parents with a more authoritative parenting style who demonstrate greater cohesion, adaptability, and warmth prior to disclosure are able to respond more positively after disclosure (Willoughby, Malik, & Lindahl, 2006) and are more involved in their child's life (Reeves et al., 2010). Research has found that parents who are Latino, immigrant, religious, or of low socioeconomic status are more likely to reject youth due to disclosure (Ryan, Russell, Huebner, Diaz, & Sanchez, 2010). Parental rejection is associated with increased substance use, depression, suicide attempts, and risky sexual behavior (Ryan, Huebner, Diaz, & Sanchez, 2009). Parental acceptance, on the other hand, is associated with greater self-esteem, social support, and overall health (Ryan et al., 2010). In addition, LGB youth report consistently higher levels of sexual and physical abuse than their heterosexual peers (Friedman et al., 2011), and youth demonstrating greater gender nonconformity experience higher rates of sexual abuse than their more conforming peers (Roberts, Rosario, Corliss, Koenen, & Austin, 2012).

Mental Health Outcomes

When addressing the mental health needs and outcomes of LGBTQ students, there are two important considerations for counselors. First, most LGBTQ students are not at risk for major mental health issues, demonstrating resilience in the face of systemic and interpersonal discrimination (de Vries, Doreleijers, Steensma, & Cohen-Kettenis, 2011; Murdock & Bolch, 2005; Robinson & Espelage, 2011). Second, because of experiences of victimization and prejudice, an "unusually large percentage of LGBTQ-identified youth are at elevated risk" (Robinson & Espelage, 2011, p. 326) for mental health issues that affect all adolescents, such as depression, substance abuse, and suicide (Duncan, Hatzenbuehler, & Johnson, 2014; Robinson & Espelage, 2011; Teasdale & Bradley-Engen, 2010; Varjas et al., 2008). That is to say, just being LGBTQ does not put students at higher risk for mental health problems or indicate that they need counseling; rather, experiences of victimization and prejudice at home and school impact students' mental health.

Higher levels of LGBTQ-related victimization are associated with negative psychosocial adjustment, including lower self-esteem, higher rates of depression, and less overall life satisfaction (Kosciw et al., 2014; Russell et al., 2011; Toomey et al., 2013). Further, "The negative impact of specifically homophobic school victimization continues into the young adult years and affects quality of life and capacity to enjoy life" (Toomey et al., 2013, p. 77). Along with experiences at school, family reactions to LGBTQ youth impact mental health outcomes, with family acceptance associated with more positive outcomes and family rejection associated with more negative outcomes (Espelage, Aragon, Birkett, & Koenig, 2008; Ryan et al., 2009, 2010; Snapp, Watson, Russell, Diaz, & Ryan, 2015). Further, research has found that LGB youth are more likely to experience emotional and physical maltreatment by their parents, particularly their fathers, than their heterosexual peers (Corliss, Cochran, & Mays, 2002).

Research has found that LGBTQ youth are at higher risk for depression and suicide than their heterosexual and cisgender peers (Eisenberg & Resnick, 2006; Grossman & D'Augelli, 2007; Marshal et al., 2013; Teasdale & Bradley-Engen, 2010). Although most of the research does not disaggregate data for transgender youth, data from clinical adolescent populations and transgender adults find transgender youth to be at very high risk for suicide (Kenagy, 2005; Skagerberg, Parkinson, & Carmichael, 2013). The high rates of depression and suicide among LGBTQ youth are explained in large part by high rates of victimization, high social stress, lack of social support, and poor family relationships (Burton, Marshal, Chisolm, Sucato, & Friedman, 2013; Eisenberg & Resnick, 2006; Shields, Whitaker, Glassman, Franks, & Howard, 2012; Teasdale & Bradley-Engen, 2010). Research suggests that these higher rates of depression and suicide continue into early adulthood, although the risk for suicide does diminish somewhat (Marshal et al., 2013). It is important to note that sexual orientation accounts for only a very small portion, if any, of the disparity in suicidality; rather, the higher levels of stress and victimization at school and home contribute to these deleterious outcomes (Eisenberg & Resnick, 2006; Marshal et al., 2013; Mustanski & Liu, 2012; Shields et al., 2012; Teasdale & Bradley-Engen, 2010).

Questioning, bisexual, and transgender students may be at increased risk for negative mental health outcomes compared with their LG, heterosexual, and cisgender peers. Research has found that questioning students experience higher levels of victimization, depression, and drug use and have more thoughts of suicide than their LGB and heterosexual peers (Birkett, Espelage, and Koenig, 2009; Espelage et al., 2008; Poteat, Aragon, Espelage, & Koenig, 2009), and students who were confused about their sexual identity were more likely to report delinquency, substance use, depression, and suicidal ideation than LG and heterosexual students (Rose, Rodgers, & Small, 2006). Other research has found that bisexual students are at significantly elevated risk for suicide, experience lower levels of school belongingness, and report greater substance use than their LG and heterosexual peers (Marshal et al., 2008, 2013; Robinson & Espelage, 2011). Finally, research has found that almost half of transgender students have seriously considered suicide (Grossman & D'Augelli, 2007), and that the mental health difficulties experienced by transgender youth continue into adulthood, with transgender adults experiencing significantly high rates of psychological distress, depression, and anxiety compared with community norms (Bockting, Miner, Swinburne Romine, Hamilton & Coleman, 2013).

Diversity Among LGBTQ Students

RACIAL AND ETHNIC DIVERSITY

Racially and ethnically diverse LGBTQ students may have unique experiences as they develop their racial/ethnic identity alongside their sexual/gender identity, although these two processes seem to occur separately and concurrently (Jamil, Harper, Fernandez, & Adolescent Trials Network for HIV/AIDS Interventions, 2009) and may not cause additive stress for these students (Kertzner, Meyer, Frost, & Stirratt, 2009). Research suggests that the developmental and life experiences related to sexuality do not differ drastically for racially and ethnically diverse LGB students as compared with their White peers, but racial and ethnic identity and experiences may impact students' comfort in disclosing their sexual orientation to others (Rosario, Schrimshaw, & Hunter, 2004). Further, research suggests that for LGBQ African Americans and Asian Americans, internalized homophobia/internalized heterosexism has a significantly greater impact on mental health outcomes than does internalized racism (Szymanski & Gupta, 2009a, 2009b), highlighting the role that LGBTQ-related victimization has on mental health outcomes for all LGBTQ students. What counselors can take away from this is that "the identity development process is very personal and involves reflection and integration of many societal and cultural messages and concepts" (Jamil et al., 2009, p. 212), and students may benefit from support in integrating multiple identities.

HOMELESSNESS, FOSTER CARE, AND JUVENILE JUSTICE

Homelessness is a major problem for LGBTQ youth. In one study of LGB youth, Rosario, Schrimshaw, and Hunter (2012) found that almost half reported experiencing an episode of homelessness, either running away or being forced out of their homes. The National Coalition for the Homeless (2009a) reports that at least 20% of homeless youth identify as LGBTQ. Once homeless, LGBTQ youth report higher rates of victimization, including sexual violence, mental health issues, suicidality, and risky sexual behavior, than their non-LGBTQ homeless peers (Cochran, Stewart, Ginzler, & Cauce, 2002; National Coalition for the Homeless, 2009a). Similarly, in reviewing the literature on LGB youth and foster care, Mitchell, Panzarello, Grynkiewicz, and Galupo (2015) report that LGB youth experience higher rates of parental abuse than their heterosexual and cisgender peers, making them more likely to become homeless or be placed in foster care; experience high rates of abuse while in foster care, likely because of their sexual orientation; and have poorer economic and psychological outcomes during the transition to adulthood. The same experiences that put LGBT youth at risk for homelessness and placement in foster care put them at risk for involvement in the juvenile justice system, with survival crimes such as robbery and prostitution being the most common reason LGBT youth become involved in the justice system (Feinstein, Greenblatt, Hass, Kohn, & Rana, 2001). The juvenile justice system lacks experienced professionals and appropriate supports to adequately work with LGBT youth, and youth may be sentenced to more restrictive facilities than their crimes warrant due to a lack of appropriate LGBT-sensitive programs (more restrictive facilities that segregate or isolate LGBT youth from the general population due to safety concerns; Feinstein et al., 2001).

DISABILITY AND SPECIAL EDUCATION

There are certainly LGBTQ students who have disabilities and receive special education services at school, but research on this population has been sparse. In a metasynthesis of research on LGBT youth with disabilities, Duke (2011) reviewed 13 studies and found that these students

- experience discrimination based on sexuality, gender identity, and disability across settings;
- often lack LGBT-inclusive curriculum in special education and supported living programs;
- have few opportunities to develop positive LGBT identities and explore relationships; and
- receive little or no sex education, which may explain why some LGBT youth with disabilities, and especially gay and bisexual young men with intellectual disabilities, are at increased risk for engaging in unsafe sex and contracting HIV/AIDS.

Youth experiencing gender dysphoria may be at elevated risk for autism spectrum disorder, with one study finding that children and adolescents referred to a clinic for gender dysphoria were 10 times more likely than the general population to meet criteria for autism spectrum disorder (de Vries, Noens, Cohen-Kettenis, van Berckelaer-Onnes, & Doreleijers, 2010). There is some speculation that there may be both biological considerations for this prevalence, such as testosterone levels in utero (de Vries et al., 2010; Jones et al., 2012), and behavioral considerations, with several specific case examples highlighting how characteristics of autism such as feelings of differentness, nonnormative sexual interests and behaviors, and preferences for certain sensory input can be hard to distinguish from aspects of gender dysphoria (de Vries et al., 2010). However, more research is necessary to understand this connection, as well as the experiences of all LGBTQ students with disabilities. The most important idea to take away from the research is that "innovative, inclusive, and LGBT-friendly special education and supported living programs can, and do, empower LGBT youth with disabilities to develop positive queer identities ... and actively participate in LGBT communities" (Duke, 2011, p. 37).

COUNSELING APPROACHES

LGBTQ students may enter counseling for a number of reasons. They may need counseling for issues directly related to their LGBTQ identity, such as confusion or identity-related distress; they may need counseling because of problems that are peripherally related to or exacerbated by their LGBTQ identity, such as victimization or rejection; or they may need counseling for issues that are completely unrelated to their LGBTQ identity, such as anger management or social skills (Ryan, 2001). What is most important is that counselors do not automatically assume that students' issues are related to an LGBTQ identity, while at the same time recognizing that issues like depression, anxiety, substance use, and school disengagement might be related to experiences of discrimination and victimization. For example, consider a female eighth-grade student who was referred to the counselor by her teacher, who had found her crying in the bathroom after school the previous afternoon. The student spoke openly to the counselor about her distress with her inability to manage her anger with her friends and described a situation that had occurred the day before at lunch. She also expressed concern about being able to manage her anger on an upcoming class trip. The student then went on to talk about how she felt about not being open about being gay at school, but that her family knew and were very supportive. A bit confused by the transition of topics, the counselor clarified by saying, "I'm a bit confused. . . . Do you think that your anger and your not being open at school are related?" The student thought about this for a minute and then responded, "I don't know," to which the counselor said, "Let's spend some time exploring your anger and talking about the class trip, and maybe by talking about it more, we'll understand better whether or not it's related to not being open with your classmates about your sexuality."

The counseling approaches addressed in this chapter relate to students who are experiencing distress that is related to their LGBTQ identity or exacerbated by their identity. However, counselors are encouraged to use general LGBTQ-affirmative strategies with all students in counseling because students will not always disclose an LGBTQ identity early on, and some students may not even be aware of these types of feelings until later in the counseling process. Although there are few evidence-based counseling strategies designed specifically for LGBTQ youth, effective and affirmative counseling approaches can be developed by drawing from the general literature base on LGBTQ youth and research on counseling with LGBTQ adults.

A Note About Medical Treatment of Transgender Students

In addition to counseling support, transgender students may seek medical treatment to change their external sex characteristics to align with their gender identity. Medical treatment may include puberty-blocking hormones that allow adolescents more time to explore their gender identity or gender dysphoria without the increased discomfort of the physical changes during puberty before taking irreversible medical action; hormone therapy to masculinize or feminize the body; or sex reassignment surgery, which includes procedures such as breast removal or corrective surgery on the genitals (de Vries & Cohen-Kettenis, 2012; Minter, 2012). Counselors are encouraged to seek more information about medical treatments that are specific to the individual transgender student being seen in counseling. This can be accomplished via Internet searches, research in medical texts or journals, and seeking consent to speak directly with the student's medical providers.

Ethical Considerations

All mental health providers in schools are guided by professional codes of ethics that highlight the need to respect the rights and dignity of all students. Some professional organizations, like the American Psychological Association and the National Association of School Psychologists (NASP), have taken a more specific and stronger stand related to the ethical and equitable treatment of LGBTQ students (American Psychological Association & NASP, 2014; NASP, 2010, 2011, 2014). In a joint resolution by the American Psychological Association and the NASP (2014), same-sex romantic and sexual attractions are considered "normal and positive variations of human sexuality" (p. 6), and diverse gender expressions and identities are considered "normal and positive variations of the human experience" (p. 6). Based on the NASP's *Principles for Professional Ethics* (2010), Fisher (2014) stated: "Counselors who lack knowledge about LGBTQ issues, feel unprepared to work with LGBTQ students, or have personal beliefs that impact their ability to provide affirmative services for LGBTQ students must seek information, training, supervision, and counseling" (p. 193) in order to ensure their competency in working with this population. That is to say, counselors cannot simply refer LGBTQ clients if they feel unable or unprepared to work with them; rather, they must take active steps to become able and prepared.

MAINTAINING CONFIDENTIALITY

Confidentiality may be one of the more challenging issues in counseling LGBTQ students. Legal and ethical guidelines require counselors to ensure all materials and records are kept confidential and secure. Because parents have access to records used to make educational decisions, and teachers and other school personnel have access to students' files, counselors should be cautious about written documentation that includes information about a student's sexual or gender identity. State laws vary about the age at which minors can seek counseling and hold privilege, and it is possible that parents can demand information about what has been discussed in counseling sessions. It is critical that counselors take the steps necessary, within the confines of the law, to protect students' privacy and not "out" students to their parents. For example, a ninth-grade male student had been talking about suicide at home and was hospitalized during a school break.

The student's mother asked the counselor to talk with him, and during that conversation, the student revealed that he thought he might be gay. He had not told his mother, and he was generally upset that she was "always on him about everything." The student denied any current suicidal ideation and agreed to continue to talk with the counselor. The mother called the counselor after the session to find out her impressions of the student. The counselor said, "He seems to be experiencing a lot of stress right now, and he seems to be trying to figure out who he is and how he fits into his new school. This is pretty typical for teenagers. They feel uncertain about who they are and often struggle with different aspects of identity and fitting in. Although his stress is clearly greater than what we typically see, I am confident that as he and I talk more, we'll develop some different strategies he can use to cope when he's feeling upset or stressed."

Conversion Therapy

Efforts to change sexual orientation and gender identity fall within what is called *conversion therapy* or *reparative therapy*. This type of therapy is recognized as unethical at best and harmful at worst by many major professional organizations, including the American Academy of Pediatrics, the American Psychological Association, the National Education Association, and the NASP (Just the Facts Coalition, 2008), and counselors should not engage in any practices to change students' sexual or gender identity. In fact, several states have enacted legislation banning conversion therapy for minors, and similar legislation is pending in other states (http://www.hrc.org/resources/the-lies-and-dangers-of-reparative-therapy).

Guidelines for Counseling

There is an absence of counseling interventions designed specifically for LGBTQ individuals (Haas et al., 2010), but researchers and clinicians with expertise working with LGBTQ youth have developed suggestions for mental health professionals to provide ethical and affirmative treatment. Adelson and the American Academy of Child and Adolescent Psychiatry (2012) provide the following list of guidelines to support the use of affirmative counseling for LGBTQ students:

- Maintain confidentiality within the confines of the law, as it is essential to allow LGBT youth to explore their identities within a safe space.
- Ask about victimization across settings that place LGBT youth at increased risk for mental health problems.
- Actively work to support healthy psychosexual development for LGBT youth.
- Eschew efforts to change sexual or gender identity.
- Help raise awareness about the needs of LGBT youth across school, community, and family contexts, being careful not to disclose private information about youth.
- Develop a list of supportive community and Internet resources for LGBT youth.

LGBTQ-Affirmative Counseling

Drawing from the literature on gay-affirmative counseling, LGBTQ-affirmative counseling is more of an approach to counseling and mindset about LGBTQ individuals in the larger sociopolitical context than it is a series of techniques or strategies (Johnson, 2012). In a review of literature on gay-affirmative counseling, Harrison (2000) highlights the following key features and considerations: Affirmative counseling requires that counselors actively challenge pathological views of LGB sexuality, including internalized homophobia, and recognize diverse sexual identities as normal and natural; take active steps to increase their self-awareness and knowledge about LGB issues, including experiences of oppression and discrimination; and integrate this information into their counseling, drawing on a range of therapeutic interventions. In considering gay-affirmative counseling for LGB youth, Crisp and McCave (2007) found it to be highly applicable in that it affirms and empowers youth; provides that all self-identities are equally valued; supports youth in recognizing the impact of heterosexism and homophobia on their lives and conceptualizes their presenting problems within this context; and is appropriate for use within different counseling contexts, including schools. Although not specific to transgender and gender-diverse students, the same concepts can be easily applied in recognizing diverse gender identities as normal and natural variations. Within this framework, counselors could challenge transphobia and help students recognize systemic and internalized transphobia.

At a basic level, counseling will be more LGBTQ-affirmative when counselors demonstrate warmth, caring, respect, and trustworthiness, and students feel accepted and validated (Israel, Gorcheva, Burnes, & Walther, 2008; Malley & Tasker, 2007). Counselors can accomplish this, in part, by actively listening to students, asking questions in a nonjudgmental manner, affirming students' experiences, being knowledgeable about LGBTQ issues, and focusing on sexual orientation and gender identity only when it directly relates to students' concerns (Holman & Goldberg, 2006; Israel et al., 2008; Malley & Tasker, 2007). This will help build a strong therapeutic relationship, which provides the basis for students to talk about difficult issues (Israel, Gorcheva, Walther, Sulzner, & Cohen, 2008). Counselors can also ensure that their offices have LGBTQ-affirming stickers, pamphlets, and student resources as a physical demonstration of their openness (Heck, Flentje, & Cochran, 2012; Pope, Bunch, Szymanski, & Rankins, 2004); this should include transgender-specific items (Holman & Goldberg, 2006).

Transgender-Specific Affirmative Counseling

Holman and Goldberg (2006), who are advanced practitioners with extensive experience working with gender-diverse and transgender adolescents, offer relevant and specific strategies for less experienced counselors. First, they recommend that counselors incorporate a question about gender into the intake process, such as "Many people struggle with gender. Is this an issue for you?"

(p. 97). If a student responds affirmatively or with uncertainty to this question, counselors can begin to determine how comfortable the student is with articulating his or her feelings and experiences related to gender diversity or transgenderism. It is important for counselors to recognize that despite increased public awareness about transgenderism, adolescents may need help to understand different terms and concepts related to transgender identity, as well as support in naming and expressing their thoughts and feelings. Throughout sessions, counselors can

- explore the nature of gender experiences (e.g., what the student feels concerned about, when the feelings began, how constant or variable feeling are, things that make the feelings better or worse, and the intensity of the feelings);
- develop an understanding of how gender diversity is impacting the student's life (e.g., assessing the student's overall well-being, determining how it is affecting peer and family relationships and school, identifying the coping strategies the student is using, and assessing the student's awareness of community resources and other sources of support);
- gain a deep understanding of the student's feelings about transgenderism (e.g., what is the student's belief structure about transgenderism; how does the student feel about the possibility of being transgender; how are the student's feelings influenced by family, religion, movies, society, etc.); and
- find out what other psychosocial or physical concerns might be contributing to the student's distress and how these concerns interact with gender identity.

Holman and Goldberg's (2006) suggestions for transgender adolescents are also highly applicable to LGBQ students. In an intake session, counselors might also include a question such as, "Some students identify as gay, lesbian, or bisexual, and other students feel uncertain or confused about their sexuality. Do any of these apply to you?" Similarly, LGB students may need support to name or articulate their feelings and experiences; may need to explore different aspects and options related to sexuality to develop greater self-understanding; and may benefit greatly from discussions focused on students' belief structures around sexuality, what has influenced those beliefs, and how their sexuality is impacting them at school and home.

Supporting Identity Development and Disclosure

The primary goal in supporting LGBTQ students' identity development is to help them discover "whatever self-identification they feel fits them" (Hunter, 2007, p. 131). This requires that counselors meet students exactly where they are in the developmental process, solicit the terms that students are comfortable using to describe themselves, and demonstrate absolute openness for what students are sharing (Hunter, 2007). Using an LGBTQ-affirmative counseling approach requires that counselors do not invest in any particular identity outcome for students; rather, they follow students' leads (Lebolt, 1999). For example, in a counseling session, an eighth-grade male student was talking about a crush he had on another student in his class in a very gender-neutral manner, using "they" instead of "he" or "she." The student indicated that he wanted to tell the counselor who the person was, but he was struggling to say the name aloud; in fact, he was physically covering his mouth with his hand each time he attempted to say the name. The counselor assured the student that he could share the name whenever he felt comfortable doing so, but the student insisted that he wanted the counselor to know. Ultimately, the student decided to write the name on a piece of paper and give it to the counselor to read. Clearly, this student was in an early stage of sexual identity development, and in further conversations with the counselor, it became clear that he did not yet identify with any sexual identity label. The content of the counseling sessions focused on the student's feelings, and he expressed both excitement and anxiety about the possibility of the other student finding out he had a crush on him. In this case, it was important that the counselor not rush the student to self-identify but instead follow his lead as he explored his feelings. As the student's comfort level increased a bit, the counselor might provide some psychoeducation about sexual identity, saying something like, "Sometimes, when people aren't sure about their sexuality, they use the word 'questioning.' I wonder how you might relate to this word." As students begin to self-identify as LGBTQ, counselors can help them explore how they view their identity, consider positive and negative images and messages they might have about their identity, and explore how this new understanding of self integrates with other aspects of their identity (Hunter, 2007). Eventually students may want to disclose their identity and seek out more contact with the LGBTQ community (Hunter, 2007).

Holman and Goldberg (2006) suggest that "youth who do not fit the dominant gender norms must still find a way to consciously articulate their difference and find language to express their identity" (p. 103). In the early states of identity development, counselors can help students explore their gender identity without any pressure to label their identity, disclose to others, or make decisions about lifestyle changes or sex reassignment (Holman & Goldberg, 2006). This exploration can be done through any medium that appeals to the student, such as talking, artwork, or poetry. With students who are generally mentally healthy and seem ready for greater exploration, counselors can "actively encourage experimentation with fluidity of gender identification and expression" (p. 104) in ways that feel comfortable to the student. This might include watching a movie that portrays gender diversity and discussing the student's thoughts and feelings, trying out different names and pronouns, experimenting with clothing and makeup, or interacting with the counselor as the student's imagined self. The focus of this is to help the student become more aware of "what feels right" (p. 104) and to develop greater self-understanding. For students who already identify as transgender, Holman and Goldberg (2006) suggest that the primary goal of counseling should be self-acceptance, and counseling can help students "reconcile discrepancies between identity and daily life" (p. 104) by exploring the range of possibilities for lifestyle changes, such as participating in transgender community activities; changing one's name or gender pronouns; and changing clothing, hairstyle, and so forth to be more congruent with gender identity. In this stage of identity development, transgender students may also decide to disclose their gender identity if they have not already done so.

Hunter (2007) reviews the literature on disclosure of LGBTQ status and provides concrete strategies that counselors can use to support students. It is important to remember that disclosure is a very personal decision that can only be made by students themselves. For students considering disclosure, it can be useful for counselors to help them consider the risks and benefits and to identify supportive resources should the disclosure go poorly. Counselors can also help students develop a disclosure statement that is "proud, affirmative, and direct" (Hunter, 2007, p. 145), leaving little room for equivocation. This script might look different depending on students' unique situations, and the counselor can use role play to ensure that students are comfortable with what they want to say. It can be helpful for the counselor to provide psychoeducation about different reactions people might have to a student's disclosure, including that it might take some people more time to be accepting and supportive (Mosher, 2001).

LGBTQ-Affirmative Cognitive-Behavioral Therapy

Adopting the general LGBTQ-affirmative counseling approach, counselors can integrate cognitive-behavioral therapy (CBT) techniques to help students develop "effective coping techniques, satisfying social support networks, and increased frequencies of positive events" (Safren, Hollander, Hart, & Heimberg, 2001, p. 220). This process begins by affirming the student's identity and explicitly discussing and validating his or her experiences of discrimination (Craig, Austin, & Alessi, 2013). Counselors can help the student make a distinction between problems that are caused primarily by the environment, such as parental rejection, and problems that stem from unhelpful thoughts that may not be accurate, such as a belief that "I'll never be happy" (Craig et al., 2013). In the case of the former, a counselor can help the student develop skills for coping with situations that may not be under the student's control and develop a helpful cognitive response, such as "I don't have control over where I live now, but I will in a year when I turn 18," or "I have dealt with worse things in the past, and I can get through this too" (Craig et al., 2013). In the case of the latter, counselors can use cognitive restructuring techniques to address unhelpful or distorted thoughts or negative core beliefs about the student, his or her value as a person, and his or her possible future (Craig et al., 2013; Safren et al., 2001).

CBT techniques may be useful to address internalized homophobia and transphobia (Safren et al., 2001), which can be thought of as internal representations of negative stereotypes and stigma associated with LGBTQ people and may involve feelings of shame and self-devaluing beliefs (Purcell, Campos, & Perilla, 1996; Russell & Bohan, 2007). In a collaborative, rather than a challenging, manner, so that students feel supported and safe, counselors can help students learn to identify their core beliefs and begin to question them in light of greater understanding about themselves and the world around them (Craig et al., 2013). Counselors can help educate students about how society's messages are impacting them and use students' strengths to help restructure and reframe some of their negative beliefs, such as "I value my uniqueness and don't want to be just like everyone else" (Craig et al., 2013; Fassinger, 2000).

Suicide Prevention and Intervention

Suicidality can include expressing suicidal thoughts, making threats of harming oneself, making suicidal gestures, and making active suicide attempts (Schwartz & Rogers, 2004). Recognizing that LGBTQ students are at increased risk for suicide, counselors must be familiar with the warning signs that students might exhibit (Robinson et al., 2013). According to Rudd and colleagues (2006), immediate actions should be taken if students threaten to harm or kill themselves; seek access to a means of killing themselves, such as pills or weapons; or express thoughts of death, dying, or suicide in their conversations or written expression. Further warning signs include expressing feelings of hopelessness, anger, or agitation; expressing thoughts of life having no meaning or feeling trapped; increasing engagement in risky behaviors; withdrawing from family and friends; and sudden changes in mood (Rudd et al., 2006). In addition, isolation increases suicide risk (Rutter & Behrendt, 2004), which may be particularly relevant for LGBTQ students who experience peer and family rejection. Counselors should not avoid raising the issue of suicide with students, because talking about it does not increase risk; in initiating these conversations, counselors can tell students that their goal in talking about suicide is to better understand them so they can do more to help them to feel better (Schwartz & Rogers, 2004). Counselors should also attend to warning signs even if students deny suicidal ideation (Rudd, 2008).

In talking with students who are expressing suicidal ideation, counselors can ask questions to determine students' thoughts about dying and suicide; their level of intent to commit suicide; whether or not they have a plan for how they will commit suicide; and their access to a means to commit suicide (Schwartz & Rogers, 2004). Schwartz and Rogers (2004) specify how counselors can conceptualize students' thoughts, behaviors, and plans to determine their overall risk of suicide:

- Students who express thoughts of suicide but have no intent or plan to act on the thoughts and do not have a history of suicide attempts are considered at low risk.
- Students who have thoughts of suicide and intent to commit suicide but have no specific plan and express motivation to feel better are considered at medium risk.

- Students who express suicidal thoughts and have a plans and means to carry out the plan are considered at high risk.
- Students who express suicidal ideation and intent, have a well-thought-out plan and means to carry it out, express intense hopelessness about the future, lack social support, and have a history of suicide attempts are considered at very high risk.

For students deemed to be at high or very high risk, immediate action must be taken by calling 911 or a local mental health assessment team if such resources are available. These students should not be left alone until they are receiving emergency treatment. For students deemed at low or medium risk, counselors can help them develop a safety plan. This plan should include a statement about when the plan should be accessed, such as when the student is feeling trapped or thinking about suicide; steps for managing the feelings, such as calling an identified supportive adult or the Trevor Lifeline (866-488-7386), which is dedicated to preventing suicide among LGBTQ youth; and steps to take if the feelings reach a crisis level, such as calling 911 or going to the emergency room (Rudd, 2008). Family involvement is important in suicide safety plans (Rudd, 2008). If students are not out to family members, suicidality and safety planning can still be addressed without revealing students' sexual or gender identity.

BEYOND THE COUNSELING OFFICE: IMPROVING SCHOOL CLIMATE

Given what is known about the potentially devastating impact of ongoing victimization and discrimination for LGBTQ students, improving school climate is critical to ensure more positive academic and mental health outcomes (Birkett et al., 2009; Murdock & Bolch, 2005) and to guarantee that LGBTQ students "have equal opportunities to participate in and benefit from educational and mental health services within school" (NASP, 2011, p. 1). Research has found that four important indicators of school climate for LGBTQ students are inclusive antibullying policies; the presence of a GSA or similar club on campus; supportive teachers and other school staff; and LGBTQ-inclusive curriculum (Kosciw et al., 2014).

Inclusive Antibullying Policies

Inclusive antibullying policies are those that specifically enumerate actual or perceived sexual orientation and gender identity/gender expression as protected groups of students. In schools with inclusive policies, LGBT students heard fewer homophobic and transphobic remarks at school, saw school staff intervening more often when these types of remarks were made, and had higher self-esteem

(Kosciw et al., 2013; Kosciw et al., 2014). In schools without inclusive policies, counselors can convene a group of stakeholders to discuss how to make existing policies more inclusive for all students (Espelage & Rao, 2013). Once policies are in place, it is important that everyone be informed about them, including students, parents, teachers, administrators, and other school staff, and that all school personnel and students receive training on "concrete and realistic strategies to both prevent and respond to anti-LGBTQ bullying and harassment" (Espelage & Rao, 2013, p. 150).

Gay-Straight Alliances

In schools with a GSA or similar club on campus, LGBT students experienced lower levels of LGBTQ-victimization, heard fewer homophobic and transphobic remarks, saw school staff intervening more often when these types of remarks were made, felt safer on campus, experienced greater school connectedness, and had higher self-esteem (Kosciw et al., 2014). Under the Equal Access Act of 1984, schools that allow any noncurricular student group to meet on campus must allow a GSA or similar club to meet as well (Orr & Komosa-Hawkins, 2013), but counselors may need to help educate school administrators about LGBTQ students' rights and help to find a supportive adult adviser for the club.

Supportive School Staff

Supportive teachers and other school staff make a difference for LGBTQ students. Kosciw et al. (2014) found that almost all LGBT students could identify at least one supportive adult at school, but less than two thirds could identify at least six supportive staff members, and in this case, quantity does matter. LGBT students who identify a high number of supportive staff felt safer at school, had better school attendance, had higher grades, felt greater school connectedness, and reported higher self-esteem (Kosciw et al., 2013; Kosciw et al., 2014). Many school professionals receive inadequate training about LGBTQ students and issues in their preparation programs and would benefit from in-service training that focuses the following (Whitman, 2013):

- knowledge about appropriate language and terminology;
- information about identity development;
- information about current issues impacting LGBTQ people;
- awareness, including biases, misconceptions, and greater understanding of personal sexual and gender identity development; and
- skills, including how to provide support for LGBTQ students, how to respond to harassment and bullying in support of school policies, and how to advocate for LGBTQ students.

Inclusive Curriculum

In schools with curriculum that includes positive representations of LGBT individuals, LGBT students heard fewer homophobic and transphobic remarks at school, felt safer at school, and had better attendance and greater school connectedness (Kosciw et al., 2014). Unfortunately, less than 20% of LGBT students reported this type of inclusive curriculum (Kosciw et al., 2014). According to Greytak and Kosciw (2013), "Inclusive curriculum validates the existence of an often invisible population, reinforcing the value of LGBTQ individuals themselves and sending a strong message to LGBTQ students about their worth" (p. 157). LGBTQ people and issues can be included in almost any subject. For example, English teachers can include books written by LGBTQ authors or that contain LGBTQ characters; science teachers can engage students in discussions about biological diversity and how ideas like "sex" are more complicated than simple binary categories; and history and social studies teachers can examine civil rights by having students work on topics such as current political issues affecting LGBTQ people or coverage of minority groups in the media (Fisher & Kennedy, 2012). Sex education is another important area in which to ensure inclusion of LGBTQ people and issues; truly inclusive sex education would integrate the entire range of sexual orientations and gender identities throughout the curriculum rather than relegating it to a special topic of discussion (Greytak & Kosciw, 2013).

Where to Begin

Fisher and Kennedy (2012) suggest that a good place to start in improving school climate and school safety for LGBTQ students is with a needs assessment, which might include surveys of students, teachers, and other key stakeholders to find out about LGBTQ-related victimization and perceptions of school climate and focus groups with key stakeholders (Draughn, Elkins, & Roy, 2002). Draughn and colleagues (2002) suggest that an informal needs assessment is also highly relevant and should determine things like the existence of inclusive school policies; expectations around respect for LGBTQ students communicated across campus; instances of homophobic/transphobic bullying or harassment that have been reported and what actions were taken in those instances; and what institutional barriers exist to creating safe climates for LGBTQ students. Fisher and Kennedy (2012) further suggest that an informal needs assessment should look for a GSA on campus; the inclusiveness of school curriculum; whether or not LGBTQ individuals are visually represented on bulletin boards and in other materials available at school; and how LGBTQ students are encouraged to seek help when they experience harassment and bullying.

RESOURCES

Advocates for Youth

www.advocatesforyouth.org or www.youthresource.org

Youth Resource is the LGBT component of Advocates for Youth, providing education, advocacy, and activism. The website is appropriate for LGBT youth, families of LGBT youth, and professionals working with LGBT youth. The website includes resources such as lesson plans, curricula, and training programs.

Gay, Lesbian, and Straight Education Network

http://www.glsen.org/

The Gay, Lesbian, and Straight Education Network is a national organization focused on creating safe and supportive schools for all youth. This organization supports extensive research, including its survey of LGBTQ students in schools. The website provides information for students, educators, and other stakeholders.

Gender Spectrum

https://www.genderspectrum.org/

Gender Spectrum provides information on important gender topics and issues, including training materials, how-to guides, and information on current research. Specific topics covered include parenting and family; teens; education; medical care; mental health; legal rights; social services; and faith.

Human Rights Campaign—Transgender Visibility Guide

http://www.hrc.org/resources/entry/transgender-visibility-guide

The Transgender Visibility Guide is a downloadable pamphlet that can be used by youth, families, and professionals to help guide youth through the process of gender identity expression. The pamphlet offers advice on finding a community of support, disclosure plans, transitioning, and communication strategies for conversations with spouses, friends, parents, and families. The pamphlet also helps to dispel myths about gender identity issues. Additionally, the Human Rights Campaign's main website (www.hrc.org) contains a variety of resources for LGBTQ youth, including research reports, legislative updates, and the "Welcoming Schools" curriculum, focused on addressing family diversity and gender stereotypes for students in kindergarten through fifth grade.

Parents, Families, Friends, and Allies United with LGBTQ (PFLAG)

http://community.pflag.org/

PFLAG is an organization that unites LGBTQ groups and allies to educate and advocate for equality and acceptance. PFLAG has numerous state chapters to help support LGBTQ persons, families, and friends.

Safe Schools Coalition

http://www.safeschoolscoalition.org/

Safe Schools Coalition is an international organization committed to creating safe schools for LGBT students. The website delineates resources by topic, type, and location and by specific people who utilize the resources, such as counselors, administrators, and families. Handouts, brochures, and posters are available to use within school settings.

TransYouth Family Allies

http://www.imatyfa.org/

TransYouth Family Allies is a website that provides gender-specific information and support for parents, youth, educators, and healthcare practitioners. Resources are provided in both English and Spanish.

6

Counseling Students Who Are Pregnant or Parenting

WITH HAYLEA DRYSDALE ■

OVERVIEW

Teen pregnancy rates in the United States have declined steadily over the past three decades, and in 2013, approximately 2.6% of girls aged 15 to 19 had a baby (Hamilton, Martin, Osterman, & Curtin, 2014). However, the overall number of teenagers continues to grow, and counselors must be prepared to effectively serve pregnant and parenting teens. Most teens do not intend to get pregnant, with research finding that more than 80% of pregnancies to young women under the age of 19 years were unintended (Finer & Zolna, 2014). From an economic perspective, teen pregnancy costs the United States approximately $9.4 billion in public health care, assistance programs, early childhood day care and education, and lost tax revenue (National Campaign to Prevent Teen and Unplanned Pregnancies, 2013). There are also negative impacts on children born to teen parents, such as premature birth and low birth weights, which are associated with higher rates of infant mortality and developmental delays (National Campaign to Prevent Teen Pregnancy, 2002). Children of teen mothers are more likely to live in poverty, experience abuse, have academic difficulties, and drop out of school (Devereux, Weigel, Ballard-Reisch, Leigh, & Cahooh, 2009; Klein & Committee on Adolescence, 2005). Further, children of teen parents are more likely to become teen parents themselves, continuing the cycle of teen pregnancy through generations (Meade, Kershaw, & Ickovics, 2008).

Given the economic and social realities of teen pregnancy, prevention should be a top priority, and characteristics of effective prevention and sex education programs are discussed at the end of this chapter. But for those teens who do become pregnant, counseling interventions that help build students' internal strengths; improve problems-solving skills; increase access to social support; promote high school completion and career planning; and develop effective parenting skills are critical to improve outcomes for teens and their children and to stop the cycle of teen pregnancy and poverty (Schuyler Center for Analysis and Advocacy, 2008). Although much of the research on teen pregnancy documents negative outcomes and the research on counseling focuses primarily on pregnancy prevention, counselors can promote more positive outcomes by adopting a collaborative and multifaceted counseling approach that focuses on the student's strengths and individual resources.

BASIC CONSIDERATIONS

The negative consequences of teen pregnancy are well documented. In the United States, teenage pregnancy is viewed as problematic, often without considering the reasons that teens become pregnant, the impact that pregnancy has on teens' development, and the possibility that teens can be effective parents. This is not to say that teen pregnancy is a positive phenomenon; rather, once a teen is pregnant, rebuking or shaming her only serves to add further to the difficulties of being a teen parent. Instead, it is important for counselors to understand the context of teen pregnancy so that they can approach counseling with an empathic and nonjudgmental stance (Luttrell, 2003).

Consequences of Teen Pregnancy

Teen girls who have a child are more likely than their nonparenting peers to have educational, behavioral, and health problems; to drop out of high school; and to be unemployed (Hoffman & Maynard, 2008). Teen mothers often experience emotional distress because their pregnancy is considered a stressful event rather than a planned and expected milestone in their lives (Milan et al., 2004). Further, due to a heightened risk of emotional distress, teen mothers are more likely to have difficulty recovering from childbirth and often lack support at home (Milan et al., 2004). Beyond the demanding reality of becoming a parent, these students face educational barriers, such as strict attendance policies, assignment deadlines, and pressure related to high-stakes testing, all of which impact their educational attainment (SmithBattle, Freed, & McLaughlin, 2015). Only about half of teen mothers obtain a high school diploma by the age of 22, compared with 89% of their nonparenting peers, and about a third of teen mothers will not complete high school or a high school equivalency program (Perper, Peterson, & Manlove, 2010). Contributing to this, teen parents are more likely to experience unstable home environments (Granger & Cryton, 1999), and without support to complete high school, any future aspirations that depend on education become less achievable (Barr, Simons, Gordon Simons, Gibbons, & Gerrard, 2013). Teen mothers are more likely to be dependent on financial assistance programs and to be poorer as adults, which is likely a result of failure to complete high school (Hoffman & Maynard, 2008).

Contributing to the aforementioned difficulties, teen mothers are at significantly increased risk for postpartum depression, with research reporting that up to 47% experience postpartum depression during the first year of their child's life (Logsdon, Birkimer, Simpson, & Looney, 2003). In addition to the normal symptoms of depression, mothers with postpartum depression can also experience difficulty sleeping when the baby sleeps, feeling numb or disconnected from the baby, having negative thoughts about the baby, worrying that they could hurt the baby, and feeling guilty about not being good parents (Center for Disease Control [CDC], 2015). Teen mothers likely experience increased risk for postpartum depression due to other risk factors, such as having unplanned pregnancies; lack of support from fathers of babies; feelings of social isolation and decreased social support; a change in weight and body shape; and a low sense of self-efficacy in parenting (Birkeland, Thompson, & Phares, 2005; Reid & Meadows-Oliver, 2007). Other factors that may contribute to symptoms of depression include low socioeconomic status (SES) and low educational attainment (Reid & Meadows-Oliver, 2007). It is important to note that a significant association exists between a perceived sense of social support and the likelihood of depressive symptoms in teen mothers, with greater social support related to having fewer depressive symptoms (Reid & Meadows-Oliver, 2007). Further, research has found that staying in school increases teen mothers' sense of social support and may improve self-efficacy and decrease feelings of isolation (Reid & Meadows-Oliver, 2007).

Factors Influencing Teen Pregnancy

SOCIOCULTURAL FACTORS

Teenagers who become pregnant come from diverse cultural backgrounds, and their experience with becoming and being pregnant will vary depending on their individual contexts. Research shows that despite declines in national teenage pregnancy rates, rates for minority youth have remained relatively constant, especially for those living in low-SES communities (Barr et al., 2013). Barr and colleagues (2013) propose the social prototype model as one way to explain this phenomenon. A social prototype can be thought of as a blueprint, where different groups of people view life events based on internalized frameworks that have been created through observations and experiences, both positive and negative.

For some minority students in lower-SES areas, teenage pregnancy may have provided women in their community with a positive experience, such as increased support from community members, access to resources, and an increased sense of self-worth (Barr et al., 2013). On the other hand, in higher-SES and traditionally White communities, the social prototype of teen pregnancy has been associated with high school dropout and a reduced likelihood of obtaining higher-paying jobs (Barr et al., 2013). In further support of this idea of social prototypes, McKay and Barrett (2010) posit that in some communities the experience of becoming pregnant while being a teenager may be met with a more positive reaction, consisting of understanding, welcoming the pregnancy, and increased social support, while in other communities, students may be met with disapproving reactions. This construct can be applied to teen fathers as well, in that males from low-SES communities may perceive higher education and higher-paying careers as inaccessible and may view becoming a father as a second chance at achieving success (Amato et al., 2008; Edin, Tach, & Mincy, 2009).

The research also indicates that students are more likely to become pregnant if they have a close family member who was a teen parent, and this risk grows exponentially if a teen girl's mother and sister both experienced teen pregnancy (East, Reyes, & Horn, 2007). It may be that growing up in a family that has already had a teen parent or currently has a teen parent influences a family's social prototype to make this experience more typical or more expected than it would be in other families.

Understanding students' social prototypes is critical for establishing a good working relationship in counseling because this will help counselors remain non-judgmental and can guide interventions. It should also be noted that it is never safe to assume that this blueprint is the same for all students from minority or low-SES backgrounds, and certainly students' perspectives may change after having their child. Rather, counselors are strongly encouraged to seek to understand what becoming or being pregnant means to individual students, the lens through which they view this experience, and how it shapes their outlook moving forward.

Development

Adolescence is a time of major developmental changes, and successfully working through the developmental tasks of adolescence results in more fulfilling adult lives (Trad, 1994). Pregnant teens must go from being a teenager to being a parent in the matter of months, and the developmental hurdles of adolescence are infinitely more difficult to manage while being pregnant or parenting (Trad, 1999). There are multiple interconnected areas of development to consider when thinking about teen pregnancy. For most adolescents, *identity development* occurs as a series of gradual and cumulative changes in which adolescents have the time to organize their thoughts; assess their own behavior; think about friendships; and explore their hobbies, interests, and talents (Moriarty, Sadler, & Reynolds, 2013). Pregnant teens have far less time to explore their own identities before they must embrace the identity of "mother." Related to this is *physical development*, as physical maturation takes a secondary role as the body prepares for gestation (Trad, 1999). Teen mothers' bodies change incredibly quickly during pregnancy, and because adolescence is a time when all teens have a heightened awareness of their body image, these physical changes may impact pregnant teens' feelings about their bodies and their ability to engage in typical teen activities (Maputle, 2006). *Cognitive development*, in which adolescents increase their capacity to use reason and logic in their decision-making skills, occurs throughout the teenage and early adult years, but for teen parents, there is increased pressure to be able to use higher-order cognitive skills in the transition to parenthood (Pietrowski, 2006).

Psychological development, in which there is growth in emotionality and personality, becomes much more complicated when one is pregnant (Woodward, Fergusson, & Horwood, 2004). Pregnancy can bring on feelings of anxiety for healthy adult women, and these feelings will likely be magnified for pregnant teenagers, overwhelming their sense of control over their identity (Trad, 1999). Further, pregnant students may feel the need to, or be pushed to, separate from their parents before they are actually ready to do so, in effect accelerating their independence (Marecek, 1987). Finally, *sexual development* comes into play for pregnant teens. Although it is important to recognize that exploring sex and sexuality is a typical part of adolescent development, which is in part why abstinence-only sex education is ineffective, teens who engage in early and risky sexual behavior are more likely to engage in other risky behaviors, affecting both the teen and the baby (Schuyler Center for Analysis and Advocacy, 2008).

Social Stigma

In the United States, teenage pregnancy is generally stigmatized, bringing to mind phases like "babies having babies," and teen mothers are often described as being relatively incapable of raising a child (SmithBattle, 2013). Despite support that pregnant teens might get in their communities, teen pregnancy is generally not viewed positively in U.S. society, with schools often responding with admonishments. Abstinence-only education plays a large role in promoting the social stigma of teen pregnancy by shaming these students and failing to provide them with appropriate and meaningful information to help them make informed decisions about their sexual health and reproduction (Beh & Diamond, 2006). Teenagers who are pregnant or parenting are well aware of this reality and are rarely met with words of encouragement or an appreciation for the awesome responsibility they are facing. Instead, they are met with disapproving looks and comments, often leading to feelings of rejection, shame, and guilt (Shanok & Miller, 2007). All of this negates the idea that it is possible for teenagers to be competent and loving parents. Certainly, the transition to adulthood is going to be more challenging for these teens, but it is important to remember that some teens find ways to balance parenthood, school, and work, especially when they receive support across family, school, and community contexts (Luttrell, 2003).

Teen Fathers

Despite the breadth of research on teenage pregnancy, there is a dearth of literature that focuses on the experiences of teenage fathers. Research has found that teen fathers generally come from lower-SES communities, have lower academic achievement and higher rates of unemployment, and are more likely to engage in risky behaviors such as smoking and drinking (Quinlivan & Condon, 2005). There is some evidence that teenage fathers are more likely than their female partners to romanticize teenage pregnancy, which relates back to the social prototype model in which they view fatherhood as a second chance to have more positive outcomes (Smith, Buzi, & Weinman, 2002). It is important to acknowledge that teen fathers come in all forms, from those in committed, loving relationships with the mothers who are likely to take responsibility as a father, to those who may have behaved in a predatory manner with the mother and are unlikely to play a role in the baby's life (Goodyear, 2002). Some teen fathers feel intense pressure to provide for their child and family, amplifying issues around staying in school and finding employment (Weinman, Smith, & Buzi, 2002). Additionally, research has found that about 4% of fathers experience depression similar to postpartum depression after the birth of a child (CDC, 2015), and this is likely true of teen fathers as well. With such little information on adolescent fathers, it is important for counselors to recognize when teen fathers are struggling, to reach out to them, and to offer support and counseling to help them transition into fatherhood. This might include helping them learn decision-making skills, parenting skills, and strategies for supporting teen mothers (Goodyear, 2002; Smith et al., 2002).

Special Populations

Certain groups of students are at increased risk for teen pregnancy, including students who are homeless, who are in foster care, or who identify as LGBT (Geiger & Schelbe, 2014; Saewyc, 2005; Thrane & Chen, 2012). Teen pregnancy risk increases when students experience feelings of abandonment, spend extended periods of time away from home, and drop out of school (Thompson, Bender, Lewis, & Watkins, 2008). Youth who are homeless or in foster care are more likely to engage in risky sexual practices, such as having survival sex, unprotected sex, and multiple sex partners (Thrane & Chen, 2012). Becoming pregnant can also lead to homelessness, as some youth are kicked out of their homes because of their pregnancy or leave home to escape a dysfunctional environment (Dworsky & Meehan, 2012; Meadows-Oliver, 2006). LGBT students are also at increased risk for teen pregnancy because these students experience higher rates of abuse, are more likely to be kicked out of their homes or run away to escape dysfunctional home environments, and may engage in survival sex or prostitution once they are homeless (Saewyc, 2005; Schantz, 2015). In counseling, it is important to consider the experiences of pregnant students who are homeless, are in the foster care system, and identify as LGBT by taking into account the multiple disruptions in their home lives, their experience of abuse, and the unique stressors they face (Meadow-Oliver, 2006; Saewyc, 2005). More information about these populations can be found in Chapters 2, 3, and 5 of this volume.

COUNSELING APPROACHES

The adverse consequences of teenage pregnancy are hard to ignore, but there are ways to improve outcomes, and it is important to acknowledge not only the negative consequences but also teenagers' inherent strengths, skills, and potential

(Wiemann, Vaughn, Berenson, & Volk, 2005). Pregnancy and parenthood take a toll on all aspects of students' lives. To reduce the likelihood of negative outcomes and to promote positive development, research suggests that counseling should focus on education, social support, parenting skills, and employment preparation (Harris & Allgood, 2009).

Legal and Ethical Issues

Few topics in society are as divisive as abortion, and counselors will likely have strong personal feelings about the pro-choice/pro-life debate. Laws about choice counseling for teens (i.e., helping a student weigh options related to abortion, adoption, or keeping the baby) and parental consent for abortion differ across states. States and school districts may also have policies about what can and cannot be discussed related to abortion at school (e.g., in a civics class) and in counseling, and it is critical for counselors to know these laws and policies. Many counselors see choice counseling as beyond the scope of their practice, and in areas with a full spectrum of community health and mental health services, referring students may be the most appropriate way to get them the help and support they need to make informed decisions about their care. When referring students, it is critical to ensure that the agencies to which students are being referred are unbiased in their approach to teen pregnancy, that is, the agencies are able to present students with the entire range of options and provide follow-up support after students have made their decisions. This will require counselors to do research about the agencies and make contact with key agency personnel to fully understand the services provided. It may also be necessary to help students organize transportation to make sure they can attend appointments.

In certain states and more rural areas, there may not be appropriate community resources for pregnant teenagers. With attention to the laws and policies within the state and district, counselors may be the most qualified professionals to provide students with choice counseling. Ethical principles from professional organizations offer guidelines that can help counselors make good decisions and feel comfortable in their approach to pregnant students. For example, using the National Association of School Psychologists' *Principles for Professional Ethics* (2010) as a guide, the following should be considered when working with students who are pregnant and uncertain about how they want to proceed: At the outset, counselors need to recognize that their *clients* are the people with whom they form professional relationships, and in this case, the word *clients* refers to students in counseling (National Association of School Psychologists, 2010). With this in mind, counselors can approach counseling in a manner that respects students' autonomy to make decisions that affect their welfare, values students' right to privacy, and protects students' confidentiality (NASP, 2010). That is to say, to be effective, counselors should believe that students will ultimately make decisions that are best for themselves, and their decisions should be respected and kept confidential within the confines of the law. In practice, this can be accomplished by being aware of personal biases related to teen pregnancy, using open-ended questions to solicit information from students rather than making suggestions, and guiding students through a decision-making model without influencing the outcome.

Being aware of personal biases can help counselors ask questions and approach counseling by staying focused on students and their needs. For example, counselors can ask open questions like "What different options have you considered?" or "How might you get additional information about what your options are?" rather than more loaded or biased questions like "Have you considered abortion?" or "Wouldn't you feel terrible if you gave your baby up for adoption?" Avoiding questions and statements that start with "Have you considered . . ." or "Don't you think . . ." and other similar phrases will keep the focus on students' rather than on counselors' beliefs.

After information has been solicited from students about what options they are considering, counselors can ask thoughtful follow-up questions that do not steer the conversation toward one particular outcome. For example, asking the following questions about each option would help students explore their thoughts and feelings, rather than direct them to the option the adult thinks is best:

- What do you know about [abortion] [adoption] [what it would be like to have a baby]?
- When you consider this option, what thoughts and feelings do you have?
- How do you think this option might impact you now and in the future?

Another way to approach choice counseling, or other difficult decisions that pregnant and parenting teens need to make, is to use a more structured decision-making framework, such as those mental health professionals might use when making ethical decisions. One such model, outlined by Corey, Corey, and Callanan (2005), goes through steps for decision-making, which have been modified here to relate to choice counseling. First, counselors help students identify the options, which can be accomplished by using the open questions as described in the previous paragraph. Students should be encouraged to think outside of the box to consider options that may not seem feasible. This step might end with a statement such as "Let me know if any other options come to mind as we work together." The second step is to identify potential issues or obstacles that will need to be addressed, which might be as simple as obtaining information or as complicated as talking with parents. It is important to identify issues and obstacles and not get bogged down with how impossible they seem to overcome. Next, counselors can help students identify individuals they can talk to for "consultation" about the situation and their options, such as an older sister or aunt. This is a good time to assess students' social support and help them recognize who they can trust to help them make difficult decisions. After students have had time to talk with trusted people, the next step is to help them consider possible courses of action. As in the first step, these possible courses of action should be solicited from students, and if students get stuck, counselors can draw on information from previous sessions, ideally even using students' own words, to enumerate possible pathways. The next step is to help students consider the consequences of various options. Using open questions can help students think about the impact each option might have, such as, "Let's suppose you decide to [keep the baby; have an abortion; put the baby up for adoption]. How do you see that impacting you now? And in the future?" The final step is for students to decide on a course of action. The counselor's role in this step is to remain nonjudgmental and supportive and to help students manage the next steps they must take toward their decision. Although students might decide on a certain course of action, it is just as likely that they will change their minds along the way. This is a very personal decision, and it may take several sessions to go through all the steps and circle back as students connect with their thoughts, emotions, and personal values.

Solution-Focused Brief Therapy

Solution-focused brief therapy (SFBT) offers benefits for counseling pregnant and parenting teens, including being brief in nature, focusing on strengths and solutions instead of problems, and teaching students a process by which to set and work toward goals. When counseling pregnant and parenting students, there may be natural time constraints and significant demands on students' time. Further, by taking a strength-based and solution-focused approach, counselors can offer teens a way to recognize their internal strengths and resources and to feel confident in their decisions despite being in a culture that may provide negative messages about teen pregnancy (Marecek, 1987). Through an SFBT approach, counselors can convey their genuine belief that students are resilient and capable of completing school and obtaining employment (Harris & Franklin, 2012). With adequate support, teen parents can have positive outcomes (e.g., completing high school, increasing self-esteem, employing positive parenting practices; Harris & Franklin, 2012; Kirkman, Harrison, Hillier, & Pyett, 2001). An SFBT approach to counseling allows teens to focus on the present and future rather than on past mistakes and to recognize solutions instead of problems (Kim & Franklin, 2009). Finally, goal setting, which is central in SFBT, is a critical component for achieving positive and sustaining outcomes in counseling pregnant teens, especially for breaking the cycle of high school dropout, unemployment, and poverty (Harris & Franklin, 2003).

When working with pregnant and parenting teens, SFBT is as much a mindset as it is a series of techniques. With this group of students, an overarching goal of counseling must be to empower them to be more capable and resourceful as individuals and parents. In theory, this requires counselors to believe that "the student is the expert on the problem [and] all students have strengths, even if they are not yet obvious to us or to the student" (Cooley, 2009, p. 21). By taking this approach, counselors are communicating that they believe students are capable and competent, thus allowing students to take greater ownership of their lives. Even during counseling activities that are not specifically solution-focused, such as parenting psychoeducation, by approaching counseling with an SFBT mindset, the focus remains on promoting competence and moving forward rather than rehashing past mistakes.

In practice, SFBT uses students' concerns to guide the content of counseling and set goals, and it helps students to find solutions for their own problems by drawing on past successes and strengths (Kim & Franklin, 2009). The core assumptions and components of SFBT are detailed in Chapter 1 of this volume; all of these might apply to working with pregnant and parenting teens, depending on each student's unique circumstances. A counselor might start a counseling session by acknowledging the student's strengths in simply coming to school and wanting to talk through things in counseling, perhaps saying something like, "It says a lot about you that you are still coming to school during this [stressful, uncertain, difficult] time. How have you managed to get here under these circumstances?" This can help set the tone and establish that the counselor is going to approach things differently than other adults, and therefore help the student feel more comfortable sharing her concerns. Aspects of SFBT, such as goal setting and the miracle question, may need to be modified for pregnant and parenting teens to account for their unique situation. For example, during goal setting, counselors can start this process by asking "Given that you are pregnant and are going to keep the baby, what are some concerns that are coming up?" This approach accounts for students' reality (i.e., pregnancy or parenting) so as to not elicit goals such as "not being pregnant."

It should be noted that SFBT might not be the appropriate approach for choice counseling. However, aspects of SFBT could easily be woven through choice counseling, such as asking, "When have you had to make a difficult decision in the past? What helped you make that decision?" SFBT might also be a good approach for pregnant students who are struggling with how to tell their parents or partner about the pregnancy, using questions like "When have you had to tell your parents or someone else something difficult? How did you go about doing that? What worked for you in that situation? What did you learn from that situation that you might apply to this situation?"

Building Social Support

Research shows that social support is important for teen mothers and their children, with support from families and partners correlating with lower psychological distress (Brosh, Weigel, & Evans, 2007; Bunting & McAuley, 2004). In contrast, having a large peer network may be related to greater distress for new teen mothers, perhaps due to increasing demands and responsibilities for teen mothers as compared with the continued freedom of their peers (Bunting & McAuley, 2004). In counseling, it is important to remember that there can be stigma associated with needing and asking for help, especially for teen parents who have already been given the message that they are not capable and that their decisions are ruining their lives (Vogel, Wester, & Larson, 2007). Counselors can help normalize that all new parents feel overwhelmed and need help; can help teens identify and seek useful support from people in their lives; and can help teens develop skills and strategies to improve communication and connection with their family, partner, and friends (Bunting & McAuley, 2004; Letourneau, Stewart, & Barnfather, 2004; Reichman & McLanahan, 2001).

Group counseling may be an effective way to build social support and enhance skill development for pregnant and parenting teens. Group counseling not only allows pregnant and parenting teens to interact with peers experiencing similar challenges but also can help teens practice skills in a safe environment (Harris & Franklin, 2007; Shechtman, 2007). Given the power of peer relationships during adolescence, teens who are navigating parenthood can serve as role models and mentors for pregnant or newly parenting teens, increasing their sense of efficacy and providing valuable guidance about challenges that may be encountered along the way. Counselors can help facilitate groups in a way that creates a greater sense of community for teens, provides realistic but hopeful expectations about what is to come, and builds on students' strengths in overcoming obstacles. Group counseling might be most effective if all group members are pregnant or parenting teens, but if this is not feasible given the population in the school or district, counselors might consider referring students to a community group if available, or carefully screening a general coping or life skills group to see if it would be appropriate for pregnant or parenting teens.

Dropout Prevention

Because school completion is directly related to improving outcomes for both parent and child, it should be an overarching goal of counseling for pregnant and parenting teens (Creen, Hightower, & Allan, 2001). Despite a lack of counseling programs specifically designed for pregnant and parenting teens, there are programs with objectives to improve educational experiences for students who are at risk for school dropout and who engage in risk-taking behaviors, and counselors can draw from these programs as these issues apply to pregnant and parenting teens. One good example of an empirically supported dropout prevention program for at-risk students is WhyTry (Moore, 2009). WhyTry is a resilience education program that aims to reduce truancy and dropout and to increase academic motivation by helping students gain insight and cope more effectively with frustration and failure (Alvarez & Anderson-Ketchmark, 2009; Baker, 2008); it is also discussed in Chapter 10 of this volume. WhyTry draws from SFBT principles and uses multisensorial learning strategies to engage students (Moore, 2009). Some aspects of WhyTry can be easily adapted for pregnant and parenting teens, such as the "Tearing Off Your Label" activity, in which students learn how to change the stigmatizing labels they have been assigned and create new, more positive labels. For pregnant teenagers, instead of being a "baby having a baby," for example, they have the opportunity to identify themselves as "teens doing their best" or "strong individuals who can handle what life brings." Another program that may be appropriate is New Chance (Quint, Bos, & Polit, 1997), which is designed to increase occupational opportunities and improve parenting skills for young mothers who have dropped out of school.

Vocational Counseling

Along with school completion, career and educational planning are critical for helping teen parents and their children have more successful outcomes (Letourneau et al., 2004). Generally, vocational counseling focuses on three key factors: students' personal attributes and self-efficacy, students' beliefs about being able to achieve and perform the requirements of a career, and students' future goals (Domenico, 2005). In practice, this requires counselors to help students explore their innate strengths, skills, and interests; to assess their motivation to obtain further education and have a career; and to help them set short- and long-term goals related to education and career development (Kiselica & Pfaller, 1992). For teen parents, it is important to encourage students to consider goals beyond the immediate experience of parenting to help them think about all aspects of their lives (Muskin, 2004). Further, it can be helpful to recognize and perhaps articulate to students that both not having a vocational plan and the process of vocational planning can feel stressful and overwhelming for all students, but that this may be especially true for students who are trying to balance parenthood, school, and other obligations along with vocational planning. Students' motivation to engage in this process and work toward their goals can be negatively affected by low self-esteem, role overload, and difficulty in managing stress (Muskin, 2004). If students are overwhelmed by where to start, or perhaps demonstrate low self-esteem when thinking about education and career planning, counselors can break these ideas down into smaller, more achievable steps, such as developing a backward timeline with incremental goals or helping students develop a résumé. The goal here is to find ways to engage students in these discussions and help them stay focused on moving forward. Finally, it is important to note that vocational counseling during pregnancy should focus on the immediate needs of students in terms of identifying and organizing shorter-term school expectations and goals rather than on future career planning (Kiselica & Pfaller, 1992).

Parenting Psychoeducation

Parenting psychoeducation to improve parenting skills will help support teen parents, alleviate some of the stressors that accompany parenting, and lead to more positive outcomes for parents and children (Innes, 1990). Parenting programs that are targeted toward adolescent parents generally focus on parent-child relations and parenting skills, health outcomes and sexuality, life skills, and social support systems (Thomas & Looney, 2004). The Nurturing Parenting Program (NPP) is an evidence-based curriculum that focuses on themes of parental resilience, building social connections and support networks, knowledge of childhood development, and supporting the social and emotional needs of children (Family Development Resources, 2015). NPP was initially designed for abusive and neglectful parents, but it has been successfully adapted for multiple populations, including teen parents (Substance Abuse and Mental Health Services Administration, 2015), and it could easily be implemented in the school setting for this population. Bavolek and Rogers (2012) outline the six core elements of NPP, which include helping teen parents develop positive self-concept and self-worth; develop and increase empathy and emotional regulation skills; understand principles and benefits of nonviolent discipline; gain awareness of self, beliefs, and cultural and family roles; develop a healthy sense of empowerment; and build positive interactions among family members.

The Taking Charge Intervention

The Taking Charge (TC) intervention is a solution-focused, school-based group counseling program for pregnant and parenting teenagers that integrates all of the counseling strategies discussed in this chapter. The TC program combines solution-focused principles with cognitive-behavioral strategies and builds coping and problem-solving skills to promote school achievement, parenting efficacy, career development, and supportive interpersonal relationships (Harris & Franklin, 2012). TC is based on a foundational belief that teen parenthood does not need to be a deleterious experience; rather, teen parents have internal resources and strengths that can help them choose to stay in school and work through the obstacles they face throughout their pregnancy and early parenthood (Harris & Franklin, 2007). This type of solution-oriented program facilitates a change in perception: there absolutely can be a positive future for pregnant and parenting teens. TC addresses important areas that will help teens begin to learn the life skills that will improve outcomes for themselves and their children, including "personal goal setting; learning and applying social problem-solving; active coping; and solution-building skills" (Harris & Franklin, 2012, p. 252). The program also provides students with a series of opportunities and incentives, which can be easily applied in a school setting, such as rewarding them for school attendance, attending counseling, completing designated parenting tasks, or doing schoolwork toward earning credits (Harris & Franklin, 2007). TC is an ideal program to use with pregnant and parenting adolescents given the integration of the most well-established and evidence-based interventions.

BEYOND THE COUNSELING OFFICE: PREGNANCY PREVENTION AND SEX EDUCATION

Nowhere does the adage about an ounce of prevention being worth a pound of cure seem more fitting than when talking about teen pregnancy. Preventing and reducing teen pregnancy requires a multifaceted approach that involves stakeholders from schools, school districts, community organizations, and health care systems (Yu, 2010). On a larger scale, preventing teen pregnancy may require a shift in how society views teens, which includes recognizing that sexuality is a natural part of the whole person and educating teens about their sexuality and health in a way that focuses on health promotion rather than pathology (UCLA Mental Health in Schools Center, 1996). According to the Child Welfare League of America (2008), effective pregnancy prevention involves both young men and women and includes the following:

- education programs that encompass the multiple variables impacting adolescent sexual health;
- direct teaching of decision-making skills;
- mentoring programs;
- building strong parent–teen relationships;
- education presented from a teen perspective;
- increased access to family planning services;
- parenting classes; and
- and mental health support.

By applying these broad strategies, counselors are in a position to help advocate for and develop prevention and educational programming in schools that is relevant and meaningful for teens. A good way to begin this process is to enlist support from key stakeholders to collect and analyze data from students and families to better understand specific areas of need (Shuger, 2012). Once this is done, counselors, along with other stakeholders, might develop a series of information sessions for parents, teachers, and administrators related to pregnancy prevention and support of pregnant and parenting teens (Shuger, 2012).

In choosing or developing prevention and education programs in schools, counselors should ensure that programs fit the needs of the student population at their school; incorporate teen perspectives; involve families as appropriate; and provide direct instruction on help-seeking behavior, problem solving, and coping skills (Sarri & Phillips, 2004). Addressing teen perspectives is a salient component to prevention because it allows educators to dispel common myths about sexual health and behavior (Minnick & Shandler, 2011; Waller, Brown, & Whittle, 1999). Counselors can partner with community health agencies to ensure that the health and sex education that teens are receiving is relevant, accurate, and comprehensive (Shuger, 2012).

Despite the findings of research about what is effective in holistic pregnancy prevention and education programs, schools tend to approach sexual health in one of two ways: through abstinence-only programs or through programs that teach about abstinence and contraception. Research has consistently shown that abstinence-only sex education is no more effective than no sex education at all (Harris & Allgood, 2009) and that abstinence-only education may actually deter contraceptive use (Boonstra, 2010). There are more promising results from programs that combine abstinence and contraception education (Bennett & Assefi, 2005), but these programs can fail to take into account the unique needs of the student body and community and do not address the entire spectrum of health promotion teens need to be able to make good decisions. Given the far-reaching impact of teen pregnancy on individuals, families, schools, and society, counselors can help educate the school community about the importance of collaborating with community stakeholders to develop and implement programming that is accurate, appropriate, and meaningful to all students.

RESOURCES

Department of Health and Human Services—Office of Adolescent Health: Pregnancy Assistance Fund

http://www.hhs.gov/ash/oah/oah-initiatives/paf

The Pregnancy Assistance Fund is a resource and training center that provides information on services and supports for pregnant and parenting teens, including physical health, mental health, substance abuse, reproductive health, relationships, and positive youth development for pregnant and parenting teens.

Healthy Teen Network

http://www.healthyteennetwork.org

The Healthy Teen Network is a resource focused on reproductive health and parenting teens. Specifically, this web source includes online modules that help teens, parents, and professionals better understand the unique aspects of teen parenthood such as supporting adolescent mothers and fathers, co-parenting at the teenage level, and pregnancy prevention among older teenagers. The Healthy Teen Network also provides information related to public policy and supporting healthy youth development within the school environment.

National Campaign to Prevent Teen and Unplanned Pregnancy

http://thenationalcampaign.org/#

The National Campaign to Prevent Teen and Unplanned Pregnancy is an organization that aims to improve the lives of children and families by reducing teenage pregnancy. The website provides numerous articles on effective prevention strategies and programs, as well as current data on teenage pregnancy trends.

National Women's Law Center

http://www.nwlc.org/our-issues/education-%2526-title-ix/pregnant-%2526-parenting-students

The National Women's law Center provides information on legal mandates regarding the education of pregnant and parenting students. Resources are provided for students, parents, and educators, including webinars and presentations on how pregnancy impacts school environments. *A Pregnancy Test for Schools* is a Title IX handbook that can help school professionals generate ideas on how to improve the educational experience for pregnant and parenting students.

Planned Parenthood

https://www.plannedparenthood.org/

Planned Parenthood is a nonprofit organization that provides reproductive health services to adolescents throughout the United States, including contraception, emergency contraception, cancer screening, pregnancy testing, pregnancy options counseling, testing and treatment for sexual transmitted infections, LGBT services, and abortion. The website itself can provide teenagers with a wealth of information regarding their sexual and reproductive health.

7

Counseling Students Who Are Gifted

OVERVIEW

Most counselors devote considerable time and resources to working with students who are the most vulnerable to low achievement and school failure. Similarly, over the last few years, educators in general have focused much attention on low-performing students who are not meeting minimal academic standards. Unfortunately, discussions among educators and counselors often overlook gifted students, as this group is often able to meet or exceed standards without extra consideration. Yet gifted students can still be a vulnerable population because without proper academic and social and emotional support, they may not reach high levels of achievement and recognize their potential in school and beyond (Pfeiffer, 2013).

Currently, there are no federal criteria for giftedness, and how students are identified as gifted varies from state to state and expert to expert. Generally, at the state level for educational purposes, giftedness is defined by high intellectual ability and/or high achievement (McClain & Pfeiffer, 2012). State criteria may also include students who demonstrate extraordinary creative, artistic, or leadership abilities, and the majority of states use the term *gifted and talented* to describe this population of students (McClain & Pfeiffer, 2012). Whatever term is used, it can be helpful to understand the idea of giftedness as a social construct that may be best explained using what Pfeiffer (2013) refers to as a "tripartite model" (p. 10), which includes students who demonstrate high intelligence, students who demonstrate outstanding academic and/or creative accomplishments, and students who demonstrate great potential to excel when provided with opportunities and resources.

Over the past few decades, giftedness has been written about extensively in educational and psychological literature, yet it is clear that educational professionals, including teachers and counselors, receive little graduate training related to giftedness and working effectively with gifted students (Robertson, Pfeiffer, & Taylor, 2011). To serve this population, counselors must understand the social and emotional development of gifted students and consider counseling approaches that may best meet their needs.

BASIC CONSIDERATIONS

Gifted students face the same developmental tasks as all other students and may experience social and emotional difficulties at various times in their development consistent with those experienced by other students (Pfeiffer, 2013). Aspects of giftedness can serve as both risk and protective factors relative to social and emotional problems, and a student's giftedness should be viewed as one important aspect of the whole person (Pfeiffer, 2013). Because gifted students' unique social and emotional needs often go unrecognized and unmet (Pfeiffer, 2013), it is important for counselors to familiarize themselves with the characteristics associated with giftedness.

The social and emotional characteristics of gifted students do not exist in isolation; rather, they interact to create different individual profiles for each student. For example, it is commonly understood that aspects of diversity, such as gender, race, language, sexual orientation, and socioeconomic status, interact for individuals as they navigate identity development in adolescence and adulthood. The same is true for gifted students, whose giftedness is another characteristic of identity that interacts with all other aspects of self. Thus, the unique social and emotional considerations of giftedness should be considered along with what counselors know about other aspects of identity, and counseling approaches may need to be tailored accordingly.

Social and Emotional Development and Needs

There has been much discussion about the social and emotional adjustment of gifted students, and the predominant conclusion is that gifted students are generally as well adjusted socially and emotionally as other groups of students (Lee, Olszewski-Kubilius, & Thomson, 2012; Reis & Renzulli, 2004; Shechtman & Silektor, 2012). Further, gifted students generally have positive perceptions of their ability to make and maintain friendships (Lee et al., 2012). This is not to say that gifted students do not have unique social and emotional needs; rather, the research suggests that these social and emotional problems most often occur as a result of environmental mismatches at home and school (Pfeiffer, 2013; Reis & Renzulli, 2004; Robinson, 2002). For example, verbally gifted students may experience greater social difficulties because of the mismatch between their highly advanced vocabularies and communication styles and those of their same-age peers (Lee et al., 2012). Further, there are several areas in which gifted students, in large part due to the very nature of their giftedness, may need greater support for their social and emotional development. These include asynchronous development, underachievement, perfectionism, and social difficulties.

Asynchronous Development

One area that can contribute to social and emotional problems for gifted students is *asynchronous development*; that is, although gifted students face the same developmental tasks as their peers, they often experience uneven development across domains, with some areas being very advanced and other areas being typical or even delayed (National Association for Gifted Children [NAGC], 2009a; Reis & Renzulli, 2004). This asynchronous development may result in adults having uniformly high expectations for gifted students across all areas, without taking into account the individual student's developmental profile (Peterson, 2009; Robinson, 2002). Further, asynchronous development may mean that students have the advanced cognitive or moral development to intensely connect with an issue (e.g., slavery), without having the commensurate coping strategies to manage the emotional responses that are evoked by the issue (e.g., intense feelings about human suffering; Peterson, 2009; Reis & Renzulli, 2004). Highly gifted students often have the most asynchronous development, which can contribute to greater social and emotional difficulties (Silverman, 2002).

Underachievement

Underachievement may be the most pernicious problem affecting gifted students, and patterns of underachievement can be seen from childhood through adulthood (Reis & Renzulli, 2004). Underachievement can result from a mismatch between gifted students and the academic environment and curriculum, particularly a lack of appropriately engaging and challenging curriculum (Moon, 2009; Reis & Renzulli, 2009). As a result, students may experience intense boredom and frustration and become unmotivated in school (Moon, 2009). Further, when curriculum is insufficiently challenging, especially during elementary school, gifted students may learn that it is easy to coast through school instead of learning how to appropriately persist and work through an academic challenge (Moon, 2009; Reis & Renzulli, 2009). Some gifted students have strong negative reactions to failure, which may make them reluctant to take risks and seek challenges (Keiley, 2002). Another factor contributing to underachievement may be peer pressure to conform, which causes gifted students to effectively "dumb down" to fit in with their peer group by denying or hiding their achievements (Reis & Renzulli, 2004; Robinson, 2002). In this way, gifted students may choose acceptance by their peer group at the expense of reaching their achievement potential.

Perfectionism

Perfectionism is not an issue unique to gifted students, but giftedness may contribute to perfectionism, as teachers, parents, and students themselves may hold higher expectations for school performance (Greenspon, 2012). Most gifted students experience a healthy motivation to achieve rather than perfectionism (Schuler, 2000); however, when students experience high levels of perfectionism, it can have serious consequences for their emotional development (Greenspon, 2012). Some scholars have discussed perfectionism as existing on a continuum, with healthy, adaptive, and desirable perfectionism at one extreme and maladaptive and undesirable perfectionism at the other (e.g., Reis & Renzulli, 2004; Schuler, 2000; Wang, Fu, & Rice, 2012). Certainly, gradations of perfectionism exist, and the impact on students can run the gamut from providing motivation to achieve at a high level to intense fear of failure and self-criticism (Schuler, 2000). Perhaps it is most useful for counselors to recognize perfectionism as a harmful and maladaptive trait, separating it from students' desires to achieve at a high level, put in concerted effort on tasks, and achieve their personal bests (Greenspon, 2012). Perfectionism in this conceptualization is characterized as a self-esteem issue stemming from deeply rooted fears of failure and feelings of never being good enough (Greenspon, 2012). Although these thoughts and feelings can appear to reflect motivation and a desire for high achievement, they are, at the core, based on intense anxiety and self-criticism (Greenspon, 2011). Further, this extreme fear of failure can create academic paralysis, in which students avoid taking academic risks and trying difficult things because failing has such devastating emotional consequences (Greenspon, 2012; Keiley, 2002). At this level, perfectionism contributes to underachievement, and at all levels, perfectionism might go unnoticed by adults at school because students are so strongly invested in maintaining the appearance that they are perfect (Peterson, 2009; Schuler, 2000).

SOCIAL DIFFICULTIES

Many gifted students experience positive social relationships and feel accepted at school, but others feel out of sync with the social environment and experience isolation (Peterson, 2009; Rimm, 2002). Students who are highly gifted seem to have the greatest social difficulties (Peterson, 2009; Rimm, 2002); for these students, the feelings of loneliness and isolation may peak in elementary school due to smaller school environments that offer fewer opportunities to interact with peers who share similar abilities and interests (Gross, 2002). The research on gifted students and bullying is mixed, with some research finding no differences in experiences of bullying and victimization for gifted students (e.g., Peters & Bain, 2011), and other research finding higher levels of bullying and victimization for gifted students (e.g., Peterson & Ray, 2006). The takeaway for counselors related to social difficulties is that some gifted students, especially those who lack social support at school, experience school as a lonely, and even hostile, place where they do not feel like they fit in with their peers.

Student Diversity

Gifted students have experiences and needs that set them apart from the general school population, and there also is great intragroup diversity among gifted students (NAGC, 2009a). Additionally, although gifted students may share some general traits (including those described in the previous section of this chapter), these traits are manifested differently in each individual student, highlighting the importance of school services that both globally and specifically address these students' social and emotional needs (NAGC, 2009a; Reis & Renzulli, 2009). Adding even more complexity, gifted students are characterized by additional dimensions of diversity, such as culture and sexual orientation, that can create greater feelings of "differentness" in the school environment and can further impact their social and emotional development.

CULTURALLY AND LINGUISTICALLY DIVERSE GIFTED STUDENTS

If it is accepted that giftedness is a social construct, then it is not surprising that there are issues with the underrepresentation of culturally and linguistically diverse (CLD) students, especially African Americans, American Indians, and Hispanics/Latinos, identified as gifted and retained in gifted programs (Ford, Grantham, & Whiting, 2011). Although it is widely recognized that this underrepresentation exists, and at least half of states have policies that explicitly address the identification of CLD students as gifted (McClain & Pfeiffer, 2012), students of color, students from linguistically diverse backgrounds, and students from lower socioeconomic statuses are consistently underrepresented in gifted programs (Ford et al., 2011; Gentry, Hu, & Thomas, 2008; NAGC, 2011; Reis & Renzulli, 2004). Research has found that underrepresentation of CLD students is often due to poor performance on IQ tests and lower teacher expectations during identification processes (Ford et al., 2011). Further, when CLD students are identified as gifted, they are less likely to be retained in gifted programs, most often due to a lack of attention to students' social, emotional, and relational needs; family concerns about students' happiness in gifted programs; and underachievement in gifted programs (Ford et al., 2011).

In addition to the social and emotional needs discussed previously, gifted CLD students may have some unique needs that require support for them to be successful in school and retained in gifted programs. Due to underrepresentation of CLD students in gifted education, gifted programs are populated predominantly by White students, and gifted CLD students in such programs may experience isolation from their culturally similar peers, may struggle more with ethnic identity development, and may feel forced to choose between their giftedness and social inclusion by their peers (Ford et al., 2011; Reis & Renzulli, 2004). Further, gifted CLD students are more successful when their families are supportive and actively involved in their education (NAGC, 2011). Thus, it is recommended that counseling interventions for CLD students focus, in part, on helping students navigate the challenges of identity development, including academic identity, and learning strategies to build resilience and effectively cope with negative peer pressure and discrimination (NAGC, 2011). Additional recommendations, which will be discussed more generally in the "Counseling Approaches" section of this chapter, include small-group counseling with other gifted students from similar cultural backgrounds, culture-specific mentoring programs, and increasing involvement of family members to help them understand and support their gifted child (NAGC, 2011).

Lesbian, Gay, Bisexual, Transgender, and Questioning Gifted Students

Lesbian, gay, bisexual, transgender, and questioning (LGBTQ) students have been recognized as being a population particularly at risk for experiencing bullying and harassment and the myriad of social and emotional consequences from these experiences (see Chapter 5 in this volume). Gifted LGBTQ students may experience greater feelings of differentness and even higher rates of bullying and harassment, leading to increased isolation and alienation at school (NAGC, 2001; Peterson & Rischar, 2000).

In meeting the social and emotional needs of gifted LGBTQ students, counselors will want to consider both the counseling approaches covered in this book that are specific to LGBTQ students and the counseling approaches in this chapter. Gifted LGBTQ students will benefit the most from practitioners who can "model openness, fairness, and sensitivity regarding sexual-orientation [and gender-identity] issues" (NAGC, 2001, p. 2). Further, when considering career counseling, discussed later in this chapter, counselors should be aware of stereotyping that can occur when considering career options for LGBTQ students and ensure that students are encouraged to explore a wide range of career choices (NAGC, 2001).

Gifted Students with Disabilities

Students who have a disability and are gifted are often referred to as *twice exceptional* (NAGC, 2009b). Twice exceptionality is most likely to occur in students with specific learning disabilities, autism spectrum disorders, and attention deficit hyperactivity disorder (under the special education disability category of "other health impaired"; NAGC, 2009b). Twice-exceptional students "are often misunderstood because their giftedness can mask their disabilities and their disabilities can camouflage their talents" (Reis & Renzulli, 2004, p. 123). Further, some common characteristics of giftedness can overlap with characteristics of disabilities, such as difficulty connecting with peers and making friends or inattention in the classroom (NAGC, 2009b). Pfeiffer (2013) points out that there are very few empirical studies related to twice-exceptional students and that the literature in this area relies primarily on case studies, anecdotes, and clinical reports.

Educational programming for twice-exceptional students is complex and often fails to meet their unique academic, social, and emotional needs, such as developing a curriculum that engages students' gifts while simultaneously accounting for remediating areas of need, providing greater support for self-directed learning, and allowing for different pacing of curriculum and instruction (Baum, Cooper, & Neu, 2001; Reis & Renzulli, 2004). As a result, twice-exceptional students may experience heightened levels of frustration and failure and lowered levels of academic confidence and self-efficacy (Baum et al., 2001). They may also need greater support to manage the social aspects of school, both in the gifted program and in the general population (Reis & Renzulli, 2004).

COUNSELING APPROACHES

Although the overall news about gifted students' social and emotional development is positive, some students will need counseling support to successfully navigate challenges that arise (Pfeiffer, 2013). In addition to the aforementioned social and emotional issues students may experience that are more directly related to or exacerbated by their giftedness, gifted students may face the same full range of mental health issues as their peers (e.g., depression, eating disorders; Pfeiffer, 2013). To date, there is little empirical research on specific approaches to counseling gifted students (NAGC, 2009a; Pfeiffer, 2013); rather, it is important for counselors to use evidence-based counseling approaches to best meet students' individual needs, which might include group counseling, social skills development, and cognitive-behavioral therapy (CBT; Pfeiffer, 2013).

Gifted students may experience similar issues and benefit from similar approaches as their peers, yet it is also important for counselors to consider the unique profiles of gifted students, along with the strengths and resources they bring to counseling (Pfeiffer, 2013). A strength-based approach that capitalizes on these resources may make counseling more engaging for gifted students and help them be active agents in addressing problems. Further, gifted students will benefit from a strong counseling relationship based on trust and rapport, feeling like the counselor understands them and their gifts and challenges, and experiencing acceptance and unconditional positive regard (Peterson, 2012; Peterson & Moon, 2008; Wood, 2009).

Just as there is overlap among the issues affecting gifted students' development and success in school, there is overlap among the counseling strategies and interventions in the next sections of this chapter. For example, counseling related to career development may intersect with perfectionism because perfectionism and fear of failure can impact career decision-making (Wood & Gavin, 2009). Counselors might want to begin by addressing an issue that the student identifies as important, thereby facilitating greater buy-in from the student and helping build a solid therapeutic relationship.

Resilience, Coping Strategies, and Social Skills

Across the literature, experts recognize that gifted students who are resilient and have effective coping strategies and social skills are more successful in school and in life (e.g., Pfeiffer, 2013; Reis & Renzulli, 2004; Robinson, 2002; Schuler, 2002). A nonexhaustive list of these skills includes the following:

- managing stress and failure (Reis & Renzulli, 2004; Schuler, 2002);
- employing effective problem-solving strategies (Reis & Renzulli, 2004);
- developing persistence and determination (Pfeiffer, 2013; Schuler, 2002); and
- building friendships and other social relationships in a variety of school settings (Reis & Renzulli, 2004; Wood, 2009).

At a basic level, the goal of all counseling is to promote resilience (Neihart, 2012). Counseling approaches that build resilience, coping strategies, and social skills do not necessarily need to differ for gifted students, as long as the student's unique development and needs are taken into account. For example, gifted students may struggle with social skills for any of the same reasons other students struggle, such as perceiving social cues or knowing appropriate social responses (Cross, 2012), but their struggles may be further complicated by their giftedness and the interplay of this with their social environment. That is to say, counselors do not necessarily need new counseling techniques or curriculum in their arsenal to work effectively with gifted students; rather, they may need to take a slightly different approach to make the counseling materials relevant to gifted students' lives.

Instead of worksheet-based or scripted curricula, gifted students would likely benefit more from an approach that allows them to discuss, investigate, and solve real problems, with the counselor acting as a facilitator and adviser (Baum, Cooper, & Neu, 2001). For example, "anthropologist in the classroom" is a social-emotional strategy to help students observe and analyze social interactions (Future Horizons Incorporated, 2003). Using this strategy, counselors can help gifted students identify areas of social interaction they want to better understand; conduct a series of observations to learn more about this social phenomenon, as an anthropologist would do; and then reports the findings back to the counselor or group, depending on if it is an individual or group counseling approach. The counselor or other group members can ask questions and work with the student to analyze and understand what was learned; discuss how to use this information to build social relationships; and decide on next steps to take, such as further investigation, creating a comic strip to demonstrate the social interaction, or trying out a new skill in class that week. With this type of interactive problem-solving approach, the possibilities are endless.

Gifted students may also benefit from learning stress reduction and relaxation techniques (Pfeiffer, 2013; Wood, 2009). Counselors can use resources they already have to teach deep breathing, progressive muscle relaxation, guided imagery, mindfulness, and meditation. Gifted students might enjoy learning about the research supporting these techniques, and because these techniques are practiced rather than perfected, discussions in counseling might focus on helping students accept whatever thoughts, feelings, or sensations are present with compassion and without judgment. It can be powerful for students to take what they have learned in counseling and teach the techniques to someone else, such as a friend, sibling, or parent. By teaching someone else how to be accepting and nonjudgmental during relaxation or meditation, students may more deeply embody these messages.

Identity development may be another important aspect to consider in counseling, especially for diverse gifted students (Ford, 2011). As previously mentioned, even when CLD students are identified as gifted, they may choose not to stay in gifted programs, in part because they may struggle both in identifying with their CLD peer group and in identifying as gifted (Ford, 2011). Counselors might help

CLD gifted students explore all aspects of their identities, including racial identity and the intersection of racial identity and giftedness (Wood, 2009). They should also strive to create a safe place for CLD gifted students to discuss issues of racism, discrimination, and conflicting identities (Wood, 2009); they may need to address these issues first, so that the student knows these are appropriate topics to discuss in counseling. It may be that CLD gifted students have never explicitly discussed feelings of conflict about different aspects of their identities, and counselors can help them better integrate these different identities. Wood (2009) recommends that these discussions include exploration of students' communities and affiliations, and how they experience social acceptance and achievement. Further, career aspirations should be considered as part of identity development (Wood & Gavin, 2009).

Perfectionism

For gifted students who are experiencing the negative emotional consequences of perfectionism, Greenspon (2012) advocates an approach to counseling that encompasses empathy, encouragement, reflection, and dialogue. Greenspon (2012) suggests that counselors start with an understanding that perfectionistic students may believe that they are flawed. Their acceptance of themselves as individuals is contingent on being successful; they may consciously or subconsciously think that if only they could be perfect, then they could finally reach acceptance. Thus, one critical goal of counseling is to build counseling relationships in which students feel "accepted, validated, and empowered to make changes" (Greenspon, 2012, p. 607). Through learning about students' worlds and witnessing the hurt students are experiencing, the counselor builds and demonstrates empathy and compassion. With this foundational rapport in place, counselors can begin to help students explore how they think and feel about situations such as receiving a less than perfect grade or letting go of absolute control during a group project. During these discussions, counselors should avoid comments focused on outcome, product, or performance; instead, they should provide encouragement by pointing out positive things they notice about students, focusing on personal qualities such as thoughtfulness, passion, effort, persistence, or willingness to take risks.

As the counseling relationship develops, Greenspon (2012) suggests that counselors can help students reflect on topics and issues that will remain even if they are able to move away from perfectionism, such as making mistakes, students' views of themselves, expectations coming from self and others, and students' positive characteristics. These discussions both begin the change process and help to deepen the counseling relationship. It is through such dialogues that students can begin to explore alternative approaches for engaging with self and others. Greenspon (2012) advocates for a flexible approach to supporting the change process rather than a prescriptive program and suggests that counselors engage students in the problem-solving process to find solutions that work for them.

Given the nature of perfectionism, it might be helpful for counselors to weave in elements of CBT. Perfectionism is based in anxiety: fear that the individual will never be good enough; that mistakes occur because the individual is flawed; and that any mistake, failure, correction, or feedback causes intolerable criticism from the self or others (Greenspon, 2012). Although Greenspon (2012) does not discuss CBT as a counseling approach for perfectionism, it is a relevant approach in that it highlights the behaviors, thoughts, and feelings associated with perfectionism. Further, CBT might appeal to gifted students' strong reasoning abilities. Counselors will want to tread lightly as they introduce CBT, focusing on a collaborative rather than challenging approach because perfectionistic students may experience challenges as criticism and the idea of irrational or maladaptive thoughts as evidence of being flawed. Perhaps some psychoeducation about the natural human tendency to highlight the negative and discount the positive could provide a good way to introduce CBT, helping to normalize rather than pathologize the student's experience.

Motivation and Underachievement

As mentioned previously, underachievement may be one of the most pressing concerns related to gifted students, in part because underachievement involves a complex interaction between students and their environments (e.g., home, school, peer). Underachievement is further complicated because there is a lack of research-based interventions that have demonstrated long-lasting success in reversing patterns of underachievement for gifted students. Current theories and research (e.g., Landis & Reschly, 2013; Rubenstein, Siegle, Reis, McCoach, & Burton, 2012) draw from educational literature on school engagement and motivation, which may offer promising practices for underachieving gifted students.

The relevance and meaning of academic tasks may be an important construct in engaging underachieving gifted students because academic tasks that are perceived as personally meaningful have been related to students' motivation to achieve in school (Rubenstein et al., 2012). Counselors might help in this area by finding out what makes school or particular tasks meaningful for an individual student (Siegle, McCoach, & Rubenstein, 2012). As will be discussed in greater detail in the next section of this chapter, early career development may be a way to help gifted students see the connection between the work they must do in school and their future goals.

School engagement, and more specifically meaningful relationships with adults at school, may also be an important piece in addressing underachievement (Landis & Reschly, 2013; Rubenstein et al., 2012). Building quality relationships with and demonstrating respect and positive regard for gifted students in counseling may be a good first step in helping them feel valued at school. Once this kind of rapport has been established, a next step may be for counselors to work with students to monitor their achievement across classes. In a study conducted by Rubenstein et al. (2012), it was found that simply by informing underachieving gifted students that their grades were going to be monitored by a caring adult at school, grades improved even before other interventions were put in place. But just letting students know their grades will be monitored is not enough to effect long-term change; researchers in the same study noted that prematurely removing the support of the caring adult may result in a return to poor grades.

In addition to being a caring adult and monitoring grades, a counselor can help students set short- and long-term academic goals and recognize obstacles to students' success (Siegle et al., 2012). One possible approach to help with this is solution-focused brief therapy (SFBT). Several aspects of SFBT seem particularly relevant to underachievement and motivation. At its core, SFBT is a student-centered, problem-solving, strength-based counseling approach. Within this framework, students are viewed as experts on the problems and on the solutions; counselors employ inquiry and investigation to help students discover solutions and try them out to see if they will work; and goals are developed by students to increase motivation and buy-in to counseling (Sklare, 2014). Further, practitioners can help students to recognize obstacles that may prevent their successful progress toward goals, so that they do not become discouraged when the first thing they try does not work (Sklare, 2014).

Career Development and Counseling

Across the literature addressing the social and emotional needs of gifted students, there is a call by experts for early career development and counseling (Kim, 2012; Nicpon & Pfeiffer, 2011; Peterson, 2009; Reis & Renzulli, 2004). For gifted students specifically, and all students more generally, career counseling should be thought of as a developmental process, in which counselors and educators help students explore their interests and make school more meaningful by connecting what students are learning in the classroom to future career goals (Kim, 2012; Wood & Gavin, 2009).

There is a great deal of literature about approaches to career counseling that can be reviewed by counselors embarking on this path, but some specific considerations are particularly important in doing this type of work with gifted students. One issue that comes up frequently is *multipotentiality*, or the idea that a gifted student may have strengths, talents, and interests that could contribute to successful careers in several different areas (Pfeiffer, 2013). The potentially positive side of multipotentiality is that students can explore a number of career possibilities; the potentially negative side is that having too many choices may be overwhelming, and students may worry about making the "right" choice instead of a "good" choice (Kim, 2012). When considering career counseling with gifted students, it is important for counselors to discuss the idea that interests change over time and encourage students to be curious and flexible about career preferences as they progress through school (Greene, 2002). It may be beneficial for a counselor to provide an example of a successful public figure whose career path changed several times throughout his or her life.

Kim (2012) outlines aspects of career development and counseling for gifted students during elementary, middle, and high school. In elementary school, Kim (2012) suggests that career development can focus on helping students to understand their strengths and talents and encouraging them to delve deeper in these areas, while at the same time helping students to recognize their limitations and providing support for areas of growth. During elementary school, it can be helpful for counselors to present information about different types of careers and/or to invite diverse professionals to talk about their work. Counselors can also help students make connections between what they are learning in school and job skills.

Career counseling in middle and high school intensifies the activities begun in elementary school. Kim (2012) suggests that it is critical during this time to help gifted students develop a deeper understanding of their strengths, limitations, and areas of interest. When working with middle school students, counselors can help connect gifted students with mentors working in their areas of interest, and these mentors can help students understand the skills of that job and the academic and career path that would prepare them to work in that field. In high school, students need more in-depth career counseling to provide information about secondary education, career planning, and important career-building skills, such as creating résumés and interviewing.

During career counseling, it can be beneficial to bring in guest speakers and mentors to talk about specific fields and career paths (Wood, 2009); in the absence of available speakers in a given field, technology, such as video conferencing, can be used to provide access to individuals in careers of interest to students. Speakers may help motivate gifted students by making school feel more relevant, and they can be asked to address other areas that impact career success, such as interpersonal skills (Pfeiffer, 2013), which will help to link career development to important coping and social skills for gifted students.

Group Counseling

Group counseling may be an effective approach for providing services to gifted students, especially if the group is composed solely of their gifted peers (Nicpon & Pfeiffer, 2011; Pfeiffer, 2013). Research suggests that students in gifted programs experience greater social success because they experience more shared interests and feel more accepted and understood by their gifted peers (Eddles-Hirsch, Vialle, McCormick, & Rogers, 2012), and this is true of gifted students in group counseling. Many topics that are important for gifted students lend themselves to a group counseling approach, such as building resilience and career development, but social skills and friendship skills are particularly suited to group-based approaches. Wood (2009) suggests that group counseling can help teach gifted students skills to communicate more effectively with peers, to take others' perspectives, and to make friends. In the group counseling format, gifted students can build self-efficacy in social skills through the use of scenarios and role plays (Wood, 2009).

There are many available counseling curricula for social skills and friendship skills that may be implemented with gifted students. When selecting and implementing programs for any counseling group, counselors should carefully consider the relevance of content, scripts, and activities to the needs and abilities of their group members, and these steps are particularly relevant when designing interventions for gifted youth.

BEYOND THE COUNSELING OFFICE

Counselors may also support gifted students' social and emotional development through providing psychoeducation for parents and by promoting and/or implementing a social and emotional learning program.

Parent Psychoeducation

It is widely recognized that parents and other family members play an important role in children's social and emotional development, and this is no different for families of gifted students. Certainly, there may be unique challenges and rewards associated with parenting a gifted student, and counselors can help support parents in their efforts, just as they expect parents to help support educators in their efforts. In the school setting, family members of gifted students may benefit from a combination of psychoeducation and group support to help parents understand their gifted children and to build a connection with other families of gifted students (Moon & Hall, 1998).

A psychoeducational and supportive approach to working with families may address all the issues touched on in this chapter (e.g., perfectionism, underachievement), as well as other topics related to gifted students, their education, and their needs within the family system. For example, parents might benefit from understanding asynchronous development in gifted children, along with a discussion with other parents about setting appropriate expectations and responding to developmental challenges (Moon & Hall, 1998). Other sessions might focus more explicitly on parenting approaches to help students manage emotional distress, engage in positive social interactions, and deal with frustration and disappointment in an appropriate manner (Olszewski-Kubilius, 2002; Pfeiffer, 2013). Pfeiffer (2013) points out that parents of gifted children should expect (and thus teach, model, and reinforce) appropriate social behavior and emotional responses rather than accepting tantrums, meltdowns, and other inappropriate behavior as a normal part of giftedness. In this way, parents are reinforcing the expectation that their children are capable of managing difficult emotions and have the social skills to work with others. He further asserts that parents have a critical role to play in promoting high achievement, but not perfection, by encouraging success in school and highlighting that success often means making mistakes along the way and managing the feelings that come with disappointments and failure. Some parents of gifted children are likely to need guidance in setting expectations and limits, teaching appropriate coping and social skills, modeling expected behaviors, and talking with their children about appropriate achievement (Pfeiffer, 2013). It is important to note that counselors who conduct these types of groups need to consider the unique needs of CLD families (Ford, 2011). Although there is likely to be overlap in terms of parenting issues with non-CLD families, there are also unique concerns and experiences that must be addressed. Given the underrepresentation of CLD students in gifted education, psychoeducational and support groups may need to draw from families with gifted children across the district to ensure that a CLD family is not the only one in a group.

Social and Emotional Learning Programs

Social and emotional learning (SEL) or affective education programs are recommended in virtually every article and chapter written on the social and emotional needs of gifted students (e.g., Eddles-Hirsch et al., 2012; NAGC, 2009a; Pfeiffer, 2013; Reis & Renzulli, 2004; Wood, 2009). SEL and affective education can take different forms, from a school-wide program, to classroom curriculum, to a counseling group of gifted students, or a combination of all three. At the school-wide and classroom levels, SEL and affective education serve to teach social skills and life skills, prevent mental health problems, and create more accepting social environments for all students (Zins, Bloodwell, Weissberg, & Walberg, 2007), but research has also shown benefits specifically for gifted students. Eddles-Hirsch et al. (2012) found that the establishment of a school-wide social and emotional development program was related to a more accepting social context for gifted students, helped them manage social stress better, and helped them feel more comfortable engaging with mixed-group peers without hiding their giftedness.

There are many existing SEL and affective education programs, with varying amounts of research on their effectiveness and impact. However, Zins et al. (2007) outlined key competencies that should be addressed in social and emotional learning programs, which are

- self-awareness;
- social awareness;
- responsible decision-making;
- self-management; and
- relationship management.

Thus, when selecting an SEL program for their school community, counselors should consider both the needs of their students and whether the program addresses these core social and emotional competencies. Further, it is important to note that the greatest impact on students occurs when effective programs are used in a coordinated manner over a longer period of time, and programs should be regularly evaluated to ensure they are having the desired impact (Zins et al., 2007).

RESOURCES

The Davidson Institute for Talent Development

http://www.davidsongifted.org/

The Davidson Institute for Talent Development is a nonprofit organization focused on gifted students. It provides a database that includes articles, information on state policies, and discussion boards.

Hoagies' Gifted Education Page

http://www.hoagiesgifted.org/

Hoagies' Gifted Education Page provides resources for parents, educators, and children and teenagers on topics such as identification and assessment of gifted and talented students, traditional and home schooling, social and emotional needs, parenting, and gifted and talented programs.

The National Association for Gifted Children

http://www.nagc.org/

The National Association for Gifted Children engages in research and development, advocacy, and collaboration with gifted and talented organizations to support gifted students. Publications are available for parents, university professionals, educators, and administrators. Resources are organized by state and include information on national standards, motivation and learning, and social and emotional needs.

Supporting Emotional Needs of the Gifted

http://www.sengifted.org/

Supporting Emotional Needs of the Gifted is an organization that focuses on the emotional needs of gifted students by providing educators and family members online support groups, seminars, and professional development opportunities.

8

Counseling Students With Incarcerated Parents

OVERVIEW

As the inmate population of the United States has grown disproportionally quickly over the past few decades, so has the number of students who have a parent in jail or prison. Between 1991 and 2007, the population of state and federal prisons grew by 92%, and the number of prisoners who were parents to minor children increased by 79% (Glaze & Maruschak, 2010). According to the U.S. Bureau of Justice, there were approximately 1.7 million children with parents incarcerated in federal or state prisons in 2007, which is roughly equivalent to 1 in 50 children, or about 2.3% of children under age 18, and nearly double the number estimated in 1991 (Glaze & Maruschak, 2010; Mumola, 2000). It is important to keep in mind that these numbers represent estimates, and there are likely more students impacted by parental incarceration, since these statistics do not include city or county jails (Bocknek, Sanderson, & Britner, 2009; Gabel, 1992; Miller, 2006). Regardless, these numbers suggest that it is highly likely that any given school is serving several students who have incarcerated parents (Bernstein, 2005).

Students with incarcerated parents are not a homogeneous group, although they likely share some characteristics and experiences. If a child has an incarcerated parent, it is more likely to be a father than a mother, and more likely that the father did not have custody of the child or adolescent prior to incarceration (Glaze & Maruschak, 2010). However, the number of incarcerated mothers is currently rising at a much faster rate than that of fathers (Glaze & Maruschak, 2010). In situations where minor children were living with the incarcerated parent, the new caregiver is most likely to be a grandparent (Glaze & Maruschak, 2010; Miller, 2006). Children with incarcerated parents are disproportionately likely to be from families of color, with Black children 7.5 times more likely and Hispanic children 2.5 times more likely than White children to have a parent in prison (Block & Potthast, 1998; Glaze & Maruschak, 2010; Mumola, 2000).

In spite of the size of this population, students with parents in jail or prison may be unknown to school staff. Given the shame and social stigma that are connected with incarceration, students and caregivers may not disclose about a parental arrest, making this a somewhat invisible risk group (Clopton & East, 2008; Eddy & Reid, 2002; Rossen, 2011). This poses a challenge for counselors, who are in an ideal position to provide needed support given the proportion of time students spend in schools (Lopez & Bhat, 2007). Unfortunately, very little research has been conducted on this population above and beyond the statistical information provided from the Bureau of Justice. A handful of studies have been conducted to examine the exact risk and protective factors involved in the lives of these youth, but very little empirical research has been conducted to examine the efficacy of interventions to support them (Kjellstrand, Cearley, Eddy, Foney, & Martinez, 2012; Lopez & Bhat, 2007; Miller, 2006; Nesmith & Ruthland, 2008).

BASIC CONSIDERATIONS

Impact of Parental Incarceration

In many ways, having a parent who is incarcerated can be broadly viewed as the loss of a parent, analogous to a death. In both situations, the child or adolescent loses access to a parent and may experience a variety of associated life changes that result from this loss, including moves, changes in caregivers, financial stress, and feeling isolated from or different from peers (Bocknek et al., 2009). From this perspective, children's reactions can be likened to bereavement; in fact, children often have many of the same reactions that would be likely after the death of a parent, including sadness, anger, developmental regression, and engagement in risky behaviors (Bocknek et al., 2009; Fisher, Jimerson, Barrett & Graydon, 2010). However, incarcerations are often more complicated and more ambiguous than other losses because these parents are alive, but children do not have immediate access to their parent and may not have control over when or how they see or interact with their parent (Breen, 1995).

PREEXISTING CONTEXTUAL RISK FACTORS

Although the arrest of a parent and the subsequent life changes can place students at risk for negative outcomes, it is very important to remember that youth with incarcerated parents are disproportionately likely to have faced a variety of preexisting risks (Bocknek et al., 2009; Eddy & Reid, 2002; Lopez & Bhat, 2007; Petch & Rochlen, 2009). In fact, some authors posit that these other factors may have at least as much impact on a child or adolescent as the incarceration itself (Gabel, 1992; Miller, 2006; Nesmith & Ruthland, 2008) and may also impact children's ability to cope with the stresses associated with the arrest (Bocknek et al., 2009; Dallaire, 2007; Petch & Rochlen, 2009). Reports from the Bureau of Justice Statistics (Glaze & Maruschak, 2010; Mumola, 2000) describe the self-reported circumstances of parents before their arrest, noting high rates of homelessness, physical or sexual abuse, medical problems, substance abuse problems, and mental health problems, with some of these rates far above those expected from the general population. For example, based on the inmate population of 2007, it is estimated that 57% of state and 43% of federal inmates reported current mental health problems, and 67% of state and 56% of federal inmates reported substance abuse or dependence (Glaze & Maruschak, 2010). Given the nature of these risks, it is also likely that this group of students may have faced these risk factors from before they were born (Eddy & Reid, 2002). Along with the more direct risks of mental illness and substance abuse, children of incarcerated parents are more likely than their peers to have been undersupervised, given the nature of having a parent with these problems (Gabel, 1992). Parents were also likely to have been living in poverty and in high-crime neighborhoods where children may have been exposed to violence (Dallaire, 2007; Miller, 2006; Petch & Rochlen, 2009), representing another type of preexisting contextual risk.

Risks Associated with Incarceration of Fathers and Mothers

In 2007, there were approximately 1.5 million minor children with an incarcerated father and about 140,000 minor children with an incarcerated mother in the United States (Glaze & Maruschak, 2010). The Bureau of Justice Statistics has noted trends in which the number of incarcerated mothers is rising at much higher rates than the number of incarcerated fathers, but there remains a large difference in the overall numbers of incarcerated mothers and fathers (Glaze & Maruschak, 2010; Mumola, 2000). However, in spite of their smaller proportional numbers, it is very important to note than when children's incarcerated parent is their mother rather than their father, they are often at disproportionally greater overall risk than children with an incarcerated father (Dallaire, 2007; Eddy & Reid, 2002; Kjellstrand et al., 2012; Miller, 2006).

When mothers are incarcerated, their children are at significantly higher risk for being arrested later in life than if their fathers are incarcerated. It is hypothesized that this differential risk is explained by the proportionally greater number of contextual risk factors found in the lives of families with an incarcerated mother (Dallaire, 2007). Specifically, mothers who are incarcerated are more likely to report additional incarcerated family members (e.g., aunts, uncles, grandparents), substance abuse, mental illness, homelessness, and physical or sexual abuse at or before the time of their arrest (Dallaire, 2007; Glaze & Maruschak, 2010).

Another potential explanation for the higher risks faced by children of incarcerated mothers is the fact that these children are much more likely to have a change in caregiver as a result of their parent's arrest. According to Glaze and Maruschak's 2010 report, about three quarters of incarcerated mothers reported that their children were living with them at the time of their arrest, compared with about one quarter of incarcerated fathers. Children with an incarcerated father are likely to continue to live with their mother after their father's arrest, whereas children with an incarcerated mother are most likely to live with grandparents or other family members or to live in nonfamilial care, such as foster care or orphanages (Dallaire, 2007; Glaze & Maruschak, 2010; Mumola, 2000). They are also more likely to have multiple changes in caregiver situations, temporary placements, and multiple moves, and to be separated from their siblings (Miller, 2006). Chapter 3 of this volume addresses risk factors associated with being in foster care. Some authors also hypothesize that, from an attachment theory perspective, the disruption in the mother-child bond resulting from maternal incarceration may explain the heightened risks found for this group (Dallaire, 2007). The difference in risk could also be framed in terms of the overall amount of life disruption caused by the arrest of a parent. If a father is arrested and the child continues to live with his or her mother, the overall amount of disruption may be relatively low; when a mother is arrested and a child is placed in a series of temporary custodial arrangements, the overall disruption to that child's life is very high (Kjellstrand et al., 2012; Miller, 2006; Rossen, 2011).

Stigma

A significant risk faced by families impacted by parental incarceration is the stigma associated with involvement in the justice system. Unfortunately, it is very common for both caregivers and children to report feeling shame, embarrassment, and social isolation related to the incarceration of a parent (Council on Crime and Justice, 2006; Miller, 2006; Rossen, 2011). Youth in particular report feeling different from their peers, not having many friends, and not feeling safe talking about their situation (Bocknek et al., 2009), and they may fear being rejected or judged based on their parent's actions and status (Miller, 2006). In some situations, stigma may be real, and in others it may be perceived, but the net impact is the same. Additionally, some children may be specifically told by their caregivers to not disclose their parent's incarceration to friends or teachers. Although this advice may come from a perspective of trying to protect the student from embarrassment or social rejection, it can have the unintended impact of isolating students from peers and adults who could provide support. Supporting students in combating the impacts of stigma and resulting feelings of social isolation is an important task in counseling. It is also important to note that in some communities where incarceration rates are high, stigma and social isolation in students with incarcerated parents may actually be lower than in other communities due to the normalization of familial incarceration.

Financial Strain

Families with incarcerated parents were disproportionately likely to be from poverty prior to the parent's arrest and are also more likely to experience further financial distress as a result of the incarceration (Council on Crime and Justice, 2006; Glaze & Maruschak, 2010; Miller, 2006; Mumola, 2000; Rossen, 2011). Even if the arrested parent was a noncustodial parent, it is likely that he or she had been a financial contributor in the child's life, and potentially the sole source of financial support, especially in the case of incarcerated mothers (Glaze & Maruschak, 2010; Miller, 2006; Mumola, 2000). This means that on top of the stresses associated with a change in caregivers, impacted families often experience additional financial strain. Additionally, the financial impact faced by these families often continues after a parent is released as a result of employment restrictions based on criminal history.

Threats to Attachment and Relationships

Naturally, when a parent is incarcerated, there is going to be some impact on the parent-child relationship. The extent of that impact, as well as whether or not it should be conceptualized as a risk factor, will be highly variable. Although it is outside the scope of this book, attachment theory and the work of attachment theorists (e.g., John Bowlby and Mary Ainsworth; Lightfoot, Cole, & Cole, 2009) provide relevant perspectives regarding potential impacts of disrupted parent-child attachments. From a broader perspective, counselors need to keep in mind that some children will experience the relative loss of their primary attachment figure as a result of an incarceration. Depending on the age of the child and the circumstances of his or her change in caregivers, reactions might include regressive developmental behaviors, sadness, fear, anxiety, and an impaired ability or desire to form attachments with others (Bocknek et al., 2009; Bruxton-McClendon, 2013; Council on Crime and Justice, 2006; Miller, 2006; Seymour, 1998).

For some families, parents will become primary caregivers again upon their release; for others, parental rights may be terminated, especially when longer sentences are involved (Miller, 2006). Another potential change in the home life and affect attachment may come in the form of marital discord or divorce, as families that were intact prior to the incarceration of a parent face a number of stressors that make these outcomes more likely (Kazura, 2000).

Reactions by Age

The impact of parental incarceration for any given child will vary by age and developmental level (Bruxton-McClendon, 2013; Eddy & Reid, 2002; Miller, 2006; Rossen, 2011). For example, one would expect very different reactions based on different abilities to understand the changes associated with a parent leaving the home for an extended period after an arrest. As with reactions to grief, a given child or adolescent's reaction will be shaped by his or her age, cognitive development, and attachment to the incarcerated person, among other factors. For very young children, reactions may include developmental regressions (e.g., loss of speech, bed-wetting), somatic complaints (e.g., stomachache, trouble sleeping), or misconceptions about the incarceration itself (e.g., parent will be home soon, arrest was child's fault; Bruxton-McClendon, 2013; Miller, 2006). Older children may still hold misconceptions about the parent's arrest and may also worry about the safety and day-to-day life of their incarcerated parent and the social stigma and teasing that may occur if classmates or friends find out (Bruxton-McClendon, 2013; Nesmith & Ruthland, 2008). In addition, school-age children may struggle in school, attempt to avoid school, become defiant or oppositional toward authority figures, or engage in aggressive or delinquent behaviors (Bruxton-McClendon, 2013). As with reactions to grief and loss, adolescents may display any of these behaviors, but they are also at risk for engaging in risky behaviors such as sexual promiscuity, substance abuse, and antisocial activity (Bruxton-McClendon, 2013; Eddy & Reid, 2002).

The Impact of Combined Risks

While the depth and breadth of risk factors faced by children and adolescents have been thoroughly described in the literature, only a handful of authors have described the possible mechanisms at play regarding how these factors interact to influence outcomes. For simplicity, it may help to separate these factors into pre-incarceration contextual factors (e.g., living in poverty, exposure to violence or drug abuse in the home) and incarceration and related factors (e.g., multiple changes in caregivers, inadequately prepared caregivers, stigma, and social isolation). From one standpoint, the incarceration can be framed as a culminating activity, with a greater emphasis placed on the contextual factors already in place before a parent's arrest as having the greatest impact on a child's or adolescent's ultimate outcome (Nesmith & Ruthland, 2008). From another, contextual factors are described as having a compounding impact on the incarceration, such that they may impact a child's ability to cope with the subsequent stressors that come after the arrest of a parent (Council on Crime and Justice, 2006; Petch & Rochlen, 2009). Finally, from her large study of incarcerated parents, Dallaire (2007) described an additive model regarding contextual risks, such that the more risks that are present prior to the arrest, the more likely it was that a child of an incarcerated parent went on to be arrested him- or herself.

Regardless of the model utilized, it is helpful to recognize which potential risk factors are involved in the life of any given student with an incarcerated parent. Although some risks are malleable (e.g., support can be provided to help new caregivers provide stability for children, students can be enrolled in mentoring programs to provide supportive adult relationships), others, especially the contextual factors present before the parent's arrest, are not.

INTERNALIZING BEHAVIORS

Students with incarcerated parents are at risk for a variety of internalizing behaviors (Bocknek et al., 2009; Council on Crime and Justice, 2006; Miller, 2006). Feelings of depression and anxiety are common reactions, especially for youth for whom the incarceration or prior contextual risks were traumatizing (Petch & Rochlen, 2009). For example, Miller (2006) found that children were more likely to develop internalizing problems if they witnessed their parent's arrest. Depending on the scenario, children may see some combination of potentially traumatizing sights such as (a) weapons pointed at their parent, (b) flashing lights or sirens on a patrol car, (c) a physical struggle between their parent and the arresting officers, and (d) their parent being taken away in handcuffs (Bruxton-McClendon, 2013). From this lens, it is easy to see how an arrest might cause symptoms of post-traumatic stress in a child, especially a young child (Bocknek et al., 2009; Petch & Rochlen, 2009).

Externalizing Behaviors

As discussed previously, students with an incarcerated parent are at increased risk for later incarceration. Much of the evidence to support this finding comes from research with incarcerated adults, who report very high rates of themselves having had a parent who was incarcerated at some point during their childhood or adolescence (e.g., Dallaire, 2007; Glaze & Maruschak, 2010; Mumola, 2000). Although this is an alarming long-term negative outcome, students are also at risk for a variety of more immediate problems, particularly externalizing behaviors such as aggression, engagement in delinquent activity, and engagement in antisocial or illegal activities, all of which may lead to involvement in the juvenile justice system (Bocknek et al., 2009; Bruxton-McClendon, 2013; Council on Crime and Justice, 2006; Eddy & Reid, 2002; Miller, 2006; Nesmith & Ruthland, 2008; Petch & Rochlen, 2009). Many authors have also described increased rates of defiance toward authority or rejection of limits and boundaries, which may manifest in the school setting as outright defiance, discipline problems, truancy, and decreased academic performance (Bruxton-McClendon, 2013; Council on Crime and Justice, 2006; Miller, 2006; Nesmith & Ruthland, 2008; Rossen, 2011). Petch and Rochlen (2009) hypothesize that behaviors such as rejection of legal or school authority figures and general defiance can be viewed as an attempt to regain control, or a result of the loss of trust in the "system" that is specific to the experience of having a parent incarcerated. Other authors note the possibility that anger and defiance are expressions of grief over the loss of their parent or the loss of the stability in their lives (Bernstein, 2005).

Resilience

Although children with incarcerated parents are often discussed as a group that faces many risks, it does not necessarily follow that all youth in this group will go on to experience negative outcomes (Bruxton-McClendon, 2013; Dallaire, 2007; Gabel, 1992; Rossen, 2011). Additionally, although many counselors tend to automatically frame the removal of a parent from the home as a negative event, it is important to remember that in some instances, the incarceration of a parent may represent the loss of a risk factor rather than the addition of one. If the parent's personal characteristics (e.g., substance abuse, violent behavior, homelessness) were creating a home environment characterized by erratic behavior, neglect, abandonment, or a general lack of safety and security, his or her arrest may lead to a general improvement in the child's life circumstances (Bruxton-McClendon, 2013; Dallaire, 2007; Gabel, 1992).

COUNSELING APPROACHES

Students with incarcerated parents are a diverse group, potentially facing a variety of risks and stressful situations in their lives. Fortunately, there are many recommendations for how counselors can work with these students to foster positive trajectories.

Counseling Considerations

Counselors will need to take extra care to establish safe and trusting relationships with these students, who may fear disclosing their familial situation and may have been told to not discuss their parent's arrest or incarceration with others (Clopton & East, 2008; Nesmith & Ruthland, 2008). Additionally, given their potential interactions with authority figures, some students may be particularly reluctant to engage in counseling if the counselor is perceived as a person with authority. Some students may also have difficulty forming trusting relationships overall, which will naturally make the establishment of a counseling relationship challenging. Establishing rapport and building trust in counseling relationships take time and effort. Murphy (2008) provides several suggestions for building cooperative counselor-client relationships that include

- treating students as experts on themselves and their circumstances;
- conveying respectful curiosity, humility, and a willingness to learn;
- dedicating time to listening, and asking and learning before offering any suggestions;
- respecting students' right to reject suggestions; and
- acknowledging students' strengths via genuine compliments.

When preparing to work with students with incarcerated parents, it may help counselors to step back and view the big picture in terms of the rights of the impacted students because, regardless of the actions of their parents, children have a number of rights that should not be taken from them (Bernstein, 2005; Council on Crime and Justice, 2006; Sazie, Ponder, & Johnson, 2003), including the right to

- know that what is happening to their parent is not their fault;
- know where their parent is and when they will be able to contact or see him or her;
- have supportive people in their lives with whom they can safely discuss their incarcerated parent and their feelings toward the parent;
- know what will be changing in their lives as a result of the incarceration;
- be seen as individuals separate from their parent's actions; and
- feel safe and supported at school.

Being cognizant of these rights does not mean that a counselor needs to be prepared to provide a student with all of the aforementioned information (e.g., be able to answer questions about where a parent is and when the student can see or speak with him or her); nevertheless, it is important to keep these rights in mind as the counseling relationship begins. For example, a counselor may make statements in an opening session that affirm that this incarceration is not the student's fault, that the student is not accountable or responsible for the parent's actions, and that the counselor will work with the student to ensure that he or she is supported at school. It would also be appropriate to acknowledge that changes may have already taken place in the student's life and that the counselor will be working in collaboration with the student and others to help him or her adjust to these changes and understand what subsequent changes may be in store. With awareness and support, much can be done to ameliorate risks and ensure that students with incarcerated parents maintain their rights and dignity.

General Counseling Strategies

Given how much students with an incarcerated parent may have to cope with, the use of a solution-focused brief therapy (SFBT) approach is strongly recommended for this population (Rossen, 2011). Asking questions that help students remember when they have been successful in dealing with stressful, difficult, or scary situations in the past can help empower them to cope with their current circumstances (Bruxton-McClendon, 2013; Rossen, 2011). Counselors can help students to develop future-oriented goals, identify internal resources, and find external sources of support, such as caring friends and teachers (Springer, Lynch, & Rubin, 2000). Another useful SFBT approach is helping students anticipate potentially stressful events (i.e., flagging the minefield) in order to develop proactive coping strategies. Such events that may be upsetting for students include upcoming court dates, visitation dates, release dates, birthdays, or holidays such as Mother's Day or Father's Day (Bruxton-McClendon, 2013; Rossen, 2011). In these cases, a counselor could ask questions such as "What might you do if your mom isn't able to call you on your birthday?" or "What might you be able to say to yourself if you find out that your father didn't get parole?"

Students may also benefit from counseling programs that teach stress management and coping skills, depending on their unique areas of need. For example, *Coping Cat* is a CBT-based intervention that helps students recognize and understand anxiety and implement coping strategies (Kendall & Hedtke, 2006). Another useful counseling program based on social-emotional learning is the *Strong Kids* series (*Strong Start; Strong Kids; Strong Teens*), which helps students understand emotions, cope with anger and stress, build skills in problem-solving, and effectively use positive thinking strategies (Merrell, Carizalez, Feuerborn, Gueldner, & Tran, 2007a, 2007b, 2007c; Merrell, Parisi, & Whitcomb, 2007). Although both *Coping Cat* and the *Strong Kids* series have research support, neither has been specifically evaluated for use with students with incarcerated parents.

For younger students, counselors may consider using play therapy techniques to help process feelings and experiences. Shillingford, Trice-Black, and Whitfield-Williams (2013) describe the application of play therapy for these youngsters, noting that when a safe and supportive environment is established, play can help children explore all the issues addressed in this chapter, including feelings of shame, stigma, or isolation; feelings about their incarcerated parent; visitation; and the re-entry of an incarcerated parent into the family.

Bibliotherapy may be another useful counseling tool for this group of students. Two commonly used books are *When a Parent Goes to Jail: A Comprehensive*

Guide for Counseling Children of Incarcerated Parents (Yaffe & Hoade, 2000) and *My Daddy Is in Jail: Story, Discussion Guide, and Small Group Activities for Grades K–5* (Bender, 2003).

Counseling Specifically Related to Incarceration

ANSWERING QUESTIONS AND CORRECTING MISCONCEPTIONS

Students with an incarcerated parent will naturally have a lot of questions. Young children may wonder why their parent is away, what it means to be arrested, and if the arrest was their fault; older children and adolescents may wonder what jail or prison is like for their parent, whether their parent is safe, when they might see their parent again, and what it will be like to visit a parent in a correctional facility (Sazie et al., 2003). Because it is very common for caregivers to not discuss the incarceration or to provide inaccurate or misleading information to children with incarcerated parents, children can experience stress and anxiety and use their imaginations and images from media to fill in the gaps incorrectly (Bocknek et al., 2009; Bruxton-McClendon, 2013; Council on Crime and Justice, 2006; Miller, 2006; Nesmith & Ruthland, 2008). One important aspect of counseling is to help students to understand more about the realities of their situation; by providing accurate information, counselors can help provide honest, age-appropriate, and accurate responses to students' questions about their parent's incarceration and how it impacts them (Council on Crime and Justice, 2006). For younger students, this might mean using terms that they can relate to (e.g., that the parent is in a type of timeout); for older students, this could mean helping them understand what the facility may look like in preparation for a visit, how the criminal justice system works, and so forth (Bruxton-McClendon, 2013). It is optimal for counselors to work with caregivers to ensure consistency in the information provided (Bruxton-McClendon, 2013), and in many situations, it may be preferable to work with caregivers to help them to provide this information directly. More information on working with caregivers is included in the "Beyond the Counseling Office" section of this chapter.

CONTACT AND VISITATION WITH AN INCARCERATED PARENT

The amount of contact students have with their incarcerated parent will depend on several factors. As discussed earlier in this chapter, the incarceration of some parents may represent an improvement in the circumstances of the student, and in those cases, maintaining contact with the incarcerated parent may be a low priority for the family (Council on Crime and Justice, 2006). In other situations, especially if the incarcerated parent had been a full-time caregiver, helping the students to maintain contact with a very important person in their life is crucial (Miller, 2006). Research suggests that visits that occur within the context of a structured intervention program, such as Girls Scouts Beyond Bars (Block & Potthast, 1998), tended to have a positive impact for children, while visits occurring outside of such interventions tended to have a negative impact (Poehlmann,

Dallaire, Booker, & Shear, 2010). Although the research is scarce, the general trend suggests that if children are going to visit their incarcerated parents, it is best if those visits occur in the context of some support. Caregivers hold the responsibility for facilitating this contact (e.g., providing transportation for visits, providing calling cards or accepting collect calls), but counselors can play a very important role by helping to prepare students for letters, calls, or visits and helping students to process their reactions after these events have occurred.

It is natural that students will have some apprehension about visiting an incarcerated parent. In addition to the fear of the unknown, many student may find the realities of the jail or prison environment (e.g., physical searches of visitors, metal detectors, Plexiglas barriers, jumpsuits, and handcuffs) to be new and frightening (Kazura, 2000; Poehlmann et al., 2010). Counselors can help prepare children by front-loading them with as much age-appropriate information about visitation as possible (Bernstein, 2005; Kazura, 2000; Nesmith & Ruthland, 2008; Poehlmann et al., 2010; Rossen, 2011). It will help students to understand when visits can occur, reasons that visits may not be possible, and what the visitation may be like, and counselors can work with caregivers to answer questions such as the following:

- What will the room look like?
- Will physical contact be allowed?
- Will their parent be in handcuffs?
- Can they play a game with their parent?
- Can they bring items like artwork to share with their parent?
- How might they feel before, after, or during the visit?

In helping students prepare for visits to jails or prisons, counselors may be at a disadvantage if they do not have familiarity with these institutions. When counseling younger students, counselors should spend time preparing for sessions by seeking out information about the facility in question. With older students, it may be appropriate to spend time researching these details together. If students are particularly anxious, role plays regarding how they might act and what they might say to their incarcerated parent may be helpful (Rossen, 2011). For students of any age, it is important to provide a safe and nonjudgmental context for students to process their feelings about contact and visits after they occur.

It is important to note that not all students will be able to visit their incarcerated parent in person, and in many instances, caregivers may not want or be able to support in-person visits, especially if the parent is incarcerated at a great distance from where they are living, or if caregivers are worried that visits may be detrimental (Bernstein, 2005; Council on Crime and Justice, 2006; Miller, 2006; Nesmith & Ruthland, 2008; Poehlmann et al., 2010; Rossen, 2011). Additionally, some facilities may have policies that prohibit visits for sentences of shorter lengths or may allow visitation only after a certain amount of time has passed (e.g., 60 days; Kazura, 2000). In these cases, counselors can help to support students who contact their parent via mail or phone calls. They can encourage students to draft letters and can use counseling time to help students brainstorm and role-play what they want to say to their parent, although counselors should be aware that the literacy level of the parent may prevent students from receiving reciprocal communication in written form (Kazura, 2000).

RE-ENTRY

The release of a parent and his or her reintegration into a student's life can be very stressful (Bruxton-McClendon, 2013; Gabel, 1992; Petch & Rochlen, 2009). As with contact and visitation, counselors who are aware up upcoming releases can help students prepare for the changes in their lives and routines, as well as help students process feelings that they may have as their family adjusts to its new structure. The stresses of re-entry will vary across families but may be particularly acute for students whose parents were involved in activities that put children at risk prior to the arrest. In other words, students may be naturally apprehensive about the return of a parent who was violent, abused drugs or alcohol, or was unable to provide a stable home environment for them (Gabel, 1992). In these cases, a counselor may wish to help students create a plan for what they might do, whom they might contact, and where they might go should they ever feel unsafe around their returning parent. Additionally, given that re-entry of an incarcerated parent represents another tumultuous time of change in students' lives, counselors should focus on providing stability and continuity of relationships and support in the school setting to the greatest extent possible (Bruxton-McClendon, 2013).

Counseling Groups

Given the risk of students with incarcerated parents experiencing a sense of isolation, group counseling is a natural fit for this population. Although there is limited empirical support for the efficacy of counseling groups in school settings for students with incarcerated parents (e.g., Lopez & Bhat, 2007; Springer et al., 2000), many authors recommend the use of group-based strategies such as support groups to help decrease feelings of isolation and provide supportive peer networks (e.g., Bernstein, 2005; Council on Crime and Justice, 2006; Rossen, 2011).

As with any form of group counseling, great care should be taken when students are being screened for a group of this type. Given the shame, fear, and stigma that can be associated with disclosing that a parent is incarcerated, it is critical that only group participants who will be capable of providing a safe and supportive context for any disclosures are selected. It is also very important that enough time is dedicated to helping groups build trust and cohesion before students are expected to share any potentially sensitive information. In their group for children with incarcerated parents, Springer and colleagues (2000) found that group members were ready for deeper discussions and more personal disclosures by the fourth and fifth group session. Both Springer et al. (2000) and Lopez and Baht (2007) recommend that groups run for approximately 12 sessions to allow time for trust to develop.

Content for counseling groups for students with incarcerated parents can be selected to meet a range of goals depending on the students' unique needs. The most commonly recommended approach is to run groups primarily as support groups, with the leader's role being to establish safety, foster a sense of community, and encourage interaction and mutual support among members (Bernstein, 2005; Council on Crime and Justice, 2006; Springer et al., 2000). Lopez and Baht (2007) reported positive results with a curriculum based on SFBT principles that also included bibliotherapy, modeling, and role play. Although group content needs to be based on the specific needs of group participants, many topics that are relevant to this population can be addressed within a group counseling format, including preparation for and reactions to visits, exploring emotions regarding changes in living arrangements or family structure, and exploring feelings related to stigma and isolation. Additionally, for children in elementary school, Burgess, Caselman, and Carsey (2009) developed a curriculum that can be used for group or individual counseling. Their book, *Empowering Children of Incarcerated Parents*, includes 10 lessons, each with a script, discussion questions, and reproducible handouts and activities. Lesson topics include (a) dealing with shame, (b) acknowledging trauma, (c) handling angry feelings, and (d) planning for the future. Each lesson also includes letters from a fictional student to his incarcerated parent for discussion.

BEYOND THE COUNSELING OFFICE

Working With the Custodial Parent or Guardian

Indirect services can be an important way in which counselors can support students. For this population, providing support or helping to locate appropriate support for caregivers can be critical to the success of students. As a foundation, counselors need to reach out to caregivers to create relationships based on trust that function as partnerships with the student's best interests in mind (Bruxton-McClendon, 2013). Given the stigma that surrounds incarceration, counselors should ensure that materials going home from the school convey a nonjudgmental message of inclusivity of all families, regardless of circumstance. Because incarcerations are not always disclosed to school teams (Eddy & Reid, 2002; Rossen, 2011), it may be that the only way a counselor becomes aware of students who may need support is that their caregivers trusted school personnel enough to disclose this information. It benefits students when caregivers feel comfortable enough to share information about the incarcerated parent, such as upcoming visit days, communication from the parent and the student's reaction to that communication, upcoming court appearances, release dates, or even the type of information that has already been shared with the student about the parent and his or her incarceration (Bruxton-McClendon, 2013; Rossen, 2011).

Some caregivers, particularly those who only became caregivers due to the incarceration, such as grandparents, will also benefit from direct service or assistance with locating services. It is important for counselors to keep in mind that not all caregivers were prepared to or wanted to become caregivers prior to the incarceration (Clopton & East, 2008). Most situations involving the incarceration of a parent will be stressful on the family unit as a whole; factors such as loss of income and care of a distressed child would create a strain on any family. Stresses on caregivers often do not go unnoticed by children or adolescents, and they can exacerbate other problems (Council on Crime and Justice, 2006). Additionally, caregivers are often the "gatekeepers" of relationships with the incarcerated parent (Council on Crime and Justice, 2006; Nesmith & Ruthland, 2008; Poehlmann et al., 2010) and may need support in making decisions about contact or in gathering the resources needed to provide access to visits, particularly if the parent is incarcerated at a distance. It should be noted that there may be multiple adults serving in caregiving roles for students; it is not uncommon for large familial and nonfamilial extended kinship communities (e.g., church members, godparents) to be involved in the lives of these youth (Bocknek et al., 2009).

Mentorship

There is some research to support the efficacy of involving students with mentoring programs (e.g., Bocknek et al., 2009; Shillingford et al., 2013). The mechanisms at play here are intuitive: Children and adolescents with incarcerated parents are in need of stable, positive role models. Mentoring programs in general aim to provide supportive, caring relationships with adults, which are well-known protective factors for youth facing a variety of risks. General mentoring programs (e.g., informal programs or programs such as Big Brothers Big Sisters) are recommended (Council on Crime and Justice, 2006), as are targeted programs created specifically for youth with incarcerated parents (e.g., Michigan Department of Mental Health's Project SEEK and Seton Youth Shelter's Mentoring Children of Prisoners; Shillingford et al., 2013). Counselors can help identify potential programs for students.

School Climate

An important noncounseling role for counselors is to work with administrators, parents, teachers, community leaders, and other stakeholders to educate others about this population and work to collectively reduce the stigma associated with having an incarcerated parent (Bruxton-McClendon, 2013; Clopton & East, 2008; Nesmith & Ruthland, 2008; Petch & Rochlen, 2009; Rossen, 2011). By offering in-service workshops, presenting at meetings, creating brochures, or providing information on school websites to educate school communities, counselors can let others know about the unique needs of this population (Nesmith & Ruthland, 2008; Petch & Rochlen, 2009; Rossen, 2011). Counselors can also help administrators and teachers to understand the importance of curricula and lessons that teach students about social justice and the diverse types of families that exist within society (Clopton & East, 2008; Petch & Rochlen, 2009). Bruxton-McClendon (2013) provides an excellent example of an inclusive lesson plan that asks students to discuss a person whom they miss (e.g., deceased person, family member or friend on military deployment, family member or friend who has moved away, family member who is incarcerated), then write a card and select artwork or schoolwork that they wish to share with that person.

Counselors can also help students with incarcerated parents get involved with after-school activities such as clubs or sports, which benefits students by providing after-school supervision, widening their peer group, and building supportive relationships with other adults at school (Bruxton-McClendon, 2013; Council on Crime and Justice, 2006; Nesmith & Ruthland, 2008).

Comprehensive Programs

A number of evidence-based comprehensive programs have been implemented to support families with incarcerated parents. One of the most frequently cited programs is Girl Scouts Beyond Bars (Block & Potthast, 1998), an intervention that provided small-group support to girls with incarcerated parents, focusing on eliminating shame and isolation and on preparing for visits. In addition, like many comprehensive programs described in the literature for this population, Girl Scouts Beyond Bars provided support for incarcerated parents regarding parenting and communicating with their children. Several other authors present positive results of similar comprehensive programs, although there is more empirical support available regarding programs that focus on helping children indirectly by providing incarcerated parents with an array of services (e.g., Kazura, 2000) than there are programs that focus on supporting children in particular. Results from these types of programs are promising; Girl Scouts Beyond Bars reported an increased number of parent-child visitations, as well as decreased externalizing behaviors in participating girls. However, comprehensive programs to support these families are rare and inconsistently offered (Bernstein, 2005). As with any multifaceted intervention, they tend to be expensive and are often funded via grant-based initiatives. Although counselors will not likely be involved with the provision of services in this type of program, it is important that they research the availability of such services in their area in order to help families access them.

RESOURCES

ANNIE E. CASEY FOUNDATION

http://www.aecf.org/resources/children-with-incarcerated-parents/

The Annie E. Casey Foundation is a private philanthropic organization that aims to improve the lives of children at risk for poor health, educational, social, and economic outcomes. The foundation's website hosts a list of select resources that includes books and research articles, as well as a comprehensive list of names and websites for programs designed to work with children with incarcerated parents.

Little Children, Big Challenges: Incarceration

http://www.sesamestreet.org/parents/topicsandactivities/toolkits/incarceration#7

Little Children, Big Challenges is a series of programs and toolkits designed by Sesame Street the TV show/brand for young children. They include a toolkit for children with incarcerated parents that includes materials for incarcerated parents and caregivers and activities for children. They also include a series of *Sesame Street* video clips featuring children coping with parental incarceration.

National Resource Center on Children and Families of the Incarcerated

http://nrccfi.camden.rutgers.edu/

The National Resource Center on Children and Families of the Incarcerated is hosted by Rutgers University–Camden. It has been working to meet the needs of this population by disseminating accurate and relevant information, preparing and inspiring those working with impacted children and families, and guiding policy and practice. The center's website hosts research articles, fact sheets, and directories of available programs and resources for each state. The center also provides an extensive list of bibliotherapy and video resources for use with children and adolescents.

9

Counseling Students in Military Families

OVERVIEW

There is a saying within the military that describes family life: "When one person joins, the whole family serves" (Park, 2011, p. 65). There are currently more than a million school-age children from military families in the United States, the majority of whom attend public schools (U.S. Department of Defense, 2013). During peacetime, military children and their families are nearly identical to civilian children and families on indices such as well-being and academic achievement (Park, 2011; Pisano, 2014). When families face deployment, however, social, emotional, academic, and behavioral problems can occur (Chandra, Martin, Hawkins, & Richardson, 2010; De Pedro et al., 2011; Garner, Arnold, & Nunnery, 2014; Guzman, 2014; Kaplow, Layne, Saltzman, Cozza, & Pynoos, 2013). The U.S. military is the most widely deployed military in the world, and approximately 2 million children have had deployed parents since 2001, many with multiple and lengthy deployments (De Pedro et al., 2011; Lester et al., 2013; Pisano, 2014), with some military personnel having an average of four or more deployments since the birth of their oldest child (Lester et al., 2011). Some deployments have come with very short notices (Carter, 2013), and they can last up to two years, although the average length is around 12 to 18 months (Aronson & Perkins, 2013).

Most children with deployed parents are resilient, but a portion display social, emotional, or behavior problems related to stress at home and concerns over both deployed and nondeployed parents (Chandra et al., 2010). Other identified sources of stress for these youth include feelings of isolation from the civilian community, relocations that may disrupt social and academic development, and the changes in family dynamics and responsibilities that come along with the extended absence of a parent (De Pedro et al., 2011; Garner et al., 2014). A number of protective factors for deployment-related stress have been identified, including supportive friends and family members, access to community mental health care, supportive school environments, access to military-specific resources, and personal strengths like coping skills (De Pedro et al., 2011), and counselors can help students build skills and access available supports.

BASIC CONSIDERATIONS

Global War on Terror

Since 2001, the United States has been involved in a number of military engagements (e.g., Operation Iraqi Freedom and Operation Enduring Freedom, which are collectively referred to as the Global War on Terror [GWOT]; Hollingsworth, 2011). The GWOT is the longest-running military operation in the history of the United States (Aronson & Perkins, 2013), and several aspects set it apart from other wars in our history, including its length, the number of deaths and service members wounded in action, the length and frequency of deployments, and the reliance on members of the Reserves and National Guard (Hardy, 2006; Huebner, Mancini, Bowen, & Orthner, 2009). For these reasons, the GWOT has been described as being particularly hard on military service members and their families, even when compared with other wars (De Pedro et al., 2011; Guzman, 2014; Ross & DeVoe, 2014).

Support Services for Military Families

Fortunately, the military provides an extensive array of services to help support its families (Huebner et al., 2009). Unfortunately, not all families have access to the supports (e.g., counselors, family programming) provided by the military (Aronson & Perkins, 2013), especially those who serve in the Reserves or National Guard and may not live on or near military facilities. Although a significant number of resources and services are available online (several of which are reviewed at the end of this chapter), many military families will seek help when needed in schools or community settings. Many civilian counselors may not be particularly familiar with the military or the unique needs of this population, and it is important that they seek this information in order to provide effective services. Hoshmand and Hoshmand (2007) note that trends regarding the lack of knowledge of or interest in the military on the part of civilian helping professionals may stem from an "ideological ambivalence toward an establishment associated with warfare" (p. 173), but they also note that counselors need to put aside these beliefs in favor of their ethical obligations to best support all students. Similarly, Carter (2013) reminds counselors that their own opinions or beliefs regarding the current war or the military in general have no place within the counseling relationship.

Education

According to the U.S. Department of Defense Demographic Report (2013), there are more than 2.2 million active military members with about 2.9 million family members (i.e., spouses, children, elderly dependents). About 42% of both active-duty (traditional branches) and Reserve or National Guard members have children, for a total of about 1.9 million children in military families, and more than 1 million of these children are school-age. About one third of these children and families reside on military bases, and the children attend schools that are operated by the Department of Defense Educational Activity (DoDEA), but the majority live in civilian communities (De Pedro et al., 2011; Hoshmand & Hoshmand, 2007). Given these numbers, it is more likely that most schools have at least a few students with one or more parents in the military (Carter, 2013). Children from military families may attend almost any school, although some schools and districts have very high percentages of these families, with about 80% of military-connected families attending 214 school districts nationwide (De Pedro et al., 2011). Because children and families may not always immediately disclose military status, professionals should routinely ask about military connections (Murphy & Fairbank, 2013).

Reserves and National Guard Families

The high levels of involvement of Reservist and National Guard service members in the GWOT (i.e., nearly half of deployed service members at some points during the recent wars; Hardy, 2006; Huebner et al., 2009) have led researchers and helping professionals to investigate the unique needs of these families. When compared with service members from more traditional branches of the military (e.g., U.S. Army, Marine Corps), members in the Reserves or National Guard are less likely to live on a military base (Harrison & Vannest, 2008). As such, they are less likely to be surrounded by the formal and informal services and community supports provided by the military and the military culture of a base community, which are most critical for family members during deployments (Chandra, Martin, Hawkins, & Richardson, 2010; De Pedro et al., 2011). Additionally, Reserve or National Guard members and their families may not receive the same type of preparation in advance of a deployment (Esposito-Smythers et al., 2011).

For these reasons, children and families involved in the Reserves or National Guard may be the most in need of support and the most likely military-involved families to seek or received support from school-based mental health professionals (Esposito-Smythers et al., 2011). Many researchers describe children and families who are experiencing the deployment of a Reservist or National Guard family member as socially isolated, and they are in need of avenues to connect with others and share experiences (e.g., Chandra et al., 2010; DePedro et al., 2011; Harrison & Vannest, 2008).

Moving and Relocation

In the time prior to the current GWOT, the aspect most counseling and educational professionals likely associated with military families was their mobility. Relocations are much more common in military families than in civilian families, with rates averaging about 33% per year, compared with 20% in the civilian population (Williams, 2013). Framed another way, between kindergarten and 12th grade, the average military family moves between six and nine times (Jackson, 2010). Next to deployment, relocations have been identified as the biggest factors influencing the academic and emotional well-being of children in military families (Garner et al., 2014).

When any family moves, there are many changes that take place for its children, particularly with regard to school. Relocations require that students adjust to new teachers, classmates, school policies, school climates, academic content, and peer groups (Pisano, 2014; Williams, 2013). Especially when moves are made during the academic year, students may be placed in classes where they have missed certain aspects of the curricula, and they may require tutoring or other academic supports to help them catch up with their classmates (Garner et al., 2014). Another challenge that may happen with moves is that school records may be lost or arrive late, causing students to not be able to enroll in programs such as honors or Advanced Placement courses or in special education (Jackson, 2010; Pisano, 2014). Additionally, students may be excluded from school-based activities such as sports teams or drama productions because they have missed tryouts or auditions (Pisano, 2014).

For all students, these transitions may cause some level of stress or anxiety, but it is important for counselors to recognize that students from military families are likely to experience these transitions many times throughout their education. Every student is unique; these frequent moves may make transitions more stressful or challenging, or they may make students more tolerant and flexible regarding such changes. For some students, relocations can be positive experiences (Park, 2011).

Fortunately, all 50 states have recently signed the Military Children's Interstate Compact (www.mic3.net). The purpose of this compact is to ensure uniform treatment of students from military families when they enroll in new districts or states. The compact covers areas such as kindergarten birthday cutoffs, state-mandated high school exit exams, and continued participation in GATE or Advanced Placement classes for students who have recently moved from another state. According to the compact, receiving schools are more flexible in how they honor course and program placements (e.g., make placements based on informal information and have longer timelines for accepting official documentation; Williams, 2013). Although school administration should be aware of the provisions of the compact as they apply within their state, it is helpful if counselors educate themselves and others at school about the compact so they are able to advocate for the needs of students from military families who relocate to their schools.

Loss or Injury of a Parent

When military parents are deployed, especially to a war zone, there is always a risk that they may be injured or killed. Although the exact risks are impossible to calculate, researchers estimate that children of deployed military families have disproportionately high fears of the death of their deployed parent (Cozza, Chun, & Polo, 2005). It is hypothesized that exposure to news and other media focused on particularly dangerous aspects of our various active combat areas play a role in students' worries (Pisano, 2014). Additionally, some children living on military bases may hear of the death or injury of one of their classmates' parents, which will naturally cause concern over the well-being of their own parent. Regardless of the foundation of these fears, the risks are real, and counselors need to be prepared for these possibilities.

When military service members are injured while on deployment, there is a possibility that they will spend a significant portion of their recovery in a hospital that is distant from their home base (Hardy, 2006). The remaining parent may need to travel to be at the hospital with the injured military member, sometimes with and sometimes without their children (Cozza et al., 2005). Children need to be prepared for what they will see when visiting their injured parent at the hospital, particularly for more significant injuries such as amputations (Cozza et al., 2005; Curry, 2012). Information about an injury or illness needs to be conveyed to the child in a developmentally appropriate way. Parents may share too much, which may unnecessarily frighten or worry a child, or too little, which may cause additional anxiety (Cozza et al., 2005).

The loss of a parent is never easy on a child, and children and adolescents in military families are no more inoculated than their civilian peers against the impact of the death of a parent. Although there is no systematic research on the grief reactions of children who have experienced the death of a deployed parent, researchers hypothesize that several factors may complicate or compound students' reactions to these losses in particular. First, grief reactions may be complicated due to prolonged separation distress experienced by the youth before a parent's death (Kaplow et al., 2013). Also, the death of a deployed parent may be ambiguous (e.g., remains are not recovered; Kaplow et al., 2013), or the family may be aware of the intentional or aggressive nature of the death itself (e.g., parent is killed directly by an enemy combatant; Cozza et al., 2005). Finally, a military family's living arrangements may make coping more difficult (e.g., family may be living far away from loved ones due to a recent relocation, or the family will have to move away from supportive networks of a military base within one year after a loss; Cozza et al., 2005; Kaplow et al., 2013).

Deployment

Deployment, or the relocation of a military member away from his or her family for service purposes, is a process that involves several distinct phases.

Deployments can happen for a variety of service-related purposes, but the literature on this population focuses on deployments to or in support of combat zones or missions. The three phases of deployment that military members and their families go through are predeployment (i.e., preparation for departure), deployment (i.e., service in a location away from family), and reintegration (i.e., service member returns home).

PREDEPLOYMENT PHASE

The predeployment phase consists of the days, weeks, or months leading up to a military deployment. This phase is often characterized by worry, fears, and anxiety about the upcoming changes the family will face (Esposito-Smythers et al., 2011; Murphy & Fairbank, 2013), as well as sadness, confusion, fear, or anger over the upcoming departure of a family member (Pisano, 2014). Families may also experience mixed emotions that include pride, but the phase is most typically characterized by stress (Pisano, 2014). In the context of the current GWOT, deployments are occurring with less preparation time or advance notice, which may increase the stress experienced during this period (Hollingsworth, 2011) because families may have to make decisions about important matters such as child care or finances within very short time frames (Carter, 2013). Additionally, given the multiple deployments that are common within the GWOT, the predeployment phase may begin before a family has fully reintegrated from the last deployment (Pisano, 2014). Common reactions to the predeployment phase found in children include confusion, guilt, anger, or worry about their parent and the upcoming changes within their family (Wilson et al., 2011).

DEPLOYMENT PHASE

The actual deployment of a parent marks the absence of that parent and often coincides with significant changes in the roles and responsibilities of family members (Williams, 2013). The length of deployments can vary significantly from a few months to a year or more; they may be viewed as having subphases (e.g., first few weeks, middle, end); and they may involve one or more brief visitation periods, in which the deployed member is home for a few days or weeks (Carter, 2013; Pisano, 2014). Visitations may be particularly stressful for some children who may be simultaneously happy to see their parent and already anticipating the next time they have to say good-bye (Murphy & Fairbank, 2013).

Reactions to deployment tend to be most intense during the first month. Depending on the age of the student, he or she may have increased responsibilities at home, including chores and child care for younger siblings (Chandra et al., 2010; Engel, Gallagher, & Lyle, 2010; Esposito-Smythers et al., 2011; Pisano, 2014). The stress level within the entire family may increase as shifts are made to compensate for the deployed parent's absence, and youth may notice and be worried about the stress levels of their nondeployed parent (Huebner, Mancini, Wilcox, Grass, & Grass, 2007). Some families may move temporarily during deployments for employment or to be closer to friends or family (De Pedro et al., 2011). School performance may decline during the deployment phase due to changes in attention or to more practical reasons such as the nondeployed parent not having time to help with homework (Engel et al., 2010; Huebner et al., 2007; Pisano, 2014). During deployment, children and adolescents are likely to experience stress resulting from concern over the safety of their deployed parent (Chandra et al., 2010; Huebner et al., 2007), which may be particularly intense if that parent is deployed to a combat zone (Curry, 2012). Older children may be more acutely aware of the dangers that their parent may face, but all children may be exposed to stories or images of the dangerous or threatening environments where their parents are deployed (Hollingsworth, 2011; Kaplow et al., 2013). Chandra et al. (2010) found that as many as 30% to 40% of students did not have thorough information about the parent's deployment, which may have led to more intense fear and worry. The ongoing risk that a parent may be killed or injured can be viewed as a pervasive sense of uncertainty (Huebner et al., 2007; Kaplow et al., 2013).

REINTEGRATION PHASE

The re-entry, reunification, or reintegration phase is when a deployed parent returns home and the family adjusts to include that family member again. This is consistently listed as one of the most difficult and stressful phases of deployment (Chandra et al., 2010; Huebner et al., 2007; Williams, 2013; Wilson et al., 2011). It often begins with relief and excitement over a family member's safe return but shifts to being a period of stress as the realities of the family's changed dynamics settle in (De Pedro et al., 2011; Esposito-Smythers et al., 2011). Reintegration can be a lengthy process as new routines are established slowly to account for changes and growth within individual family members during the deployment period (Pisano, 2014). Additionally, the military member may need to readjust to civilian life (Murphy & Fairbank, 2013). This process can also be viewed as particularly taxing because they have already lived through the prolonged periods of stress that occurred during the deployment itself and may have suffered physical or psychological harm (DePedro et al., 2011).

Although the stresses associated with reintegration can be related to academic and behavioral challenges, including depression, anger, oppositional behaviors, or needy/attention-seeking behaviors in youth (DePedro et al., 2011; Riggs & Riggs, 2011; Wilson et al., 2011), some families are able to see positive aspects of this experience (Pisano, 2014). Some children report that their family felt closer than before or that they were being treated as more grown up after their deployed parent returned, given the additional responsibilities they had taken on during the parent's absence (Wilson et al., 2011).

IMPACT ON CHILDREN AND ADOLESCENTS

Parental deployment has been linked to academic, emotional, and behavioral changes in children and adolescents (Cole, 2012; Pisano, 2014). Across studies and samples, youth with deployed parents have higher internalizing and externalizing behavior problems than their civilian peers, particularly behaviors consistent with depression and anxiety (Esposito-Smythers et al., 2011; Huebner et al., 2007; Lester et al., 2013; Wilson, Wilkum, Chernichky, MacDermid Wadsworth, &

Broniarczyk, 2011). Some authors report slight differences in reactions across genders (e.g., with somatic complaints and internalizing behaviors being more common in females, and anger and aggression more common in males; Carter, 2013; Chandra et al., 2010; Hollingsworth, 2011), and others report similar conduct and emotional symptoms (Lester et al., 2011). Signs of particularly maladaptive reactions to deployment may include intense, prolonged anger or developmental regressions (Kaplow et al., 2013). Carter (2013) provides the following list of behaviors, adapted from the U.S. Department of Defense Educational Opportunities Directorate, that educators and other professionals in school settings should be cognizant of as indicators that students with deployed parents are in need of counseling or other support services: "(a) difficulty resuming normal classroom assignments and activities; (b) intense emotional reactions such as frequent crying and intense sadness; (c) depression, withdrawal, and being noncommunicative; (d) inattention and lack of concentration; (e) expression of violent or depressed feelings in 'dark' drawings or writings; (f) self-injury or threats to others; (g) significant and rapid weight changes; (h) reduced self-care; and (i) substance abuse" (p. 178).

Students' academic performance may also be negatively impacted by deployment (De Pedro et al., 2011; Pisano, 2014). Engel et al. (2010) found modest but significant differences in the test scores of military students with and without deployed parents. These authors also found that the lower scores associated with a deployment tended to dissipate after parents reunited with their families. Another way to view potential academic challenges faced by this population focuses around the overall stress experienced by these families. Stress may make routine challenges or concerns more difficult than they were in its absence (Pisano, 2014). For example, disagreements with classmates or struggles with difficult homework may appear more daunting or more serious due to the higher stress children are facing during deployment.

Many theoretical approaches have been applied as explanations for youth reactions to parental deployment. From a developmental perspective, a child's understanding of the length of a parent's absence, reasons behind that absence, stresses placed upon their remaining parent, the potential dangers faced by a deployed parent, and war or combat in general will all shape a response to deployment (Carter, 2013; Kaplow et al., 2013; Riggs & Riggs, 2011). From an attachment perspective, youth's reactions are likely to depend on the attachment to both the deployed and the remaining parent (Esposito-Smythers et al., 2011; Riggs & Riggs, 2011). Huebner et al. (2007, 2009) describe deployment as an ambiguous form of loss, explaining that reactions are similar to grief reactions but are complicated by the fact that many factors surrounding the deployment (e.g., parent's safety, length of absence) are unknown to them.

Although the potential negative reactions to the deployment cycle are important for counselors to be aware of, it is equally important to keep in mind that the majority of children and families cope very well with deployment (Chandra et al., 2010; De Pedro et al., 2011; Esposito-Smythers et al., 2011; Park, 2011; Pisano, 2014; Wilson et al., 2011). In fact, research suggests that some children and adolescents will actually benefit from deployments and the opportunities for increased independence and responsibility that they provide (Engel et al., 2010; Park, 2011). However, there is also evidence that children's resilience may wear down with multiple deployments, such that a student who copes well on a first deployment may struggle more with subsequent ones (Chandra et al., 2010; Pisano, 2014).

Regardless of the exact symptoms a student may be exhibiting, it is important to keep in mind that some reaction to deployment is normal and healthy. Any child or adolescent is likely to experience some changes in mood or behavior as a result of a change as drastic as the removal of a parent for an extended period of time, and it is natural that those reactions may be intensified by the stress placed on families and concern over the safety of the deployed parent. Reactions that are more intense and that linger for more than a few weeks may require attention.

Impact on Parents

Deployment impacts entire families. Given the stresses inherent in a deployment cycle, the deployment of a family member is also likely to exacerbate any preexisting family problems (Chandra et al., 2010). Although the physical and psychological impact of deployment to a combat zone is outside the realm of this chapter, it can be concluded that the potential impact on the deployed parent is likely to be profound. Current rates of suicide and post-traumatic stress disorder (PTSD) among returning military members are very high (e.g., between 2001 and 2009, suicides of military members increased by 71%; Carter, 2013; Cozza et al., 2005). Returning veterans are also at risk for sleep disturbances and substance abuse problems (Riggs & Riggs, 2011). Negative impacts of deployment on the military member of a family will make the reintegration phase more complicated for the entire family unit; psychological problems such as PTSD are linked with higher levels of interpersonal conflict, lower levels of effective interpersonal communication, and decreased cohesion in families (Cozza et al., 2005; Riggs & Riggs, 2011). Parents returning from deployment are also at risk for child maltreatment and domestic violence, and factors such as social isolation, lack of access to mental health treatment, financial stresses, exposure to violence during deployment, and maladaptive family dynamics and communication styles make these negative behaviors more likely (De Pedro et al., 2011; Esposito-Smythers et al., 2011; Hoshmand & Hoshmand, 2007). Sadly, rates of child maltreatment have increased in military families during the GWOT, and all practitioners working with these families need to be cognizant of the possibilities of violence, abuse, and neglect (DePedro et al., 2011).

Understandably, deployments place a great deal of stress on nondeployed or nonmilitary spouses, co-parents, or caregivers in military families. These families and caregivers have been found to have higher levels of depression, anxiety, and overall levels of distress than the general population (Lester et al., 2011, 2013). Findings indicate that the health and stability of the caregiving parent during a deployment is critical to the well-being of children and adolescents (Curry, 2012; Pisano, 2014). Distress or unhealthy reactions in the remaining parent may result in "incompetent and role-reversing parenting practices, and enmeshed family processes" (Riggs & Riggs, 2011, p. 679) or emotional withdrawal from children (Harrison & Vannest, 2008), which puts youth at risk of developing internalizing problems such as anxiety or depression (Riggs & Riggs, 2011). The importance of parental responses to deployment highlights the need to work with entire families rather than with just students in this population. Strategies for supporting caregivers through deployments are presented in the "Beyond the Counseling Office" section of this chapter.

COUNSELING APPROACHES

There is an alarming lack of empirically supported counseling techniques for children in military families (Esposito-Smythers et al., 2011; Guzman, 2014; Park, 2011). With the exception of one comprehensive family intervention offered to families directly through the military (i.e., Families OverComing Under Stress, discussed in the "Beyond the Counseling Office" section of this chapter), the programs or strategies presented in this chapter are recommended either based on minimal research support or because they are broadly evidence based for treating populations with similar concerns or behaviors. To prepare to work effectively with children of military families, counselors need to familiarize themselves with military culture, including military branches, terminology, history, and resources (Esposito-Smythers et al., 2011). It would also be helpful to be in contact with any local military school liaisons (Aronson & Perkins, 2013; see the "Beyond the Counseling Office" section of this chapter).

The primary strategies recommended for counseling students from military families, particularly those with deployed parents, are psychoeducation and skill building. Several authors recommend strengths-based approaches (e.g., Guzman, 2014; Park, 2011), although no specific strategies are presented in the literature. A general frame of working with a student's existing strengths and assets, as well as building on weaker skills, fits well with what is known about this population and its needs. Although psychoeducation can be accomplished via individual counseling, the best fit for most students with deployed parents would be a group-based format. Another recommended broad strategy is to help students connect with after-school activities, sports, or clubs; students who are coping with deployment report that these activities provide helpful distractions from the stresses they face at home, as well as helping with the development of informal support networks of friends and teachers (Huebner & Mancini, 2008).

Build General Coping Skills

Many students who are struggling with the deployment of a military parent could benefit from counseling techniques designed to teach and help them master skills for healthy coping. Counseling sessions may focus on building, modeling, and practicing skills such as problem-solving, relaxation, effective communication, and on affect regulation, such as skills for managing anxiety (Cole, 2012; Esposito-Smythers et al., 2011; Murphy & Fairbank, 2013). Counselors can select from a variety of counseling materials for these. A few strategies that practitioners may consider include (a) the SNAP technique (i.e., "State the problem; Name the goal; All possible solutions; Pick the best one and try it out"; Lester et al., 2011, p. 22); (b) creating a strength box to combat feelings of sadness or anxiety (i.e., students decorate a box and fill it with ideas and strategies that help then feel better or more relaxed (Wilson et al., 2011); (c) using a feelings thermometer (i.e., using a picture of a thermometer to help identify and communicate emotional reactions, especially with family members; Lester et al., 2012); and (d) activities that help students share feelings, especially with the deployed parent (e.g., "one thing that I was proud of when you were gone," "one thing that made me sad while you were gone"; Wilson et al., 2011, p. 228).

Students may also benefit from participating in a general strength-based social-emotional learning curriculum such as the Strong Kids series (*Strong Start; Strong Kids; Strong Teens*), which helps students cope with anger and stress, build skills in problem-solving, understand their emotions, and effectively apply positive thinking strategies (Merrell, Carizalez, Feuerborn, Gueldner, & Tran, 2007a, 2007b, 2007c; Merrell, Parisi, & Whitcomb, 2007). Because the purpose of this group-based intervention is broad, groups need not be limited to other children from military families. Alternatively, a counselor may wish to explore the various skill-building activities contained in these curricula to see if any activities may be modified for individual counseling sessions.

Address Specific Symptoms

Although the majority of students with a deployed parent demonstrate resilience or may benefit from general counseling to build coping skills, a small portion will need more intensive counseling to address a more significant issue, such as depression or anxiety. Counselors will need to use professional judgment to identify students needing more intensive counseling services and proceed accordingly. For example, if a student's reaction to deployment has developed into generalized anxiety disorder, treatments with empirical support for that diagnosis should be implemented (Esposito-Smythers et al., 2011).

Cognitive-behavioral therapy (CBT) is the most commonly recommended strategy for students with more intense needs (Esposito-Smythers et al., 2011; Guzman, 2014), and many evidence-based CBT counseling programs exist to address students' specific needs. Using the aforementioned example, a counselor might use *Coping Cat* (Kendall, & Hedtke, 2006) in counseling for a student with more generalized anxiety. Skill-building techniques and other more cognition-based aspects of CBT (e.g., challenging cognitive distortions) can also be used with this population. For example, counselors could apply CBT to help students whose reactions to deployment are being shaped by maladaptive thoughts or inaccurate beliefs (Esposito-Smythers et al., 2011; Murphy & Fairbank, 2013). For instance, a student may feel unsafe at home because she has learned that her parent is in a dangerous location. In this case, a counselor could help the student to check that thought by asking questions such as "What evidence is there to suggest that you are safe at home?," "How do you know when you are safe and unsafe?," and "How could you check to see if you are safe or unsafe?"

Grief Counseling

Counselors should apply their general training on working with grief and loss when working with military students who have experienced the death of a parent. A review of counseling strategies for children who have experienced grief and loss is beyond the scope of this chapter. However, there are many resources that counselors can use to guide their work with children who have lost a military parent. Books such as *Why Did You Die? Activities to Help Children Cope With Grief and Loss* (Leeuwenburgh & Goldring, 2008) and *Counseling Children and Adolescents Through Grief and Loss* (Fiorini & Mullen, 2006) may be helpful, and counselors should be mindful of the potential complications of a combat-related death, which were discussed earlier in this chapter. Additionally, grief and loss curricula such as the *Mourning Child Grief Support Group Curriculum* series (Lehmann, Jimerson, & Gaasch, 2001a, 2001b, 2001c) may be modified for individual use or implemented in small-group settings. If group counseling is judged to be an appropriate intervention by the counselor, group members should consist of only military-connected youth if possible.

In addition to providing direct counseling for students, counselors can assist the surviving parent in returning to normal family routines, help school teams provide routine and consistency for students, and help parents to understand normal grief reactions and recognize signs of problematic grief (Pisano, 2014). Some more specific reactions that counselors may watch for in military children include possible jealously or anger toward other students with military parents who have not experienced a loss, worries about pain or fear involved in the parent's death, or anger directed at the enemy combatant (e.g., al-Qaeda) or the military (Kaplow et al., 2013). The latter may be difficult for a student to express in the wake of a combat-related death, especially given the effluence of patriotic support that is likely from friends, family, and the general community (Kaplow et al., 2013).

Group Counseling

Experts who work with students and families facing deployment frequently recommend psychoeducation and coping groups (e.g., Cole, 2012; Esposito-Smythers et al., 2011; Guzman, 2014; Huebner et al., 2007; Pisano, 2014; Rush & Akos, 2007). Group-based formats allow participants to build support networks and learn that they are not alone in their experiences and reactions, helping to decrease feelings of isolation (Cole, 2012; Esposito-Smythers et al., 2011; Guzman, 2014). This may be particularly helpful for students in families without formal military communities, such as families with Reserve or National Guard service members. Although psychoeducational and coping groups are presented separately in the following discussion, they can easily be blended into a single group experience, depending on the needs of the students.

Psychoeducational Groups

Groups that are focused on psychoeducation seek to teach students information that will help normalize their experiences and increase self-awareness of their reactions to deployment (Esposito-Smythers et al., 2011). Psychoeducation-based groups may cover topics such as information on the deployment cycle, common reactions to various stages of the deployment cycle, signs and symptoms of mental health problems, and how students can seek greater support (Esposito-Smythers et al., 2011; Huebner et al., 2007).

Support Groups

Similar to psychoeducational groups, support groups for this population are created to help students understand their emotional reactions and develop skills to better cope with parental deployment. Support groups provide a safe place for students to share their reactions and experiences, which can help both to foster a support network and to normalize their experiences (Pisano, 2014; Rush & Akos, 2007). Support groups may also have sessions that use modeling, observation, and practice to teach or enhance social, coping, or problem-solving skills (Esposito-Smythers et al., 201; Guzman, 2014; Rush & Akos, 2007).

Rush and Akos (2007) present a 10-week hybrid psychoeducation and support group counseling intervention for children with parents in the military, with sessions on topics including (a) sharing about the deployed parent, (b) identifying and sustaining beneficial or productive routines, (c) redeployment, and (d) identifying community-based resources. Simmonds (n.d.) provides a downloadable group curriculum (*Children in Change: A Group Curriculum for Kids ages 8–14 who are Experiencing Family Change*) that covers topics such as exploring feelings related to change, anger, and worries, and working through grief. Counselors may wish to review these or other group curricula to find topics and ideas that meet the needs of their group participants.

BEYOND THE COUNSELING OFFICE

Only a small portion of military children and their families will need direct counseling services to cope with the stresses associated with relocation and deployment. The remainder of these children and families can be assisted in a variety of ways that fall outside of the traditional counseling role. Counselors can assist in the creation and provision of comprehensive school-based support systems that address school climate, curriculum, teacher training, and the needs of parents or caregivers (Harrison & Vannest, 2008).

School-wide Support

Counselors can play a large role in helping their schools to create supportive and welcoming climates for students in military families. One important step to take is to make sure that schools are ready to welcome students at any point during the year. Schools can support these families by creating welcome packets containing all the information that parents usually receive during back-to-school or other annual events (Collins, 2009; Williams, 2013). Pisano (2014) also recommends that schools develop buddy programs for new students and work with coaches, advisers, and program directors to ensure that military students entering throughout the school year are able to participate in teams, clubs, or theater productions, even if they missed tryouts or auditions. Tutoring or homework support are also beneficial, especially because military students may have missed portions of curricula due to school transfers (Collins, 2009; Harrison & Vannest, 2008; Pisano, 2014; Williams, 2013). School-based professionals should also work with military liaisons if possible and stay abreast of the military units that the school's families are connected with, in order to know in advance about deployments, homecomings, or losses (Collins, 2009).

Classroom-based Supports

The creation of military-inclusive curricula and classrooms can help students feel more comfortable and supported at school (De Pedro et al., 2011). Teachers may discuss deployment areas in the world across subjects, including math, history, and geography. For example, classes could calculate geographical distances to deployment areas, learn time zones relevant to deployment areas, or study the history of these regions (Carter, 2013; Harrison & Vannest, 2008). Teachers should also allow students to express their feelings, both regarding deployment and regarding their deployed family member via activities such as poetry, journaling, writing personal letters or emails, or participating in pen pal programs (Carter, 2013; Harrison & Vannest, 2008; Pisano, 2014). Carter (2013) also recommends that teachers maintain structure, routines, and high expectations for students in military families because this consistency can help when they are coping with changes at home.

Teacher and Staff Training

It is important that teachers and other school staff be trained regarding military youth, including learning about the deployment cycle, reactions and behaviors to expect, and what type of concerning behaviors necessitate a consultation or referral to the counselor (Collins, 2009; De Pedro et al., 2011; Harrison & Vannest, 2008; Huebner & Mancini, 2008; Pisano, 2014). Many training materials are available on the various websites that are reviewed at the end of this chapter.

Supporting Families

As discussed earlier in this chapter, many families may not have access to supports provided by the military. Therefore, counselors should be prepared to provide appropriate services or referrals to parents and caregivers in addition to students (Collins, 2009). Counselor can assist families by providing resources and information to help them support their child's academic success (Cole, 2012). Psychoeducation can address topics such as

- the deployment cycle;
- how to support students when they are sad or anxious;
- how to support students when they are struggling academically;
- navigating the school-based support systems (e.g., special education referrals, Student Study Teams, 504 plans);
- how to limit exposure to news; and
- how to share accurate information about deployment in age-appropriate ways (Esposito-Smythers et al., 2011; Huebner & Mancini, 2008; Kaplow et al., 2013; Pisano, 2014).

Parents and caregivers may also benefit from learning about self-care, problem-solving, and stress management strategies, either in individual or in group settings (Esposito-Smythers et al., 2011; Huebner & Mancini, 2008).

Connecting With Resources

Much of the research on supporting military spouses and caregivers during deployments mentions the importance of informal supports (e.g., family, friends, church members, teachers), especially for Reserve or National Guard families who are not directly connected with military communities (e.g., Huebner et al., 2009; Murphy & Fairbank, 2013). Counselors can help facilitate informal supports in several ways. First, informal support networks sometimes arise from formal supports (e.g., parents may meet at a PTA meeting or support group and develop personal friendships; Huebner & Mancini, 2008), which highlights the importance of connecting with military parents and inviting them to campus for such events. Additionally, if a counselor has a working relationship with a military school liaison, he or she can connect parents with that person to help access resource networks (Aronson & Perkins, 2013).

Families OverComing Under Stress

Although a few programs that aim to support military families, especially during deployments, have been developed and are being evaluated for efficacy (e.g., Strong Families; Ross & DeVoe, 2014), only one has extensive research support. Families OverComing Under Stress (FOCUS; www.focusproject.org) is a standardized and manualized secondary prevention program involving parent, child, and combined sessions that consist of psychoeducation and the development of skills such as goal setting, emotional regulation, and problem-solving (Esposito-Smythers et al., 2011; Lester et al., 2012; Murphy & Fairbank, 2013). In 2015, FOCUS was available to all military families (e.g., families involved in any stage of deployment; Guzman, 2014) and was provided at 17 military facilities in the United States and 3 in Japan (www.focusproject.org). Participation in FOCUS has been demonstrated to decrease parental distress and unhealthy family functioning, increase a family's use of social supports, and reduce clinical symptoms in children (Lester et al., 2011). If it is available and applicable, counselors may recommend that families utilize this resource.

RESOURCES

4-H MILITARY PARTNERSHIPS

http://4-hmilitarypartnerships.org/

4-H Military Partnerships represent a collaborative effort between military organizations (e.g., Department of Defense, Office of the Secretary of Defense, Navy Child and Youth Programs), nonmilitary organizations (e.g., National Institute of Food and Agriculture, U.S. Department of Agriculture), and the 4-H organization to support and provide 4-H programs to military-connected youth at home and overseas. The website contains links to clubs and day, week, and extended camps offered for military youth.

KIMOCHIS MILITARY FAMILY RESOURCES

http://www.kimochis.com/

Kimochis are emotion-based character dolls and animals that counselors and parents may use to discuss feelings and teach skills. This company sells kits designed to support military connected youth that focus on enhancing familial communication and building resilience. Kits are available for educators and parents, and a limited number of discounted or donated kits for families are available.

MILITARY CHILD EDUCATION COALITION

http://www.militarychild.org/

The Military Child Education Coalition is a national organization that seeks to provide quality and inclusive educational opportunities for children from military families. Its website hosts a wealth of resources for parents and educators. Parents can find links to videos on a variety of topics regarding supporting students in schools, as well as resources such Military Student Transition Consultants, who are available to answer questions and provide support for parents experiencing relocations. The educators' section of the website includes a variety of online professional development topics (e.g., "Responding to the Military Child With Exceptional Needs," "Supporting Military Children Through School Transitions") that provide continuing education units.

Military Child Initiative

http://www.jhsph.edu/research/centers-and-institutes/military-child-initiative/

The Military Child Initiative is hosted by Johns Hopkins University and the Johns Hopkins University Bloomberg School of Public Health. This organization aims to enhance the education of military-connected youth by providing information, training, and support to parents and educational professionals. It hosts a best practices library with resources on topics such as deployment and supporting students in emotional crisis, as well as a free web course ("Building Resilient Kids") that qualifies for continuing education units.

Military One Source

http://www.militaryonesource.mil/

Military One Source, which describes itself as a "central hub" of information for the military community, provides information on benefits, relocations, deployments, parenting, and retirement. It provides links to resources such as mentoring programs, summer camps, and youth and teen programs. It also hosts resources for challenging topics such as the death of a service member, domestic violence, and child abuse. Military One Source also provides free telephone, Internet, video, and in-person nonmedical counseling for military-connected adults and children.

National Guard Family Program

https://www.jointservicessupport.org/FP/Default.aspx

The National Guard Family Program is a nationwide program that aims to support and educate families. Its website provides information such as forms needed for counseling services and links to *Sesame Street* content (i.e., kits, videos, interactive materials) for young people regarding deployment (i.e., *Sesame Street Talk Listen, Connect: Deployments, Homecomings, Changes*).

10

Counseling Students to Increase Motivation and School Completion

WITH BRIANNA MESHKE MCLAY ■

OVERVIEW

Graduation rates in the United States are increasing (Stark & Noel, 2015), with nearly four out of five students who started ninth grade in 2008 finishing high school in 2012 (Stetser & Stillwell, 2014). However, this also means that at least one out of five students who started ninth grade did not finish high school, and certain groups of students, including most culturally and linguistically diverse students, students with disabilities, and many of the student populations addressed in this book, are at disproportionally greater risk for lack of school completion (Stark & Noel, 2015; Stetser & Stillwell, 2014). Most educators working in secondary schools see firsthand the impact that low motivation and poor academic achievement have on some high school students, and despite their best efforts to engage these students, they fail to reverse students' trajectory toward school dropout.

As a society, high school completion is viewed as an important accomplishment and milestone in the transition from adolescence to adulthood, and the negative consequences of failing to complete school (i.e., dropping out) are experienced on both an individual and a systemic level. High school dropouts earn less money in the workforce, are more likely to be incarcerated, have poorer physical health, and report less happiness than their peers who graduated from high school (Messacar & Oreopoulos, 2013). On a societal level, failure to complete high school has economic implications in that high school dropouts are more likely to live in poverty and are unable to participate in the labor force of skilled workers that allows the United States to keep up with the demands of the global economy (Petrick, 2014). This is further supported by the U.S. Department of Education's 2015 report on dropout, which states that individuals who dropped out of school were less likely to be actively involved in the labor force in any capacity, regardless of job type

(Stark & Noel, 2015). High school completion is also a requirement for college entrance, and college graduates drive economic growth (Levin & Rouse, 2012). In short, whether viewed as a social justice issue due to disparate graduation rates or through an economic lens for the collective benefit of the United States, more students need to graduate high school.

Lack of motivation and low academic achievement are among many potential reasons that a student may fail to complete school. Unfortunately, many of the factors that contribute to low academic motivation and dropping out are developmental (e.g., preschool attendance, grade retention in elementary school) and may not be malleable by the time a student comes to a counselor's attention. This means that counseling services are often the last intervention attempted, or that a school community has already missed many opportunities to intervene and change a student's trajectory by the time a student may be seen for counseling due to dropout risk. This makes counseling both potentially challenging and, in many ways, crucially important.

BASIC CONSIDERATIONS

At-Risk Populations

According to data provided by the U.S. Department of Education's National Center for Education Statistics (NCES), the gap between graduation rates of White students and students of color has narrowed in recent years, yet the disparity remains significant (Stark & Noel, 2015; Stetser & Stillwell, 2014). With a national average graduation rate of 80% in 2012, White (84%) and Asian (87%) students have above-average rates, whereas Black (67%), Hispanic (71%), and American Indian/Pacific Islander (65%) students have graduated at much lower rates (Stetser & Stillwell, 2014). Students from low-income or economically disadvantaged families also have lower-than-average graduation rates (70%) compared with their peers, whose rates for 2013 were estimated at 88.2% (Stark & Noel, 2015). Students with disabilities (59%) and those who are English language learners (ELL; 57%) have the lowest graduation rates of the groups presented by the NCES (Stark & Noel, 2015).

As can be seen from the preceding statistics, group membership can be a risk factor for dropout. Specifically, non-Asian students of color, students with disabilities, low-income students, and ELL students are all at higher risk for dropout than their peers. Research on the causes of school dropout is complicated by the fact that although at-risk populations can be identified via group dropout rates, very few studies work at the individual level to identify the factors involved in any given student's decision to drop out. A policy brief prepared by Rumberger and Lim (2008) reviewed 25 years of dropout research in an attempt to pinpoint the specific reasons that students drop out of high school; it revealed that individual factors that contributed to dropout included the student's academic performance, behavior, outlook, and personal history. Family, school, and community factors also play a vital role in whether a student makes it to graduation (Rumberger & Lim, 2008).

Individual Risks

ACADEMIC PERFORMANCE AND HISTORY

Academic performance is the most well-documented contributing factor to dropout. Factors such as academic achievement, grade retention, and school transience are all related to school completion and dropout (Bowers, Sprott, & Taff, 2013; Rumberger & Lim, 2008). Students who drop out not only are likely to have poor current achievement in high school but also are likely to have had a history of academic struggles throughout their educational careers. For example, grade retention in elementary school is significantly related to high school dropout, and participation in preschool is related to greater school completion (Rumberger & Lim, 2008). The developmental and historical nature of these risks makes intervening at the high school level very challenging, but it highlights the need for counselors desiring to impact graduation rates to advocate for early intervention efforts.

BEHAVIORAL RISKS

Behavioral factors related to dropout include conduct both in and out of the classroom environment and encompass school attendance, homework completion, and participation in extracurricular activities, which may collectively be referred to as *school engagement* (Rumberger & Lim, 2008). Factors such as suspensions, participation in school fights, and absenteeism are also related to dropout risk (Suh & Suh, 2007). Suh and Suh (2007) also noted that students who live in metropolitan areas are more at risk for school-related behavioral difficulties.

ECOLOGICAL FACTORS

Ecological factors that may impact high school completion include characteristics of the student's family, school, and community. In terms of family structure, students who live with both parents tend to have higher graduation rates than those who live with one parent or in a different arrangement (Rumberger & Lim, 2008). As mentioned previously, students from middle- to high-income families have higher rates of high school completion than their lower-income peers, mainly due to accessibility of resources and different parenting practices (Rumberger & Lim, 2008). Students who attend schools with more middle- to high-income students also have higher graduation rates; however, the size of the school itself does not have an impact on graduation rates, nor does teacher preparation (Rumberger & Lim, 2008). School climate does matter, however, and schools with more class disruptions and less academic rigor tend to have more students drop out (Rumberger & Lim, 2008). The community in which the student resides also plays a vital role in terms of academic success; students tend to be more successful when they have ample community resources and positive role models (Rumberger & Lim, 2008).

BELIEFS, ATTITUDES, AND MOTIVATION

Rumberger and Lim (2008) reported that there has been little research connecting student attitudes and academic achievement to dropping out of high school;

however, there is some evidence that students who hold higher educational expectations and self-perceptions that they are able to succeed are less at risk for dropping out. Although beliefs and attitudes do not have a strong research correlation to dropout per se, they are highly correlated with risk factors such as academic achievement and school engagement, which makes them relevant in this discussion. For example, low motivation is associated with low school engagement, which is a risk factor for dropout (Crumpton & Gregory, 2011; Smith & Thomson, 2014). The relationships among these variables, as well as their relationships with achievement, are complicated and often multidirectional (Crumpton & Gregory, 2011). For example, a student who is chronically struggling in school may eventually internalize that lack of success, disengage from school, and potentially associate school with negative emotions (Smith & Thomson, 2014). Similarly, a fear of failure may play a role in some students' low achievement because it might lead to self-protecting behaviors such as school or work avoidance (De Castella, Byrne, & Covington, 2013).

Rowell and Hong (2013) provide a detailed explanation of motivation as it relates to achievement and engagement. From their perspective, motivation is composed of a variety of beliefs and feelings, such as autonomy (i.e., sense of control over one's own learning), self-efficacy (i.e., belief in one's ability to accomplish goals and tasks), and attributional beliefs (i.e., one's internal beliefs regarding how to explain successes and failures). Attributions can vary among three dimensions: (a) stability (i.e., caused by either a stable trait or something that may vary), (b) locus of control (i.e., caused by factors from within or outside of the student), and (c) controllability (i.e., caused by factors that are either uncontrollable or controllable). From this perspective, if students attribute their poor performance on a test to factors that were uncontrollable (e.g., that test was too hard, nobody could have passed it), stable (e.g., I'm just not smart enough), or due to factors solely external to student (e.g., the teacher hates me), they would not likely have a lot of motivation to try hard on the next test. In contrast, factors that are internal (e.g., I didn't read the study guide), unstable (e.g., I have the ability to study next time if I want to), and controllable (e.g., next time, I can stay home and study before a test) are more likely to be associated with higher motivation.

Multiple Risk Factors

Although research on dropout risk has identified a plethora of risk factors, there is no solitary factor that precisely predicts whether a student will drop out (Dockery, 2012). Therefore, it is imperative that counselors monitor both individual and ecological factors to identify students who are truly at risk for dropping out. By analyzing data from the National Longitudinal Survey of Youth, Suh and Suh (2007) found that grade point average, socioeconomic status, and behavioral factors all had a large impact on dropout rates when examined individually. According to the authors, being exposed to multiple risk factors increases the likelihood of dropout. This suggests that students with multiple indicators during the high school years, including most of the populations addressed in this book, may benefit from targeted interventions to boost their motivation to attend and complete high school.

Skill Versus Performance Deficit

When a student is struggling or failing academically, is chronically truant, or is otherwise at risk for dropping out, it is important for counselors to determine if these behaviors are related to learning needs, such as having an academic skills deficit or learning disability. In other words, it is critical to determine whether or not a student *can't*, or simply *doesn't*, do the academic task at hand. In the academic, behavioral, and social skills intervention literature, this distinction is often referred to as *skills/acquisition deficits* versus *performance deficits* (e.g., Duhan et al., 2004; Gresham, Van, & Cook, 2006). For example, if a student is failing her math class, it is important for a counselor to know if she is capable of the work but choosing not to complete it (i.e., *doesn't* do), or unable to complete the work because it is too challenging or she lacks the foundational skills to be successful at this level of math (i.e., *can't* do). The difference between these two potential explanations for a lack of successful academic progress has a huge impact on how a counselor might decide to support this student. If the student doesn't do the work, the counselor may explore her motivation or other issues impeding her progress. However, if she lacks the skills to be able to be successful, academic skills–focused interventions, such as tutoring, must be put in place.

Students may also have a significant and diagnosable learning need, such as a learning disability or attention deficit hyperactivity disorder. School psychologists and some other professionals in the school setting are very familiar with these types of learning needs. If a counselor suspects a student is at risk of dropping out because he or she lacks the skills or abilities to complete academic work, the counselor needs to inform the school team so that it can develop appropriate academic interventions and/or assess the student for special education. For example, a counselor working with a 17-year-old student at a juvenile detention center may notice that his client has very low reading abilities (i.e., *can't* do) for his age, is struggling with class content, and is in danger of failing. The counselor needs to advocate for his client by informing the school team so that it can determine if there are additional academic interventions that can support the student and if the student needs to be evaluated for a potential disability.

Although the *can't* do and *doesn't* do descriptions are often perceived as a dichotomy, it is important to keep in mind that for many at-risk students, it is likely some combination of the two factors that best describes why they are not achieving academically. Therefore, counselors should carefully evaluate the reasons why students are not being successful, being cognizant of areas where they may need additional support (e.g., tutoring, academic interventions, special education) in order to meet academic standards, while also determining which factors (e.g., motivation, goal setting, study skills) may be appropriate targets for counseling interventions.

COUNSELING APPROACHES

For students at risk for dropping out, motivation and other academic enabling skills are factors that may be amenable to counseling. That is to say, neither students nor the most gifted counselors will be able to change variables such as ethnicity, disability, poverty, preschool attendance, or grade retention in elementary school. Unfortunately, there is very little research about the role of counseling intervention in dropout prevention, and there is only slightly more available on the impacts of counseling on academic motivation and achievement. As stated earlier in this chapter, these factors often represent only a fraction of a given student's reasons for potentially dropping out, but when applied in combination with methods for reducing negative outcomes from other risk scenarios (e.g., homelessness, living in foster care, pregnancy), a more holistic approach to supporting students at risk of leaving school before completion can be developed. At the individual counseling level, interventions will need to focus not just on motivation but also on whatever other risks and conditions are inhibiting educational success for each student. For example, one student may be very unmotivated to complete homework because her home life is very stressful, while another may be identified as being unmotivated by a teacher but may struggle from debilitating test anxiety, and yet another may appear unmotivated but actually lack adequate academic or study skills to be successful in class. Counselors need to thoroughly investigate the needs of students before proceeding with intervention.

Increasing Motivation

Almost by definition, students who are referred for counseling due to a lack of motivation are likely to be reluctant participants in the counseling process. Although these students are not likely to be mandatory participants like some other student populations (e.g., juvenile offenders), counselors need to pay particular attention to students' resistance to counseling and assess their readiness for change. In a five-stage model of change developed by Prochaska and DiClemente (1982), resistance, or simply not recognizing the need for change, is the earliest stage of the change process and is considered a typical part of the behavior change process. It is in this *precontemplation* stage (Prochaska & DiClemente, 1982) that most students who lack motivation and are at serious risk for school dropout will enter counseling, and the first task of the counselor must be to engage students exactly where they are in a way that allows them to develop their own motivation. That is to say, these students have likely been advised, lectured, disciplined, and coerced by parents, teachers, and school administrators without any positive impact on their school engagement and motivation to achieve. Simply repeating these tactics within a counseling session will almost certainly have no impact whatsoever; counselors must take a different approach to have any chance of reaching these students to engage them in the counseling process and to have any hope of building greater internal motivation to succeed in school. For these students, the best place to start in counseling may be through using motivational interviewing (MI) to meet them in this precontemplation stage (i.e., not recognizing the need for change) and work effectively with their resistance.

Motivational Interviewing

MI is a specialized counseling approach in which counselors collaborate with clients to build understanding of their values and motivations; to evoke intrinsic motivation for change; and, ultimately, to allow clients to choose whether or not to make changes (Hettema, Steele, & Miller, 2005; Miller & Rollnick, 2002, 2004). MI is client directed in that counselors use specific approaches to help clients articulate their reasons for wanting to change, and it is clients, not counselors, who develop the arguments for wanting to change (Hettema et al., 2005). That is to say, "The least desirable situation, from the standpoint of evoking change, is for the counselor to advocate for change while the client argues against it" (Miller & Rollnick, 2002, p. 39).

MI was initially developed as a pretreatment for individuals struggling with substance abuse and has since been found to be an effective treatment approach in its own right for addressing a number of psychological and physiological behaviors that negatively impact health and well-being (Miller & Rollnick, 2004; Miller & Rose, 2009). Although there is scant research on using MI with students who are at risk for school dropout, the few studies that are available have found that MI-based interventions positively impact school attendance, grades, class participation, and other indicators of school engagement (Atkinson &Woods, 2003; Enea & Dafinoiu, 2009; Strait, Smith, McQuillin, Swan, & Malone, 2012). Given these preliminary results and the well-established research on MI in addressing other extremely challenging and harmful behaviors (e.g., drug abuse, cigarette use, diet changes for diabetes management; Rubak, Sandboek, Lauritzen, & Christensen, 2005), MI may have the potential to engage highly resistant students in counseling with the ultimate goal of helping them find the motivation to complete high school.

Miller and Rollnick (2002) outline the four guiding principles of MI. The first is the expression of empathy using reflective, respectful listening and acceptance. The goal here is to genuinely seek to understand clients and accept them for who they are. This does not mean that counselors should agree with clients' choices; rather, they should not judge clients for their choices. The second principle is to develop discrepancy. This is done in an intentional way "to create and amplify, from the client's perspective, a discrepancy between present behavior and his or her broader goals and values" (p. 38). Developing discrepancy focuses on the importance of change rather than the gap between where the client is currently and where he or she must go to reach the goal. The third principle is to expect, accept, and reframe resistance, as opposed to trying to convince clients that they should change. Research has shown that resistance increases when counselors are directive and authoritative with clients and decreases when counselors are empathic and reflective (Miller & Rollnick, 2004). The final principle outlined by Miller and Rollnick (2002) is to nurture self-efficacy so that clients believe in their ability to successfully make changes and feel hopeful for the future. This requires that counselors actually believe in clients' ability to change, and it further reinforces that MI is client-directed at all levels.

Most of the actual methods used in MI will be familiar to counselors, but effectively applying these methods using an MI framework requires additional training. The methods used are open-ended questioning, reflecting, affirming, summarizing, and evoking change talk (Miller & Rollnick, 2002). Extrapolating from Miller and Rollnick (2002), each of these methods will be briefly described and demonstrated as they might apply to students at risk for school dropout.

Open-ended Questioning
MI requires that students do much of the talking in counseling sessions; the use of open-ended questions helps to accomplish this. Questions should be primarily neutral; explore all sides of the issue; and center around school, classes, behaviors, and other aspects of the student's life that may be impacting motivation and achievement such as family and peer relations. Some questions for early sessions might include "Tell me about school. What do you like about it?," "What don't you like about it?," and "How have your thoughts and feelings about school changed over the years?" Later sessions might include more targeted questions such as "What are reasons you might want to finish high school?," "How do you envision your future if you graduate from high school?," or "How do you envision your future if you drop out of school?"

Reflecting
Early in MI, counselors should use a lot of reflective statements. They require counselors to go beyond the actual words that students are using and to make a guess about the underlying meaning. The reflection is given as a statement, not a question, because a statement does not require a response and is not as likely to be resisted by students. Further, the reflection should try to move students forward in their discussion of the problem, focusing on certain aspects of what they are talking about and ignoring other aspects. For example, if a student is talking about how deep in the hole he is at school in relation to his grades and work, a possible reflective statement might be "It's overwhelming to think about everything you would have to do to get caught up, but it would feel better if you knew where to start."

Affirming
Affirming students' strengths and efforts helps build rapport and encourages continued exploration. Using the previous example of the student who feels overwhelmed by the amount of work he would have to do to catch up, affirmations

might include "I appreciate you being so open with me about school" and "I've enjoyed getting to know you better today."

Summarizing

The purpose of summarizing is to "reinforce what has been said, show that [the counselor has] been listening carefully, and prepare the [student] to elaborate further" (Miller & Rollnick, 2002, p. 74). When summarizing, counselors should include references to change talk, described next, so that students can again hear their own ideas about change. Summaries can bring together several ideas that students have talked about, link ideas together to help students explore the relationship among topics, or help transition from one topic to the next.

Evoking Change Talk

Change talk is a major component of MI. It can be thought of as clients' own reasons and desires to make changes. At a basic level, counselors encourage change talk by using the other methods described previously to help students articulate the disadvantages of staying in their current situation (e.g., failing school), the advantages of changing, feelings of hope for making changes, and intentions to make changes. Examples of questions to evoke change talk include "What do you think will happen if you drop out of school?," "What would be good about staying in school?," "If you decided to stay in school, what strengths do you have that would help you to succeed?," and "Of the ideas we've talked about, what would you be willing to try?"

As counseling is successful in reducing resistance to change and students begin to engage in more change talk, they can be supported to move into the next stages of change, *contemplation, preparation,* and *action* (Prochaska & DiClemente, 1982). Counselors can continue to use MI techniques to work with students in these stages, and because MI has been found to be effectively integrated with other treatment approaches, counselors might also consider infusing elements of MI with other evidence-based counseling techniques like cognitive-behavioral therapy (CBT) and solution-focused brief therapy (SFBT) to help students identify small, accomplishable goals and make plans for action to help them toward their goals (Miller & Rollnick, 2002, 2004).

COGNITIVE-BEHAVIORAL THERAPY

CBT strategies may be useful when addressing motivational issues related to self-efficacy and attributional beliefs, and CBT can be used to encourage students to explore their thoughts and beliefs and how these are impacting their behaviors. For example, a student who attributed her struggles in school to stable, uncontrollable factors, such as "I'm not smart enough" or "I'm just not good at math," could be gently challenged by the counselor to generate alterative explanations that incorporate unstable and controllable factors that lead to a greater sense of control and motivation. More adaptive, replacement thoughts might include "I just have to work harder in math" or "I'm smart *and* this is hard for me." In this way, CBT can be integrated with other counseling techniques to address individual students' specific issues and needs.

Solution-Focused Brief Therapy

Similarly, SFBT strategies may be integrated to help increase students' motivation. Relationship questions may be particularly helpful in working with students at risk of school failure or dropout (Franklin, Kim, & Tripodi, 2013). This strategy involves asking questions from the point of view of someone the student cares about (e.g., teacher, coach, parent, grandparent). Example questions for this population include "What would your coach say if you studied hard for this test?," "What might your grandmother notice if you were working toward passing your biology class?," "How might your teacher respond if you completed your work for one week?," and "What do you think your girlfriend might say if you came to school every day?" If applicable, these types of questions may help foster motivation by allowing students to see how their current behavior or trajectories may be impacting those they care about, and how these important individuals might respond to changes in behavior.

Increasing Academic Enabling Skills

Broadly defined, academic enabling skills are attitudes and behaviors that facilitate learning and allow students to access and benefit from the academic curriculum (DiPerna, 2006; DiPerna, Volpe, & Elliott, 2002). Research suggests that two academic enablers, motivation and study skills, are particularly relevant for secondary students and are related to increased academic achievement (DiPerna, 2006; DiPerna et al., 2002). Motivation, discussed in the previous section of this chapter, refers to students' beliefs about their ability to complete tasks, their willingness to complete tasks, and their interest in the tasks (DiPerna, 2006). Study skills refer to intentional activities that students engage in to acquire, make meaning from, remember, and apply academic information effectively and efficiently (DiPerna, 2006). Examples of these skills include taking notes, time management, prioritizing learning tasks, and test-taking strategies. For secondary students, after it is determined that they have no significant academic skills deficit, counselors should begin to assess and remediate their motivation and study skills (DiPerna, 2006). This remediation can be addressed in individual or group counseling.

Study Skills

Gettinger and Seibert (2002) provide a comprehensive review of the research on study skills as they relate to academic competence, offering four broad categories that can be targeted for intervention. The first category, *repetition- or rehearsal-based study skills*, focuses on the basic strategies of "repetition, rereading, or rehearsal of information" (p. 355). These strategies are good for helping students remember small amounts of information or information that is used frequently, such as vocabulary words or math facts. Counselors can also teach students how to use strategies, such as mnemonic devices and imagery of keywords, to learn and retain this type of information. The next category, *procedural or organization-based study skills*, involves processes like time management, organization of work, development of study routines, and the ability to adapt to the fluctuating demands of school. Counselors can help students develop daily, weekly, and monthly plans for how and when they are going to study; can help students recognize when they are most focused so they can choose to do more difficult tasks at that time; break longer projects and assignments into smaller parts; and reschedule study time when necessary. The third category, *cognitive-based study skills*, involves how students make information they are learning meaningful by drawing on past knowledge, connecting information to what they already know, and creating new schemata to help integrate new information with existing knowledge. Counselors can help students learn how to make and use cognitive maps, or visual representations of the details and connections among information and knowledge, to organize and understand what they are learning. The last category, *metacognitive-based study skills*, relates to how students determine the need to study, implement a plan to study, and evaluate how their plan worked. That is, "Metacognitive strategies relate to how students select, monitor, and use strategies in their repertoire" (p. 358). Counselors can help students develop a study plan, choose what strategies they are going to use, evaluate how their plan worked, and revise their plan if needed.

Counseling Strategies

There are specific strategies that counselors can use to help students increase their academic enabling skills. For students with a skill deficit (e.g., they do not know specific study skills), counselors can use *modeling* and *coaching* to teach specific skills (DiPerna, 2006). For students with a performance deficit (e.g., they know specific study skills but do not apply them appropriately or consistently), counselors can use *behavioral rehearsal* and *reinforcement* to increase use of the skills (DiPerna, 2006).

Modeling

Counselors can use modeling to "demonstrate a behavior so a student can observe and learn how to perform the same behavior" (DiPerna, 2006, p. 14). As the skill is modeled, it is ideal for counselors to talk though their thought processes and describe the actions they are taking so that students can better understand when and why to use the skill, which helps them apply use of the skill to different learning situations (Gettinger & Seibert, 2002). Once the student has seen the skill modeled, he or she can practice it in front of the counselor, with the counselor providing praise (DiPerna, 2006; Gettinger & Seibert, 2002).

Coaching

Coaching is a scaffolded approach that involves the counselor and student talking about the skill, including what it looks like and when it would be good to use it, and then practicing the skill with counselor feedback in different settings

(DiPerna, 2006). As the student gets better at using the skill, the counselor gradually provides less support until the student has mastered the skill on his or her own (Gettinger & Seibert, 2002).

Behavioral Rehearsal

Behavioral rehearsal involves the student practicing the skill with counselor support (DiPerna, 2006). This could be done by having the student visualize the steps of the skill, verbalize the steps, or role-play the steps (DiPerna, 2006). Hill (2014) provides steps for role-playing a skill, as follows: (a) The student and counselor talk about a situation in which the student could have used the skill but did not; (b) the student and counselor identify a behavioral goal related to using the skill; (c) the student and counselor generate and evaluate several possibilities of skills the student might want to use to reach the goal, ultimately choosing one that seems like the best option; (d) the counselor models the use of the skill for the student; (e) the student practices the skill with coaching and feedback from the counselor; and (f) the student determines when he or she will try the skill in the coming week and then reports back to the counselor about how it worked.

Reinforcement

Positive reinforcement should be used throughout the counseling process, but it can be particularly helpful for counselors to use when students know strategies but are not consistently using them (DiPerna, 2006). Reinforcement can be as simple as praising students for using a strategy they already know, trying a new strategy, sticking to their plan, or making a small step toward their goal. Counselors can also help motivate students to use strategies by reinforcing them with preferred activities, such as playing a game at the end of the counseling session, or by providing small tangible rewards when students have reached a desired goal or level of proficiency with using a skill on their own (DiPerna, 2006).

COGNITIVE-BEHAVIORAL THERAPY

There is some evidence to suggest the efficacy of CBT-based interventions on enhancing academic achievement. Sapp, Farrell, and Durand (1995) found that a CBT-based intervention that included psychoeducation on study and academic success skills was related to increases in grade point average or class grades, as well as reductions in missed classes. Further, Zyromski (2008) recommends that CBT be applied to metacognitive skills (e.g., self-monitoring, planning) to enhance academic achievement. Additionally, CBT could also be implemented for other problems that inhibit a student's ability to be successful in school, such as anxiety, depression, or social stress (Zyromski, 2008).

CBT principles could also be applied in helping students identify maladaptive thoughts and underlying beliefs that are hindering their academic behaviors. A catch, check, and change, or "three Cs," approach, as described in Creed, Reisweber, and Beck (2011, p. 71) may be applied to various thoughts that are associated with unmotivated behaviors (e.g., truancy, not studying, not completing homework). In this approach, counselors teach students how to identify their maladaptive thoughts, challenge the accuracy and truth of those thoughts, and change the thoughts into more adaptive ones. For example, students may be struggling academically because they are not understanding concepts in class but also are not asking questions, and therefore are not able to complete independent classwork or homework. When prompted to identify their thoughts, they might say something like, "If I ask a question, people might think I'm stupid" or "If I don't get everything right away, I'm not smart enough to ever get it." A counselor could help a student to challenge these thoughts by asking questions such as "If your best friend asked a question, would you think that she was stupid?," "What does this thought do for you?," or "Are there things that even the smartest people on earth have to work at before they understand them?" The next step in this process would be to help the student identify replacement thoughts, or thoughts that replace the current thoughts but are related to more positive behavioral outcomes. In this case, more appropriate thoughts might include "I am not the only one who has this question" or "It's okay to not get it right on the first try."

SOLUTION-FOCUSED BRIEF THERAPY

SFBT strategies can also be utilized when counselors are working with students on enhancing study skills. Specific SFBT strategies noted by Franklin et al. (2013) as important for working with at-risk students include the miracle question, relationship questions, scaling, and goal setting. Goal setting allows counselors to keep sessions future oriented; when combined with scaling, it may provide students with opportunities to take responsibility for small increments of change. For example, a counselor could track a student's progress in implementing time management or studying strategies by utilizing scaling questions (e.g., "How well were you able to apply your study strategies this week, on a scale from 1 to 10?").

Group Counseling

Group counseling can be an effective and efficient way to address some of the risk factors associated with low motivation and school dropout, and the majority of group approaches described in the empirical literature focus on building skills for academic success, which have shown some benefits in improving factors such as school attendance and grades (e.g., Blum & Adelle, 1993; Brannigan, 2007; Kayler & Sherman, 2009). When screening students for groups, it is important for counselors to consider where students are in their resistance or readiness for change; a group that consists solely of students who are adamantly opposed to changing their behaviors and school attitudes will not likely be effective (Catterall, 1987). Additionally, the inclusion of a few particularly unmotivated students may alter the cohesion and ultimate success of a group intervention (Kayler & Sherman, 2009). In such cases, it might be more effective to work with these students individually to increase motivation and then introduce them to a group once they are beginning to engage in change talk. Group counseling can take different forms depending on the specific goals of the group. Groups can easily adopt an MI,

CBT, or SFTB focus; can support academic success through building academic enabling skills; or can use a specific curriculum to build resilience and motivation.

Motivational Interviewing

Young (2013) suggests that MI strategies can be incorporated into a group format. Techniques such as asking open questions, making affirmations, reflecting on and restating students' comments to ensure understanding, and summarizing input throughout the session may assist counselors in establishing rapport and facilitating an environment of trust, especially in the early stages of the group. Additionally, MI may be used to resolve feelings of uncertainty and to encourage group participation, which may be particularly useful in working with students who are not motivated to make changes to succeed academically. Once a group leader determines that participants are ready and willing for change to occur, they can help facilitate goal setting by asking important questions and taking note of any self-change statements that are made throughout the group sessions.

Academic Success Groups

Psychoeducational groups targeting academic enabling skills are fairly common in school settings. These groups tend to focus on classroom and study skills and strategies (e.g., making flash cards, taking notes), planning and organization skills (e.g., time management, use of a planner), test-taking skills (e.g., elimination strategies for multiple-choice exams, prioritizing known or easy items, relaxation strategies if anxiety is a problem), self-advocacy skills (e.g., identifying sources of help, asking the teacher for clarification), and understanding the link between education and one's future goals (e.g., Brannigan, 2007; Blum & Adelle, 1993; Kayler & Sherman, 2009; Langberg et al., 2011). Research on the long-term effectiveness of these groups is limited; however, given that these types of group interventions do show some efficacy in increasing factors associated with achievement, such as grades (Brannigan, 2007; Blum & Adelle, 1993; Kayler & Sherman, 2009), counselors may wish to consider them, particularly for younger students or those newly identified as being potentially at risk for academic failure.

WhyTry

WhyTry (www.whytry.org) is an evidence-based intervention aimed at enhancing students' resilience. It is a manualized and standardized intervention, with training provided through the website (www.whytry.org). This curriculum, which is based on both CBT and SFBT principles (Joye & Alvarez, 2010), is organized around a series of 10 lessons in the form of pictorial analogies, which are integrated with discussion questions, activities, and music. The primary areas targeted by WhyTry are (a) resisting peer pressure; (b) decision-making; (c) problem-solving; (d) building a support network; and (e) motivation to succeed by gaining "opportunity, freedom, and respect" (Alvarez & Anderson-Ketchmark, 2009, p. 59). WhyTry has been widely researched and found to have beneficial impacts on motivation and grades, as well as on internalizing and externalizing behavior problems (Alvarez & Anderson-Ketchmark, 2009; Joye & Alvarez, 2010).

BEYOND THE COUNSELING OFFICE

Given that the majority of risk factors for dropout are status variables (e.g., group membership) or developmental or historical (e.g., grade retention, preschool attendance), it is not surprising that counselors desiring to reduce dropout rates will be doing a lot of work outside of the counseling office.

Advocacy

Counselors working within school settings should advocate for a variety of system-level changes. First, counselors could work with school administration by discussing the risks associated with grade retention (see Jimerson et al., 2006). Next, counselors can advocate to ensure that their districts and communities provide ample and effective alternative education opportunities for students who are not successful in traditional high school settings. Options such as alternative educational schools, online or distance learning programs, or Middle College programs (http://mcnc.us/) may all be appropriate. However, these options need to be able to provide quality education and have the resources to meet the needs of students with long histories of academic struggles and other risk factors. Additionally, programs that provide alternatives to traditional school settings tend to lack opportunities for engagement and participation, particularly in sports, clubs, or other extracurricular activities such as theater productions. Because these programs may be important for school engagement, counselors may elect to advocate for students in alternative education settings to have such activities or have access to those provided at other sites. Other areas for advocacy include early intervention for academic achievement and efforts to identify and close the achievement gaps that exist across racial and linguistic groups.

Check and Connect

Check and Connect (http://checkandconnect.umn.edu/) is a K–12 intervention that targets school engagement, problem-solving, persistence, and social and relational skills. In this program, at-risk students are assigned an adult monitor who systematically reviews student data such as attendance, grades, and behavioral referrals (i.e., *check* their progress); the adult also meets regularly with the student in a mentoring relationship to give individualized attention, feedback, and encouragement (i.e., *connect* with the student). Mentors in the high school version of this program meet with students about twice a month to discuss progress and provide additional intensive interventions (e.g., help with homework, provide tutoring, provide social skills and problem-solving training). This program has empirical support for reducing dropout rates (U.S. Department of Education, 2015). Check and Connect is a standardized intervention that requires attendance at specialty training to plan for implementation, train mentors, and ensure fidelity of implementation. Even with the advocacy of a counselor, many districts will not have the resources to implement a comprehensive program like Check and Connect. However, many schools are able to create and implement mentor programs that follow the general approach of providing close monitoring and support to at-risk students. For example, Blum and Adelle (1993) describe combining a mentoring program with their group intervention for at-risk students.

Special Considerations for the Ninth-Grade Year

Researchers agree that ninth grade is an important year to support high school completion because many students transitioning from eighth to ninth grade demonstrate a decrease in academic performance and an increase in absenteeism and problem behaviors (McCallumore & Sparapani, 2010). Recognizing the critical nature of the ninth-grade year, Roderick, Kelley-Kemple, Johnson, and Beechum (2014) described a successful intervention to reduce school failure by focusing on ninth graders in the Chicago public schools. The basic premise of the intervention was to track ninth-grade students' academic progress and provide school staff with monthly reports so that they could intervene with students at risk for failure before they fell too far behind. Results showed that more 9th graders were on track for graduation, most students remained on track during 10th and 11th grades, and the district had higher graduation rates. The findings of the study indicate that early and accurate detection may be the key to effectively preventing dropout.

RESOURCES

GRADNATION: AMERICA'S PROMISE ALLIANCE

http://gradnation.org/

GradNation is composed of concerned individuals and organizations (e.g., educators, community members, nonprofit organizations, businesses) whose main focus is on improving timely graduation rates throughout the United States. GradNation's ultimate goal is to achieve a 90% nationwide high school graduation rate by the year 2020. The foundational principles of GradNation are referred to as its five promises, which are (a) caring adults, (b) safe places, (c) a healthy start, (d) effective education, and (e) opportunities to help others. Aside from providing information about dropout, including statistics, the GradNation website supports the organization of community-based GradNation summits, which are local events that involve community members and stakeholders working together to develop action plans to support youth in their area.

NATIONAL DROPOUT PREVENTION CENTER/NETWORK

http://dropoutprevention.org/effective-strategies/

The National Dropout Prevention Center/Network at Clemson University works to improve opportunities available to enhance the academic, social, and life skills necessary for success in high school and beyond. This network functions as a resource center for parents, educators, and other stakeholders looking for information on successful programs and policies related to dropout prevention. Aside from its online resources, this organization also hosts conferences (e.g., "2016 At-Risk Youth National Forum"; "2016 National Forum on Dropout Prevention for Native and Tribal Communities") and offers to partner with districts, Local Education Agencies, or other agencies needing support with grant applications or research.

REFERENCES

Ackerman, S. J., & Hilsenroth, M. J. (2003). A review of therapist characteristics and techniques positively impacting the therapeutic alliance. *Clinical Psychology Review*, *23*(2), 1–33. Retrieved from www.journals.elsevier.com/clinical-psychology-review/

Adelson, S. L., & the American Academy of Child and Adolescent Psychiatry. (2012). Practice parameter on gay, lesbian, or bisexual sexual orientation, gender nonconformity, and gender discordance in children and adolescents. *Journal of the American Academy of Child and Adolescent Psychiatry*, *51*(9), 957–974. doi:10.1016/j.jaac.2012.07.004

Altena, A. M., Brilleslijper-Kater, S. N., & Wolf, J. M. (2010). Effective interventions for homeless youth: A systematic review. *American Journal of Preventive Medicine*, *38*(6), 637–645. doi:10.1016/j.amepre.2010.02.017

Alvarez, M., & Anderson-Ketchmark, C. (2009). Review of an evidence-based school social work intervention: WhyTry. *Children and Schools*, *31*(1), 59–61. Retrieved from http://cs.oxfordjournals.org/

Amato, P. R., Landale, N. S., Havasevich-Brooks, T. C., Booth, A., Eggebeen, D. J., Schoen, R., & McHale, S. M. (2008). Precursors of young women's family formation pathways. *Journal of Marriage and Family*, *70*(5), 1271–1286. doi:10.111.j.1741-3737.2008.00565.x

American Psychological Association & National Association of School Psychologists. (2014). *Resolution on gender and sexual orientation diversity in children and adolescents in schools*. Retrieved from http://www.nasponline.org/about_nasp/resolution/gender_sexual_orientation_diversity.pdf

American Psychiatric Association. (2013). *Diagnostic and statistical manual of mental disorders* (5th ed.). Washington, DC: Author.

American School Counselor Association. (2010). *Ethical standards for school counselors*. Alexandria, VA: Author. Retrieved from http://www.schoolcounselor.org/asca/media/asca/Resource%20Center/Legal%20and%20Ethical%20Issues/Sample%20Documents/EthicalStandards2010.pdf

Annie E. Casey Foundation. (2011) *Kids count data snapshot on foster care placement*. Retrieved from http://www.aecf.org/resources/kids-count-data-snapshot-on-foster-care-placement/

Aragon, S. R., Poteat, V. P., Espelage, D. L., & Koenig, B. W. (2014). The influence of peer victimization on educational outcomes for LGBTQ and non-LGBTQ high school students. *Journal of LGBT Youth*, *11*(1), 1–19. doi:10.1080/19361653.2014.840761

Arnold, E. M., Kirk, R. S., Roberts, A. C., Griffith, D. P., Meadows, K., & Julian, J. (2003). Treatment of incarcerated, sexually-abused adolescent females: An outcome study. *Journal of Child Sexual Abuse, 12*(1), 123–139. doi:10.1300/J070v12n01_06

Aronson, K. R., & Perkins, D. F. (2013). Challenges faced by military families: Perceptions of United States Marine Corps school liaisons. *Journal of Child and Family Studies, 22*(4), 516–525. doi:10.1007s10826-012-9605-1

Atkins, D. L., Pumariega, A. J., Rogers, K., Montgomery, L., Nybro, C., Jeffers, G., & Sease, F. (1999). Mental health and incarcerated youth. I: Prevalence and nature of psychopathology. *Journal of Child and Family Studies, 8*(2), 193–204. doi:1062-1024/99/0600-0193516.00/0

Atkinson, C., & Woods, K. (2003). Motivational interviewing strategies for disaffected secondary school students: A case example. *Educational Psychology in Practice, 19*(1), 49–64. doi:10.1080.0266736032000061206

Avery, R. J., & Freundlich, M. (2009). You're all grown up now: Termination of foster care support at age 18. *Journal of Adolescence, 32*(2), 247–257. doi:10.1016/j.adolescence.2008.03.009

Aviles, A., & Helfrich, C. (2004). Life skill service needs: Perspectives of homeless youth. *Journal of Youth and Adolescence, 33*(4), 331–338. doi:10.1023/B:JOYO.0000032641.82942.22

Aviles de Bradley, A. M. (2011). Unaccompanied homeless youth: Intersections of homelessness, school experiences and educational policy. *Child and Youth Services, 32*(2), 155–172. doi:10.1080/0145935X.2011.583176

Baker, D. (2008). *Examining the effectiveness of the Why Try Program for children receiving residentially based services and attending a non-public school* (Doctoral dissertation). Retrieved from ProQuest. (Accession No. 3331194)

Barr, A. B., Simons, R. L., Gordon Simons, L., Gibbons, F. X., & Gerrard, M. (2013). Teen motherhood and pregnancy prototypes: The role of social context in changing young African American mothers' risk images and contraceptive expectations. *Journal of Youth and Adolescence, 42*(12), 1884–1897. doi:10.1007/s10964-013-9912-x

Baum, S. M., Cooper, C. R., & Neu, T. W. (2001). Dual differentiation: An approach for meeting the curricular needs of gifted students with learning disabilities. *Psychology in the Schools, 38*(5), 477–490. doi:10.1002/pits.1036

Bavolek, S. J., & Rogers, M. S. (2012). *The Nurturing Parenting Programs and the six protective factors*. Park City, UT: Family Development Resources.

Becker, A. B. (2014). Employment discrimination, local school boards, and LGBT civil rights: Reviewing 25 years of public opinion data. *Journal of Public Opinion Research, 26*(3), 342–351. doi:10.1093/ijpor/edu003

Beh, H. G., & Diamond, M. (2006) The failure of abstinence-only education: Minors have the right to honest talk about sex. *Columbia Journal of Gender and Law, 15*(1), 16–62. Retrieved from cjgl.cdrs.columbia.edu

Bender, J. (2003). *My daddy is in jail: Story, discussion guide, and small group activities for grades K–5*. Chapin, SC: Youth Light.

Bender, K., Thompson, S. J., McManus, H., Lantry, J., & Flynn, P. M. (2007). Capacity for survival: Exploring strengths of homeless street youth. *Child and Youth Care Forum, 36*(1), 25–42. doi:10.1007/s10566-006-9029-4

Bennett, S. E., & Assefi, N. P. (2005). School-based teenage pregnancy prevention programs: A systematic review of randomized controlled trials. *Journal of Adolescent Health, 36*(1), 72–81. doi:10.1016/j.jadohealth.2003.11.097

Bernier, A., Carlson, S. M., & Whipple, N. (2010). From external regulation to self-regulation: Early parenting precursors of young children's executive functioning. *Child Development, 81*(1), 326–339. doi:10.1111/j.1467-8624.2009.01397.x

Bernstein, N. (2005). *All alone in the world: Children of the incarcerated.* New York, NY: New Press.

Biggar, H. (2001). Homeless children and education: An evaluation of the Stewart B. McKinney Homeless Assistance Act. *Children and Youth Services Review, 23*(12), 941–969. doi:10.1016/S0190-7409(01)00176-1

Birkeland, R., Thompson, K., & Phares, V. (2005). Adolescent motherhood and postpartum depression. *Journal of Clinical and Child Adolescent Psychology, 34*(2), 292–300. doi:10.1207/s5374424jccp3402_8

Birkett, M., Espelage, D. L., & Koenig, B. (2009). LGB and questioning students in schools: The moderating effects of homophobic bullying and school climate on negative outcomes. *Journal of Youth Adolescence, 38*(7), 989–1000. doi:10.1007/s10964-008-9389-1

Block, K., & Potthast, M. (1998). Girl Scouts Behind Bars: Facilitating parent-child contact in correctional settings. *Child Welfare, 77*(5), 561–578. Retrieved from http://www.cwla.org/child-welfare-journal/

Blum, D. J., & Adelle, J. L. (1993). Academic growth group and mentoring program for potential dropouts. *School Counselor, 40*(3), 207–217. Retrieved from http://www.schoolcounselor.org/

Bockneck, E., Sanderson, J., & Britner, P., IV (2009). Ambiguous loss and posttraumatic stress in school-age children of prisoners. *Journal of Child and Family Studies, 18*, 323–333. doi:10.1007/s10826-008-9233-y

Bockting, W. O., Miner, M. H., Swinburne Romine, R. E., Hamilton, A., & Coleman, E. (2013). Stigma, mental health, and resilience in an online sample of the US transgender population. *American Journal of Public Health, 103*(5), 943–951. doi:10.2105/AJPH.2013.301241

Boonstra, H. D. (2010). Sex education: Another big step forward—and back. *Guttmacher Policy Review, 13*(2), 27–28. Retrieved from https://www.guttmacher.org

Borum, R. (2006). *Assessing and managing violence risk in juveniles.* New York, NY: Guilford Press.

Bowers, A. J., Sprott, R., & Taff, S. (2013). Do we know who will drop out? A review of the predictors of dropping out of high school. Precision, sensitivity, and specificity. *High School Journal, 96*(2), 77–100. Retrieved from http://soe.unc.edu/hsj/

Bowman, D., & Popp, P. A. (2013). Students experiencing homelessness. In E. Rossen & R. Hull (Eds.), *Supporting and educating traumatized students: A guide for school-based professionals* (pp. 73–92). New York, NY: Oxford University Press.

Brannigan, M. (2007). A psychoeducational group model to build academic competence in new middle school students. *Journal for Specialists in Group Work, 32*(1), 61–70. doi:10.1080/01933920600978554

Breen, P. (1995). Bridging the barriers. *Corrections Today, 57*, 98–99. Retrieved from http://www.aca.org/ACA_Prod_IMIS/ACA_Member/Publications/Corrections_Today_Magazine/ACA_Member/Publications/CT_Magazine/CorrectionsToday_Home.aspx?hkey=08c84ce7-094c-4ae8-836d-d43cd22c656f

Brosh, J., Weigel, D., & Evans, W. (2007). Pregnant and parenting adolescents' perception of sources and supports in relation to educational goals. *Child and Adolescent Social Work Journal, 24*(6), 565–578. doi:10.1007/s10560-007-0170-8

Bruskas, D. (2008). Children in foster care: A vulnerable population at risk. *Journal of Child and Adolescent Psychiatric Nursing, 21*(2), 70–77. doi:10.1111/j.1744-6171.2008.00134.x

Bruxton-McClendon, J. K. (2013). Students with incarcerated parents. In J. R. Curry & L. J. Fazio-Griffith (Eds.), *Integrating play techniques in comprehensive school counseling programs* (p. 167–184). Charlotte, NC: Information Age Publishing.

Bunting, L., & McAuley, C. (2004). Research review: Teenage pregnancy and motherhood: The contribution of support. *Child and Family Social Work, 9*, 207–215. doi:10.1111/j.1365-2206.2004.00328.x

Burgess, S., Caselman, T., & Carsey, J. (2009). *Empowering children of incarcerated parents.* Chapin, SC: Youth Light.

Burley, M., & Halpern, M. (2001). Educational attainment of foster youth: Achievement and graduation outcomes for children in state care (Report No. 01-11-3901). Retrieved from http://www.wsipp.wa.gov/ReportFile/773/Wsipp_Educational-Attainment-of-Foster-Youth-Achievement-and-Graduation-Outcomes-for-Children-in-State-Care_Full-Report.pdf

Burton, C. M., Marshal, M. P., Chisolm, D. J., Sucato, G. S., & Friedman, M. S. (2013). Sexual minority-related victimization as a mediator of mental health disparities in sexual minority youth: A longitudinal analysis. *Journal of Youth Adolescence, 42*, 394–402. doi:10.1007/s10964-012-9901-5

Carter, C. (2013). Students from military families. In E. Rossen & R. Hull (Eds.), *Supporting and educating traumatized students: A guide for school based professionals* (pp. 173–185). New York, NY: Oxford University Press.

Cary, C. E., & McMillen, J. C. (2012). The data behind the discrimination: A systematic review of trauma-focused cognitive behavioral therapy for use with children and youth. *Children and Youth Services Review, 34*, 748–757. doi:10.1016/j.childyouth.2012.01.003

Catterall, J. S. (1987). An intensive group counseling dropout prevention intervention: Some caution on isolating at-risk adolescents within high schools. *American Education Research Journal, 24*(4), 521–540. Retrieved from http://www.jstor.org/stable/1163178

Centers for Disease Control. (2015). Depression among women of reproductive age. Retrieved from http://www.cdc.gov/reproductivehealth/depression/index.htm

Cepukiene, V., & Pakrosnis, R. (2011). The outcome of solution-focused brief therapy among foster care adolescents: The changes of behavior and perceived somatic and cognitive difficulties. *Children and Youth Services Review, 33*(6), 791–797. doi:10.1016/j.childyouth.2010.11.027

Chandra, A., Martin, L. M., Hawkins, S., & Richardson, A. (2010). The impact of parental deployment on child social and emotional functioning: Perspectives of school staff. *Journal of Adolescent Health, 46*(3), 218–223. doi:10.1016/j.jadhealth.2009.10.009

Child Welfare League of America. (2008). Teen pregnancy preventions. Retrieved from 66.227.70.18/advocacy/2008leagenda.14.htm

Chipungu, S. S., & Bent-Goodley, T. B. (2004). Meeting the challenges of contemporary foster care. *Future of Children, 14*(1), 75–93. doi:10.2307/1602755

Clark, H., & Unruh, D. (2010). Transition practices for adjudicated youth with E/BDs and related disabilities. *Behavioral Disorders, 36*(1), 43–51. Retrieved from http://www.ccbd.net/publications/behavioraldisorders

Clausen, J. M., Landsverk, J., Ganger, W., Chadwick, D., & Litrownik, A. (1998). Mental health problems of children in foster care. *Journal of Child and Family Studies, 7*(3), 283–296. doi:10.1023/A:1022989411119

Clopton, K., & East, K. (2008). "Are there other kids like me?": Children with a parent in prison. *Early Childhood Education Journal, 36*, 195–198. doi:10.1007/s10643-008-0266-z

Cochran, B. N., Stewart, A. J., Ginzler, J. A., & Cauce, A. M. (2002). Challenges faced by homeless sexual minorities: Comparison of gay, lesbian, bisexual, and transgender homeless adolescents with their heterosexual counterparts. *American Journal of Public Health, 92*(5), 773–776. Retrieved from ajph.aphapublications.org

Cohen, J. A., & Mannarino, A. P. (2010). Psychotherapeutic options for traumatized children. *Current Opinion in Pediatrics, 22*(5), 605–609. doi:10.1097/MOP.0b013e32833e14a2

Cole, R. (2012). Professional school counselors' role in partnering with military families during the stages of deployment. *Journal of School Counseling, 10*(7), 1–23. Retrieved from jsc.montana.edu

Collins, M. E. (2014). Youth development and transitional living services. In G. P. Mallon & P. M. Hess (Eds.), *Child welfare for the twenty-first century: A handbook of practices, policies, and programs* (2nd ed., pp. 467–477). Thousand Oaks, CA: Sage.

Collins, M. E., Paris, R., & Ward, R. L. (2008). The permanence of family ties: Implications for youth transitioning from foster care. *American Journal of Psychiatry, 78*(1), 54–62. doi:10.1037/0002-9432.78.1.54

Collins, M. E., Spencer, R., & Ward, R. (2010). Supporting youth in the transition from foster care: Formal and informal connections. *Child Welfare: Journal of Policy, Practice, and Program, 89*(1), 125–143. Retrieved from www.cwla.org/child-welfare-journal/

Collins, R. (2009). Five things school leaders can do to build connections. Alexandria, VA: American Association of School Administrators. Retrieved from http://www.aasa.org/content.aspx?id=9014

Cooley, L. (2009). *The power of groups: Solution-focused group counseling in schools.* Thousand Oaks, CA: Sage.

Corcoran, J. (1997). A solution-oriented approach to working with juvenile offenders. *Child and Adolescent Social Work Journal, 14*, 277–288. Retrieved from http://www.springer.com/psychology/personality+%26+social+psychology/journal/10560

Corcoran, J. (2004). *Building strengths and skills: A collaborative approach to working with clients.* New York, NY: Oxford University Press.

Corliss, H. L., Cochran, S. D., & Mays, V. M. (2002). Reports of prenatal maltreatment during childhood in a United States population-based survey of homosexual, bisexual, and heterosexual adults. *Child Abuse and Neglect, 26*, 1165–1178. doi:10.1016/S0145-2134(02)00385-X

Corey, G., Corey, M. S., & Callanan, P. (2005). An approach to teaching ethics courses in human services and counseling. *Counseling and Values, 49*(3), 193–207. doi:10.1002/j.2161-007x.2005.tb01022.x

Council on Crime and Justice. (2006). *Children of incarcerated parents.* Minneapolis, MN: Author.

Courtney, M. E., & Dworsky, A. (2006). Early outcomes for young adults transitioning from out-of-home care in the USA. *Child and Family Social Work, 11*(3), 209–219. doi:10.1111/j.1365-2206.2006.00433.x

Cozza, S. J., Chun, R. S., & Polo, J. A. (2005). Military families and children during operation Iraqi Freedom. *Psychiatric Quarterly, 76*(4), 371–378. doi:10.1007/s11126-005=4974-y

Craig, S. L., Austin, A., and Alessi, E. (2013). Gay affirmative cognitive behavioral therapy for sexual minority youth: A clinical adaptation. *Clinical Social Work Journal, 41*, 258–266. doi:10.1007/s10615-012-0427-9

Creed, T. A., Reisweber, J., & Beck, A. T. (2011). *Cognitive therapy for adolescents in school settings*. New York, NY: Guilford Press.

Creen, H. F., Hightower, A. D., & Allan, M. J. (2001). School-based child care for children of teen parents: Evaluation of an urban program designed to keep young mothers in school. *Evaluation and Program Planning, 24*(3), 267–275. doi:10.1016/S0149-7189(01)000018-0

Crisp, C., & McCave, E. L. (2007). Gay affirmative practice: A model for social work practice with gay, lesbian, and bisexual youth. *Child and Adolescent Social Work Journal, 24*, 403–421 doi:10.1007/s10560-007-0091-z

Cross, J. R. (2012). Peer relationships. In T. L. Cross & J. R. Cross (Eds.), *Handbook for counselors serving students with gifts and talents* (pp. 409–425). Waco, TX: Prufrock Press.

Crumpton, H., & Gregory, A. (2011). "I'm not learning": The role of academic relevancy for low-achieving students. *Journal of Educational Research, 104*, 42–53. doi:10.1080/00220670903567398

Curry, J. (2012). Using play therapy techniques in counseling children with deployed parents. In E. Rossen & R. Hull (Eds.), *Supporting and educating traumatized students: A guide for school based professionals* (pp. 105–123). New York, NY: Oxford University Press.

Cutuli, J. J., Desjardins, C. D., Herbers, J. E., Long, J. D., Heistad, D., Chan, C. K., . . . Masten, A. S. (2013). Academic achievement trajectories of homeless and highly mobile students: Resilience in the context of chronic and acute risk. *Child Development, 84*(3), 841–857. doi:10.1111/cdev.12013

Daining, C., & DePanfilis, D. (2007). Resilience of youth in transition from out-of-home care to adulthood. *Children and Youth Services Review, 29*(9), 1158–1178. doi:10.1016/j.childyouth.2007.04.006

Dallaire, D. (2007). Incarcerated mothers and fathers: A comparison of risks for children and families. *Family Relations, 56*, 440–453. doi:10.1111/j.1741-3729.2007.00472.x

D'Amico, E. J., Houck, J. M., Hunter, S. B., Miles, J. V., Osilla, K. C., & Ewing, B. A. (2015). Group motivational interviewing for adolescents: Change talk and alcohol and marijuana outcomes. *Journal of Consulting and Clinical Psychology, 83*(1), 68–80. doi:10.1037/a0038155

Day, A., Riebschleger, J., Dworsky, A., Damashek, A., & Fogarty, K. (2012). Maximizing educational opportunities for youth aging out of foster care by engaging youth voices in a partnership for social change. *Children and Youth Services Review, 34*(5), 1007–1014. doi:10.1016/j.childyouth.2012.02.001

De Castella, K., Byrne, D., & Covington, M. (2013). Unmotivated or motivated to fail? A cross-cultural study of achievement motivation, fear of failure, and student disengagement. *Journal of Educational Psychology, 105*(3), 861–880. doi:10.1037/a0032464

De Jong, P., & Berg, I. (2008). *Interviewing for solutions* (3rd ed.). Bellmont, CA: Thomson Higher Education.

DeLamater, J., & Friedrich, W. N. (2002). Human sexual development. *Journal of Sex Research, 39*(1), 10–14. Retrieved from http://www.informaworld.com/smpp/title~content=t775653667

De Pedro, K. T., Astor, R. A., Benbenishty, R., Estrada, J., Smith, G. D., & Esqueda, M. C. (2011). The children of military service members: Challenges, supports, and future educational research. *Review of Educational Research, 81*(4), 566–618. doi:10.3102/0034654311142353

Dettlaff, A. J., & Cardoso, J. B. (2010). Mental health need and service use among Latino children of immigrants in the child welfare system. *Children and Youth Services Review, 32*(10), 1373–1379. doi:10.1016/j.childyouth.2010.06.005

Devereux, P. G., Weigel, D. J., Ballard-Reisch, D., Leigh, G., & Cahooh, K. L. (2009). Immediate and longer-term connections between support and stress in pregnant/parenting and non-pregnant/non-parenting adolescents. *Child Adolescent Social Work, 26*, 431–446. doi:10.1007/s10560-009-1075-2

de Vries, A. L. C. & Cohen-Kettenis, P. T. (2012). Clinical management of gender dysphoria in children and adolescents: The Dutch approach. *Journal of Homosexuality, 59*, 301–320. doi:10.1080/00918369.2012.653300

de Vries, A. L. C., Doreleijers, T. A. H., Steensma, T. D., & Cohen-Kettenis, P. T. (2011). Psychiatric comorbidity in gender dysphoric adolescents. *Journal Child Psychology and Psychiatry, 52*(11), 1195–1201. doi:10.1111/j.1469-7610.2011.02426.x

de Vries, A. L. C., Noens, I. L. J., Cohen-Kettenis, P. T., van Bercklelaer-Onnes, I. A., & Doreleijers, T. A. (2010). Autism spectrum disorders in gender dysphoric children and adolescents. *Journal of Autism and Developmental Disorders, 40*(1), 930–936. doi:10.1007/s10803-010-0935-9

DiPerna, J. C. (2006). Academic enablers and student achievement: Implications for assessment and intervention services in the schools. *Psychology in the Schools, 43*(1), 7–17. doi:10.1002/pits.20125

DiPerna, J. C., Volpe, R. J., & Elliott, S. N. (2002). A model of academic enablers and elementary reading/language arts achievement. *School Psychology Review, 31*(3), 298–312. Retrieved from http://eds.a.ebscohost.com/eds/pdfviewer/pdfviewer?sid=33d10eca-d153-4171-9262-0b78aa1628c6%40sessionmgr4003&vid=4&hid=4213

Dockery, D. J. (2012). School dropout indicators, trends, and interventions for school counselors. *Journal of School Counseling, 10*(12), 1–33. Retrieved from http://jsc.montana.edu/

Domenico, D. M. (2005). Career aspirations of pregnant and parenting adolescents. *Journal of Family and Consumer Science Education, 25*(1), 24–33. Retrieved from www.natefacs.org/FJCSE/jfcse.htm

Dore, M. M. (2014). Mental health care for children and youth. In G. P. Mallon & P. M. Hess (Eds.), *Child welfare for the twenty-first century: A handbook of practices, policies, and programs* (pp. 115–144). New York, NY: Columbia University Press.

Dorsey, S., Briggs, E. C., & Woods, B. A. (2011). Cognitive behavioral treatment for posttraumatic stress disorder in children and adolescents. *Child and Adolescent Psychiatric Clinics of North America, 20*(2), 1–16. doi:10.1016/j.chc.2011.01.006

Dorsey, S., Pullmann, M. D., Berliner, L., Koschmann, E., McKay, M., & Deblinger, E. (2014). Engaging foster parents in treatment: A randomized trial of supplementing trauma-focused cognitive behavioral therapy with evidence-based engagement strategies. *Child Abuse and Neglect, 38*(9), 1508–1520. doi:10.1016/j.chiabu.2014.03.020

dosReis, S., Zito, J. M., Safer, D. J., & Soeken, K. L. (2001). Mental health services for youths in foster care and disabled youths. *American Journal of Public Health, 91*(7), 1094–1099. doi:10.2105/AJPH.91.7.1094

Drapeau, S., Saint-Jacques, M., Lépine, R., Bégin, G., & Bernard, M. (2007). Processes that contribute to resilience among youth in foster care. *Journal of Adolescence, 30*(6), 977–999. doi:10.1016/j.adolescence.2007.01.005

Draughn, T., Elkins B., & Roy, R. (2002) Allies in the struggle. *Journal of Lesbian Studies*, 6(3–4), 9–20. doi:10.1300/J155v06n03_02

Drescher, J. (2010). Queer diagnoses: Parallels and contrasts in the history of homosexuality, gender variance, and the *Diagnostic and Statistical Manual. Archives of Sexual Behavior, 39*, 427–460. doi:10.1007/s10508-009-9531-5

Duhan, G., Noell, G, Witt, C., Freeland, J., Dufrene, B., & Gilbertson, D. (2004). Identifying academic skill and performance deficits: The experimental analysis of brief assessments of academic skills. *School Psychology Review, 33*(3), 429–443. Retrieved from http://www.nasponline.org/resources-and-publications/periodicals/spr-volume-44-no-4-%282015%29

Duke, T. S (2011). Lesbian, gay, bisexual, and transgender youth with disabilities: A meta-synthesis. *Journal of LGBT Youth, 8*, 1–47. doi:10.1080/19361653.2011.519181

Duncan, D. T., Hatzenbuehler, M. L., & Johnson, R. M. (2014). Neighborhood-level LGBT hate crimes and current illicit drug use among sexual minority youth. *Drug and Alcohol Dependence, 135*, 65–70. doi:10.1016/j.drugalcdep.2013.11.001

Dworsky, A., & Courtney, M. E. (2010). The risk of teenage pregnancy among transitioning foster youth: Implications for extending state care beyond age 18. *Children and Youth Services Review, 32*(10), 1351–1356. doi:10.1016/j.childyouth.2010.06.002

Dworsky, A., & Meehan, P. (2012). The parenting experiences of homeless adolescent mothers and mothers-to-be: Perspectives from a shelter sample. *Children and Youth Services Review, 34*, 2117–2122. doi:10.1016/j.childyouth.2012.07.004

Dworsky, A., Napolitano, L., & Courtney, M. (2013). Homelessness during the transition from foster care to adulthood. *American Journal of Public Health: Research and Practice, 103*(2), 318–323. doi:10.2105/AJPH.2013.301455

East, P. L., Reyes, B. T., & Horn, E. J. (2007). Association between adolescent pregnancy and a family history of teenage births. *Perspectives on Sexual and Reproductive Health, 39*(2), 108–115. doi:10.1363/3910807

Eddles-Hirsch, K., Vialle, W., McCormick, J., & Rogers, K. (2012). Insiders or outsiders: The role of social context in the peer relations of gifted students. *Roper Review, 34*(1), 53–62. doi:10.1080/02783193.2012.627554

Eddy, J. M., & Reid, J. B. (2002, January). *The antisocial behavior of the adolescent children of incarcerated parents: A developmental perspective*. Paper prepared for the Prison to Home Conference funded by the U.S. Department of Health and Human Services.

Edin, K., Tach, L., & Mincy, R. (2009). Claiming fatherhood: Race and the dynamics of paternal involvement among unmarried men. *Annals of the American Academy of Political and Social Science, 621*(1), 149–177. doi:10.1177/0002716208325548

Eisenberg, M. E., & Resnick, M. D. (2006). Suicidality among gay, lesbian and bisexual youth: The role of protective factors. *Journal of Adolescent Health, 39*(5), 662–668. doi:10.1016/j.jadohealth.2006.04.024

Elliot, W. (2002). Managing offender resistance to counseling: The "3 r's." *Federal Probation, 66*(3), 43–49. Retrieved from http://www.uscourts.gov/statistics-reports/publications/federal-probation-journal

Enea, V., & Dafinoiu, I. (2009). Motivational/solution-focused intervention for reducing school truancy among adolescents. *Journal of Cognitive and Behavioral Psychotherapies, 9*(2), 185–198. Retrieved from jcbp.psychotherapy.ro

Engel, R., Gallagher, L., & Lyle, D. (2010). Military deployments and children's academic achievement: Evidence from Department of Defense Education Activity Schools. *Economics of Education Review, 29*, 73–82. doi:10.1016/j.econedurev.2008.12.003

Espelage, D. L., Aragon, S. R., Birkett, M., & Koenig, B. W. (2008). Homophobic teasing, psychological outcomes, and sexual orientation among high school students: What influence do parents and schools have? *School Psychology Review, 37*(2), 202–216. Retrieved from http://www.nasponline.org/publications/spr/pdf/spr372espelage.pdf

Espelage, D. L. & Rao, M. A. (2013). Safe schools: Prevention and intervention for bullying and harassment. In E. S. Fisher & K. Komosa-Hawkins (Eds.), *Creating safe and supportive learning environments: A guide for working with lesbian, gay, bisexual, transgender, and questioning youth and families* (pp. 140–155). New York, NY: Routledge.

Esposito-Smythers, C., Wolff, J., Lemmon, K. M., Bodzy, M., Swenson, R. R., & Spirito, A. (2011). Military youth and the deployment cycle: Emotional health consequences and recommendations for intervention. *Journal of Family Psychology, 25*(4), 497–507. doi:10.1037/a0024534

Family Development Resources. (2015). The Nurturing Parenting programs. Retrieved from www.nurturingparenting.com

Fantuzzo, J. W., LeBoeuf, W. A., Chen, C. C., Rouse, H. L., & Culhane, D. P. (2012). The unique and combined effects of homelessness and school mobility on the educational outcomes of young children. *Educational Researcher, 41*(9), 393–402. doi:10.3102/0013189X12468210

Fassinger, R. E. (2000). Applying counseling theories to lesbian, gay, and bisexual clients: Pitfalls and possibilities. In R. M. Perez, K. A. DeBord, & K. J. Bieschke (Eds.), *Handbook of counseling and psychotherapy with lesbian, gay, and bisexual clients* (pp. 107–131). Washington, DC: American Psychological Association. doi:10.1037/10339-005

Fausto-Sterling, A. (2012). The dynamic development of gender variability. *Journal of Homosexuality, 59*, 398–421. doi:10.1080/00918369.2012.653310

Feinstein, R., Greenblatt, A., Hass, L., Kohn, S., & Rana, J. (2001). *Justice for all? A report on lesbian, gay, bisexual and transgender youth in the New York juvenile justice system*. Retrieved from http://www.hivlawandpolicy.org/sites/www.hivlawandpolicy.org/files/justiceforallreport.pdf

Finer L. B., & Zolna, M. R. (2014). Shifts in intended and unintended pregnancies in the United States, 2001–2008. *American Journal of Public Health, 104*(1): 43–48. doi:10.2105/AJPH.2013.301416

Fiorini, J., & Mullen, J. (2006). *Counseling children and adolescents through grief and loss*. Champaign, IL: Research Press.

Fisher, E. S. (2014). Best practices in supporting students who are lesbian, gay, bisexual, transgender, and questioning. In P. L. Harrison & A. Thomas (Eds.), *Best practices in school psychology* (6th ed., pp. 191–203). Bethesda, MD: National Association of School Psychologists.

Fisher, E. S., Jimerson, S. R., Barrett, B. N., & Graydon, K. S. (2010). Crisis: Helping children cope with grief and loss. In A. S. Canter, L. Paige, & S. Shaw (Eds.), *Helping children at home and school: Handouts from your school psychologist* (3rd ed., S9H3). Bethesda, MD: National Association of School Psychologists.

Fisher, E. S., & Kennedy, K. S. (2012). *Responsive school practices to support lesbian, gay, bisexual, transgender, and questioning students and families*. New York, NY: Routledge.

Fitzgerald, M. M., & Cohen, J. A. (2012). Trauma-focused cognitive behavior therapy for school psychologists. *Journal of Applied School Psychology, 28*(3), 294–315. doi:10.1080/15377903.2012.696037

Ford, D. Y. (2011). *Multicultural gifted education*. Waco, TX: Prufrock Press.

Ford, D. Y., Grantham, T. C., & Whiting, G. W. (2011). Culturally and linguistically diverse students in gifted education: Recruitment and retention issues. In T. C. Grantham, D. Y. Ford, M. S. Henfield, M. Trotman-Scott, D. A. Harmon, S. Porchèr, & C. Price (Eds.), *Gifted and advanced black students in school: An anthology of critical works* (pp. 323–347). Waco, TX: Prufrock Press.

Fowler, P. J., Toro, P. A., & Miles, B. W. (2009). Pathways to and from homelessness and associated psychosocial outcomes among adolescents leaving the foster care system. *American Journal of Public Health, 99*(8), 1453–1458. doi:10.2105/AJPH.2008.142547

Franklin, C., Kim, J. S., & Brigman, K. S. (2012). Solution-focused brief therapy in school settings. In C. Franklin, T. Trepper, W. Gingerich, & E. McCollum (Eds.), *Solution-focused brief therapy: A handbook of evidence-based practice* (pp. 231–244). New York, NY: Oxford University Press.

Franklin, C., Kim, J., & Tripodi, S. (2013). Solution-focused, brief therapy interventions for students at risk to drop out. In C. Franklin, M. Harris, & P. Allen-Meares (Eds.), *The school services sourcebook: A guide for school-based professionals* (2nd ed., pp. 691–704). New York, NY: Oxford University Press.

Franklin, C., Trepper, T. S., Gingerich, W. J., & McCollum, E. E. (Eds.). (2012). *Solution-focused brief therapy: A handbook of evidence-based practice*. New York, NY: Oxford University Press.

Friedman, M. S., Marshal, M. P., Guadamuz, T. E., Wei, C., Wong, C. F., Saewyc, E. M., & Stall, R. (2011). A meta-analysis of disparities in childhood sexual abuse, parental physical abuse, and peer victimization among sexual minority and sexual nonminority individuals. *American Journal of Public Health, 101*(8), 1481–1492. doi:10.2105/AJPH.2009.190009

Future Horizons Inc. (Producer). (2003). *Dr. Tony Attwood: Asperger's syndrome* [DVD]. Available from http://fhautism.com/

Gabel, S. (1992). Children of incarcerated and criminal parents: Adjustment, behavior, and prognosis. *Bulletin of the American Academy of Psychiatry and Law, 20*(1), 33–45. Retrieved from http://www.jaapl.org/

Gagnon, J., & Barber, B. (2010). Characteristics of and services provided to youth in secure care facilities. *Behavioral Disorders, 36*(1), 7–19. Retrieved from http://www.ccbd.net/publications/behavioraldisorders

Garland, A. F., Landsverk, J. L., Hough, R. L., & Ellis-Macleod, E. (1996). Type of maltreatment as a predictor of mental health service use for children in foster care. *Child Abuse and Neglect, 20*(8), 675–688. doi:10.1016/0145-2134(96)00056-7

Garner, J., Arnold, P., & Nunnery, J. (2014). Schoolwide impact of military-connected student enrollment: Educators' perceptions. *Children and Schools, 36*(1), 31–39. doi:10.1093/cs/cdt026

Garrett, S. B., Higa, D. H., Phares, M. M., Peterson, P. L., Wells, E. A., & Baer, J. S. (2008). Homeless youths' perceptions of services and transitions to stable housing. *Evaluation and Program Planning, 31*(4), 436–444. doi:10.1016/j.evalprogplan.2008.04.012

Geenen, S., & Powers, L. E. (2006). Are we ignoring youths with disabilities in foster care? An examination of their school performance. *Social Work, 51*(3), 233–241. doi:10.1093/sw/51.3.233

Geenen, S., & Powers, L. E. (2007). "Tomorrow is another problem": The experiences of youth in foster care during their transition into adulthood. *Children and Youth Services Review, 29*(8), 1085–1101. doi:10.1016/j.childyouth.2007.04.008

Geiger, J. M., & Schelbe, L. A. (2014). Stopping the cycle of child abuse and neglect: A call to action to focus on pregnant and parenting youth in and aging out of the foster care system. *Journal of Public Child Welfare, 8*(1), 25–50. doi:10.1080/15548732.2013.824398

Gentry, M., Hu, S., & Thomas, A. T. (2008). Ethnically diverse students. In J. A. Plucker & C. M. Callahan (Eds.), *Critical issues and practices in gifted education: What the research says* (pp. 195–212). Waco, TX: Prufrock Press.

Gettinger, M., & Seibert, J. K. (2002). Contributions of study skills to academic competence. *School Psychology Review, 31*(3), 350–365. doi:10.1.1.466.9214

Gilligan, R. (2000a). The importance of listening to the child in foster care. In G. Kelly & R. Gilligan (Eds.), *Issues in foster care* (pp. 40–58). Philadelphia, PA: Jessica Kingsley.

Gilligan, R. (2000b). Promoting resilience in children in foster care. In G. Kelly & R. Gilligan (Eds.), *Issues in foster care* (pp. 107–126). Philadelphia, PA: Jessica Kingsley.

Glaze, L., & Maruschak, L. (2010). *Bureau of Justice Statistics special report: Parents in prison and their minor children.* Washington, DC: U.S. Department of Justice.

Glick, B., & Gibbs, J. (2015). *Aggression replacement training: A comprehensive intervention for aggressive youth.* Champaign, IL: Research Press.

Glover, J. A., Galliher, R. V., & Lamere, T. G. (2009). Identity development and exploration among sexual minority adolescents: Examination of a multidimensional model. *Journal of Homosexuality, 56*(1), 77–101. doi:10.1080/00918360802551555

Goodenow, C., Szalacha, L., & Westheimer, K. (2006). School support groups, other school factors, and the safety of sexual minority adolescents. *Psychology in the Schools, 43*, 573–589. doi:10.1002/pits.20173

Goodrich, K. M., & Gilbride, D. D. (2010). The refinement and validation of a model of a family functioning after child's disclosure as lesbian, gay, or bisexual. *Journal of LGBT Issues in Counseling, 4*(2), 92–121. doi:10.1080/15538605.2010.483575

Goodyear, R. K. (2002). A concept map of male partners in teenage pregnancy: Implications for school counselors. *Professional School Counseling, 5*(3), 186–193. Retrieved from www.questia.com/library/professional-school-counseling

Gramkowski, B., Kools, S., Paul, S., Boyer, C. B., Monasterio, E., & Robbins, N. (2009). Health risk behavior of youth in foster care. *Journal of Child and Adolescent Psychiatry, 22*(2), 77–85. doi:10.1111/j1744-6171.2009.00176.x

Granello, P. F., & Hanna, F. J. (2003). Incarcerated and court-involved adolescents: Counseling an at-risk population. *Journal of Counseling and Development, 81*(1), 11. Retrieved from http://onlinelibrary.wiley.com/journal/10.1002/%28ISSN%291556-6676

Granger, R. C., & Cryton, R. (1999). Teenage parent programs: A synthesis of the long-term effects of the New Chance Demonstration, Ohio's learning, earning and parenting program, and the teenage parent demonstration. *Evaluation Review, 23*(2), 107–145. Retrieved from erx.sagepub.com

Greene, M. J. (2002). Career counseling for gifted and talented students. In M. Neihart, S. M. Reis, N. M. Robinson, & S. M. Moon. (Eds.), *The social and emotional development of gifted children: What do we know?* (pp. 223–236). Waco, TX: Prufrock Press.

Greenspon, T. S. (2012). Perfectionism: A counselor's role in a recovery process. In T. L. Cross & J. R. Cross (Eds.), *Handbook for counselors serving students with gifts and talents* (pp. 597–613). Waco, TX: Prufrock Press.

Gresham, F., Van, M., & Cook, C. (2006). Social skills training for teaching replacement behaviors: Remediating acquisition deficits in at-risk students. *Behavioral Disorders*, *31*(4), 363–377. Retrieved from www.ccbd.net/publications/behavioraldisorders

Greytak, E. A., & Kosciw, J. G. (2013). Responsive classroom curriculum for lesbian, gay, bisexual, transgender, and questioning students. In E. S. Fisher & K. Komosa-Hawkins (Eds.), *Creating safe and supportive learning environments: A guide for working with lesbian, gay, bisexual, transgender, and questioning youth and families* (pp. 156–174). New York, NY: Routledge.

Greytak, E. A., Kosciw, J. G., & Boesen, M. J. (2013). Putting the "T" in "resource": The benefits of LGBT-related school resources for transgender youth. *Journal of LGBT Youth*, *10*(1–2), 45–63. doi:10.1080/19361653.2012.718522

Gross, M. U. (2002). Social and emotional issues for exceptionally intellectually gifted students. In M. Neihart, S. M. Reis, N. M. Robinson, & S. M. Moon. (Eds.), *The social and emotional development of gifted children: What do we know?* (pp. 19–30). Waco, TX: Prufrock Press.

Grossman, A. H., & D'Augelli, A. R. (2006). Transgender youth: Invisible and vulnerable. *Journal of Homosexuality*, *51*(1), 111–128. doi:10.1300/J082v51n01_06

Grossman, A. H., & D'Augelli, A. R. (2007). Transgender youth and life-threatening behavior. *Suicide and Life-Threatening Behavior*, *37*, 527–537. doi:10.1521/suli.2007.37.5.527

Grov, C., Bimbi, D. S., Nanín, J. E., & Parsons, J. T. (2006). Race, ethnicity, gender, and generational factors associated with the coming-out process among gay, lesbian, and bisexual individuals. *Journal of Sex Research*, *43*(2), 115–121. doi:10.1080/00224490609552306

Guerra, N., Kim, T., & Boxer, P. (2008). What works: Best practices with juvenile offenders. In N. Guerra & P. Boxer (Eds.), *Treating the juvenile offender* (pp. 79–102). New York, NY: Guilford Press.

Gurland, S. T., & Grolnick, W. S. (2008). Building rapport with children: Effects of adults' expected, actual, and perceived behavior. *Journal of Social and Clinical Psychology*, *27*(1), 226–253. Retrieved from guilfordjournals.com/loi/jscp

Guzman, C. (2014). School-age children of military families: Theoretical applications, skills training, considerations, and interventions. *Children and Schools*, *36*(1), 9–14. doi:10.1093/cs/cdt023

Haas, A. P., Eliason, M., Mays, V. M., Mathy, R. M., Cochran, S. D., D'Augelli, A. R., ... Clayton, P. J. (2010). Suicide and suicide risk in lesbian, gay, bisexual, and transgender populations: Review and recommendations. *Journal of Homosexuality*, *58*(1), 10–51. doi:10.1080/00918369.2011.534038

Hamilton, B. E., Martin, J. A., Osterman, M. J. K., & Curtin, S. C. (2014). Births: Preliminary data for 2013. *National Vital Statistics Reports*, *63*(2). Hyattsville, MD: National Center for Health Statistics. Retrieved from http://www.cdc.gov/nchs/data/nvsr63/nvsr63_02.pdf

Harden, B. (2004). Safety and stability for foster children: A developmental perspective. *Future of Children*, *14*(1), 30–47. doi:10.2307/1602753

Hardy, L. (2006). When kids lose parents in our war in Iraq. *Education Digest: Essential Readings Condensed for Quick Review*, *72*(4), 10–12. Retrieved from http://www.eddigest.com/

Harper, G. W., Brodsky, A., & Bruce, D. (2012). What's good about being gay? Perspectives from youth. *Journal of LGBT Youth, 9*, 22–41. doi:10.1080/19361653.2012.628230

Harris, M. B., & Allgood, J. G. (2009). Adolescent pregnancy prevention: Choosing an effective program that fits. *Children and Youth Services Review, 31*, 1314–1320. doi:10.1016/j.childyouth.2009.06.002

Harris, M. B., & Franklin, C. G. (2003). Effects of a cognitive-behavioral, school-based, group intervention with Mexican American pregnant and parenting adolescents. *Social Work Research, 27*(2), 71–83. doi:10.1093/swr/27.2.71

Harris, M. B., & Franklin, C. (2007). *Taking Charge: A school-based life skills program for adolescent mothers.* New York, NY: Oxford University Press.

Harris, M. B., & Franklin, C. (2012). Taking Charge: A solution-focused intervention for pregnant and parenting adolescents. In C. Franklin, T. Trepper, W. Gingerich, & E. McCollum (Eds.), *Solution-focused brief therapy: A handbook of evidence-based practice* (pp. 247–263). New York, NY: Oxford University Press.

Harrison, J., & Vannest, K. (2008). Educators supporting families in times of crisis: Military reserve deployments. *Preventing School Failure, 52*(4), 17–23. Retrieved from http://www.tandfonline.com/toc/vpsf20/current

Harrison, N. (2000). Gay affirmative therapy: A critical analysis of the literature. *Journal of Guidance and Counseling, 28*(1), (37–53). doi:10.1080/030698800109600

Haskett, M. E., Nears, K., Ward, C. S., & McPherson, A. V. (2006). Diversity in adjustment of maltreated children: Factors associated with resilient functioning. *Clinical Psychology Review, 26*, 796–812. doi:10.1016/j.cpr.2006.03.005

Heck, N. C., Flentje, A., & Cochran, B. N. (2012). Intake interviewing with lesbian, gay, bisexual, and transgender clients: Starting from a place of affirmation. *Journal of Contemporary Psychotherapy, 43*(1), 23–32. doi:10.1007/s10879-012-9220-x

Henggeler, S. W., Schoenwald, S., Borduin, C., Rowland, M., & Cunningham, P. (2009). *Multisystemic therapy for antisocial behavior in children and adolescents* (2nd ed.). New York, NY: Guilford Press.

Herbers, J. E., Cutuli, J. J., Lafavor, T. L., Vrieze, D., Leibel, C., Obradović, J., & Masten, A. S. (2011). Direct and indirect effects of parenting on the academic functioning of young homeless children. *Early Education and Development, 22*(1), 77–104. doi:10.1080/10409280903507261

Hettema, J., Steele, J., & Miller, W. R. (2005). Motivational interviewing. *Annual Review of Clinical Psychology, 1*, 91–111. doi:10.1146/annurev.clinpsy.1.102803. 143833

Higa, D., Hoppe, M. J., Lindhorst, T., Mincer, S., Beadness, B., Morrison, D. M., ... Mountz, S. (2012). Negative and positive factors associated with well-being of lesbian, gay, bisexual, transgender, queer, and questioning (LGBTQ) youth. *Youth and Society, 46*(5), 1–25. doi:10.1177/0044118X12449630

Hill, C. E. (2014). *Helping skills: Facilitating exploration, insight and action* (4th ed.). Washington, DC: American Psychological Assocation.

Himelstein, S. (2011). Engaging the moment with incarcerated youth: An existential–humanistic approach. *Humanistic Psychologist, 39*(3), 206–221. doi:10.1080/088737267.2011.592436

Hoffman, S. D., & Maynard, R. A. (2008). *Kids having kids: The economic costs and social consequences of teen pregnancy* (2nd ed.). Washington, DC: Urban Institute Press.

Hofmann, S. G., Asnaani, A., Vonk, I. J. J., Sawyer, A. T., & Fang, A. (2012). The efficacy of cognitive behavioral therapy: A review of meta-analyses. *Cognitive Therapy and Research, 36*, 427–440. doi:10.1007/s10608-012-9476-1

Hogan, K. A., Bullock, L. M., & Fritsch, E. J. (2010). Meeting the transition needs of incarcerated youth with disabilities. *Journal of Correctional Education, 61*(2), 133–147. Retrieved from http://www.ceanational.org/Journal/

Hollin, C. R. (2003). Aggression Replacement Training: Putting theory and research to work. *Reclaiming Children and Youth: The Journal of Strength-Based Interventions, 12*(3), 132–135. Retrieved from http://cecp.air.org/resources/journals/jebp.asp

Hollingsworth, W. G. (2011). Community family therapy with military families experiencing deployment. *Contemporary Family Therapy, 33*, 215–228. doi:10.1007/s10591-011-9144-8

Holman, C. W., & Goldberg, J. M. (2006). Ethical, legal, and psychosocial issues in care of transgender adolescents. *Guidelines for Transgender Care, 1*, 95–108. doi:10.1300/J485v09n03_05

Holmqvist, R., Hill, T., & Lang, A. (2009). Effects of aggression replacement training in young offender institutions. *International Journal of Offender Therapy and Comparative Criminology, 53*(1), 74–92. doi:10.1177/0306624X07310452

Hoshmand, L., & Hoshmand, A. (2007). Support for military families and communities. *Journal of Community Psychology, 35*(2), 171–180. doi:10.1002/jcop.20141

Houchins, D. E. (2001). Developing the self-determination of incarcerated students. *Journal of Correctional Education, 52*(4), 141–147. Retrieved from http://www.ceanational.org/Journal/

H.R. Rep. No. HEHS-00-13. (1999). Retrieved from GAO's Federal Digital System: http://www.gao.gov/assets/230/228309.pdf

Huebner, A. J., & Mancini, J. A. (2008). Supporting youth during parental deployment: Strategies for professionals and families. *Prevention Researcher, 15*, 10–13. Retrieved from www.TPRonline.org

Huebner, A. J., Mancini, J. A., Bowen, G. L., & Orthner, D. K. (2009). Shadowed by war: Building community capacity to support military families. *Family Relations, 58*(2), 216–228. doi:10.1111/j.1741-3729.2008.00548.x

Huebner, A. J., Mancini, J. A., Wilcox, R. M., Grass, S. R., & Grass, G. A. (2007). Parental deployment and youth in military families: Exploring uncertainty and ambiguous loss. *Family Relations, 56*(2), 112–122. doi:10.1111/j.1741-3729.2007.00445.x

Hunter, S. (2007). *Coming out and disclosures: LGBT persons across the life span.* Binghamton, NY: Haworth Press.

Hussey, D. L., & Guo, S. (2005). Characteristics and trajectories of treatment of foster care youth. *Child Welfare League of America, 84*(4), 485–506. Retrieved from www.cwla.org/child-welfare-journal/

Innes, R. S. (1990). *Developing and instituting a parenting course for parents of children ages 3–4 years* (Unpublished doctoral dissertation). Nova Southeastern University, Fort Lauderdale, FL.

Israel, T., Gorcheva, R., Burnes, T. R., & Walther, W. A. (2008). Helpful and unhelpful therapy experiences of LGBT clients. *Psychotherapy Research, 18*(3), 294–305. doi:10.1080/10503300701506920

Israel, T., Gorcheva, R., Walther, W. A., Sulzner, J. M., & Cohen, J. (2008). Therapists' helpful and unhelpful situations with LGBT clients: An exploratory study. *Professional Psychology: Research and Practice, 39*(3), 361–368. doi:10.1037/0735-7028.39.3.361

Jackson, M. (2010). Education support for military families. *Leadership, 39*(4), 12–14. Retrieved from http://lea.sagepub.com/

Jamil, O. B., Harper, G. W., Fernandez, M. I., & Adolescent Trials Network for HIV/AIDS Interventions. (2009). Sexual and ethnic identity development among gay-bisexual-questioning (GBQ) male ethnic minority adolescents. *Cultural Diversity and Ethnic Minority Psychology, 15*(3), 203–214. doi:10.1037/a0014795

Jaycox, L. H., Kataoka, S. H., Stein, B. D., Langley, A. K., & Wong, M. (2012). Cognitive Behavioral Intervention for Trauma in Schools. *Journal of Applied School Psychology, 28*(3), 239–255. doi:10.1080/15377903

Jimerson, S., Pletcher, S., Graydon, K., Schnurr, B., Nickerson, A., & Kundert, D. (2006). Beyond grade retention and social promotion: Promoting the social and academic competence of students. *Psychology in the Schools, 43*(1), 85–97. doi:10.1002/pits.20132

Johnson, S. J. (2012). Gay affirmative psychotherapy with lesbian, gay, and bisexual individuals: Implications for contemporary psychotherapy research. *American Journal of Orthopsychiatry, 82*(4), 516–522. doi:10.1111/j.1939-0025.2012.01180.x

Jonson-Reid, M., Williams, J. H., & Webster, D. (2001). Severe emotional disturbance and violent offending among incarcerated adolescents. *Social Work Research, 25*(4), 213–22. doi:1070-5309/01

Jones, R. M., Wheelwright, S., Farrell, K., Martin, E., Green, R., DiCeglie, D., & Baron-Cohen, S. (2012). Brief report: Female-to-male transsexual people and autistic traits. *Journal of Autism and Developmental Disorders, 42*(1), 301–306. doi:10.1007/s10803-011-1227-8

Joye, E., & Alvarez, M. (2010). Tier 2 case example: WhyTry. In J. Clark and M. Alvarez (Eds.), *Response to intervention: A guide for school social workers* (pp. 95–111). New York, NY: Oxford University Press.

Just the Facts Coalition. (2008). *Just the facts about sexual orientation and youth: A primer for principals, educators, and school personnel*. Washington, DC: American Psychological Association. Retrieved from www.apa.org/pi/lgbc/publications/just-thefacts.html.

Kamieniecki, G. W. (2001). Prevalence of psychological distress and psychiatric disorders among homeless youth in Australia: A comparative review. *Australian and New Zealand Journal of Psychiatry, 35*(3), 352–358. doi:10.1046/j.1440-1614.2001.00910.x

Kaplow, J., Layne, C., Saltzman, W., Cozza, S., & Pynoos, R. (2013). Using multidimensional grief theory to explore the effects of deployment, reintegration, and death on military youth and families. *Clinical Child and Family Psychology Review, 16*(3), 322–340. doi:10.1007/s10567-013-0143-1

Kar, N. (2011). Cognitive behavioral therapy for the treatment of post-traumatic stress disorder: A review. *Neuropsychiatric Disease and Treatment, 7*, 167–181. doi:10.2147/NDT.S10389

Karabanow, J., & Clement, P. (2004). Interventions with street youth: A commentary on the practice-based research literature. *Brief Treatment and Crisis Intervention, 4*(1), 93–108. doi:10.1093/brief-treatment/mhh007

Kataoka, S., Jaycox, L. H., Wong, M., Nadeem, E., Langley, A., Tang, L., & Stein, B. D. (2011). Effects on school outcomes in low-income minority youth: Preliminary findings from a community-partnered study of a school trauma intervention. *Ethnicity and Disease, 21*(301), 1–12. Retrieved from https://www.ethndis.org

Kayler, H., & Sherman, J. (2009). At-risk ninth-grade students: A psychoeducational group approach to increase study skills and grade point averages. *Professional School Counseling, 12*(6) 434–439. Retrieved from http://www.schoolcounselor.org/

Kazura, K. (2000). Family programming for incarcerated parents. *Journal of Offender Rehabilitation, 32*(4), 67–83. doi:10.1300/J076v32n04_05

Keiley, M. K. (2002). Affect regulation and the gifted child. In M. Neihart, S. M. Reis, N. M. Robinson, & S. M. Moon. (Eds.), *The social and emotional development of gifted children: What do we know?* (pp. 41–50). Waco, TX: Prufrock Press.

Kenagy, G. P. (2005). Transgender health: Findings from two needs assessment studies in Philadelphia. *Health and Social Work, 30*, 19–26. doi:10.1093/hsw/30.1.19

Kendall, P. C. (Ed.). (2011). *Child and adolescent therapy: Cognitive-behavioral procedures* (4th ed.). New York, NY: Guilford.

Kendall, P. C., & Hedtke, K. (2006). *Cognitive-behavioral therapy for anxious children: Therapist manual* (3rd ed.). Ardmore, PA: Workbook Publishing.

Kennedy, K. G., & Fisher, E. S. (2010). Bisexual students in secondary schools: Understanding unique experiences and developing responsive practices. *Journal of Bisexuality, 10*(4), 427–485. doi:10.1080/15299716.2010.521061

Kerker, B. D., & Dore, M. M. (2006). Mental health needs and treatment of foster youth: Barriers and opportunities. *American Journal of Orthopsychiatry, 76*(1), 138–147. doi:10.1037/0002-9432.76.1.138

Kertzner, R. M., Meyer, I. H., Frost, D. M., & Stirratt, M. J. (2009). Social and psychological well-being in lesbians, gay men, and bisexuals: The effects of race, gender, age, and sexual identity. *American Journal of Orthopsychiatry, 79*(4), 500–510. doi:10.1037/a0016848

Keuroghlian, A. S., Shtasel, D., & Bassuk, E. L. (2014). Out on the street: A public health and policy agenda for lesbian, gay, bisexual, and transgender youth who are homeless. *American Journal of Orthopsychiatry, 84*(1), 66–72. doi:10.1037/h0098852

Kidd, S. A., & Carroll, M. R. (2007). Coping and suicidality among homeless youth. *Journal of Adolescence, 30*(2), 283–296. doi:10.1016/j.adolescence.2006.03.002

Kidd, S. A., Miner, S., Walker, D., & Davidson, L. (2007). Stories of working with homeless youth: On being "mind-boggling." *Children and Youth Services Review, 29*(1), 16–34. doi:10.1016/j.childyouth.2006.03.008

Kidd, S., & Shahar, G. (2008). Resilience in homeless youth: The key role of self-esteem. *American Journal of Orthopsychiatry, 78*(2), 163–172. doi:10.1037/0002-9432.78.2.163

Kiselica, M. S., & Pfaller, J. (1992). Helping teenage parents: The independent and collaborative roles of counselor educators and school counselors. *Journal of Counseling and Development, 72*(1), 42–48. doi:10.1002/j.1556-6676.1993.tb02275.x

Kim, J. S., & Franklin, C. (2009). Solution-focused brief therapy in schools: A review of the outcome literature. *Children and Youth Services Review, 31*(4), 464–470. doi:10.1016/j.childyouth.2008.10.002

Kim, M. (2012). Career planning. In T. L. Cross & J. R. Cross (Eds.), *Handbook for counselors serving students with gifts and talents* (pp. 529–541). Waco, TX: Prufrock Press.

Kinscherff, R. (2012). *A primer for mental health practitioners working with youth involved in the juvenile justice system.* Washington, DC: Technical Assistance Partnership for Child and Family Mental Health. Retrieved from http://www.tapartnership.org/docs/jjResource_mentalHealthPrimer.pdf

Kirkman, M., Harrison, L., Hillier, L. & Pyett, P. (2001). "I know I'm doing a good job": Canonical and autobiographical narratives of teenage mothers. *Culture, Health and Sexuality, 3*(3), 279–294. doi:10.1080/1391050010026097

Kjellstrand, J., Cearley, J., Eddy, J., Foney, D., & Martinez, C., Jr. (2012). Characteristics of incarcerated fathers and mothers: Implications for preventive interventions targeting children and families. *Children and Youth Services Review, 34,* 2409–2415. doi:10.1016/j.childyouth.2012.08.008

Klein, J. D., & Committee on Adolescence. (2005). Adolescent pregnancy: Current trends and issues. *Pediatrics, 116,* 281–286. doi:10.1542/peds.2005-0999

Kohler, P. D., & Field, S. (2003). Transition-Focused Education: Foundations for the future. *Journal of Special Education, 37*(3), 174–1783. doi:10.1177/00224669030370030701

Koob, J. J., & Love, S. M. (2010). The implementation of solution-focused therapy to increase foster care placement stability. *Children and Youth Services Review, 32*(10), 1346–1350. doi:10.1016/j.childyouth.2010.06.001

Koocher, G. P., & Kinscherff, R. T. (2016). Ethical issues in psychology and juvenile justice. In K. Heilbrun (Ed.), *APA Handbook of psychology and juvenile justice* (pp. 693–714). Washington, DC: American Psychological Association.

Kort-Butler, L. A., & Tyler, K. A. (2012). A cluster analysis of service utilization and incarceration among homeless youth. *Social Science Research, 41*(3), 612–623. doi:10.1016/j.ssresearch.2011.12.011

Kosciw, J. G., Greytak, E. A., & Diaz, E. M. (2009). Who, what, where, when, and why: Demographic and ecological factors contributing to hostile school climate for lesbian, gay, bisexual, and transgender youth. *Journal of Youth and Adolescence, 38*(7), 976–988. doi:10.1007/s10964-009-9412-1

Kosciw, J. G., Greytak, E. A., Palmer, N.A., & Boesen, M. J. (2014). *2013 National school climate survey: The experiences of lesbian, gay, bisexual and transgender youth in our nation's schools.* New York, NY: GLSEN.

Kosciw, J. G., Palmer, N. A., & Kull, R. M. (2015). Reflecting resiliency: Openness about sexual orientation and/or gender identity and its relationship to well-being and educational outcomes for LGBT students. *American Journal of Community Psychology, 55*(1–2), 167–178. doi:10.1007/s10464-014-9642-6

Kosciw, J. G., Palmer, N. A., Kull, R. M., & Greytak, E. A. (2013). The effect of negative school climate on academic outcomes for LGBT youth and the role of in-school supports. *Journal of School Violence, 12*(1), 45–63. doi:10.1080/15388220.2012.732546

Kurtz, P. D., Lindsey, E. W., Jarvis, S., & Nackerud, L. (2000). How runaway and homeless youth navigate troubled waters: The role of formal and informal helpers. *Child and Adolescent Social Work Journal, 17*(5), 381–402. doi:10.1023/A:1007507131236

Landis, R. N., & Reschly, A. L. (2013). Reexamining gifted underachievement and dropout through the lens of student engagement. *Journal for the Education of the Gifted, 36*(2), 220–249. doi:10.1177/0162353213480864

Landmark, L. J., Ju, S., & Zhang, D. (2010). Substantiated best practices in transition: Fifteen plus years later. *Career Development for Exceptional Individuals, 33*(3), 165–176. doi:10.1177/0885728810376410

Langberg, J., Vaughn, A., Williamson, P., Epstein, J., Girgio-Herrera, E., & Becker, S. (2011). Refinement of an organizational skills intervention for adolescents with ADHD for implementation by school mental health providers. *School Mental Health*, *3*, 143–155. doi:10.1080/1391050010026097

Lawrence, C. R., Carlson, E. A., & Egeland, B. (2006). The impact of foster care on development. *Development and Psychopathology*, *18*(1), 57–76. doi:10.1017/S0954579406060044

Lebolt, J. (1999). Gay affirmative psychotherapy: A phenomenological study. *Clinical Social Work Journal*, *27*(4), 355–368. doi:10.1023/A:1022871029582

Lee, S. Y., Olszewski-Kubilius, P., & Thompson, D. T. (2012). Academically gifted students' perceived interpersonal competence and peer relationships. *Gifted Child Quarterly*, *56*(2), 90–104. doi:10.1177/0016986212442568

Leeuwenburgh, E., & Goldring, E. (2008). *Why did you die? Activities to help children cope with grief and loss.* Oakland, CA: New Harbinger Publications.

Legault, L., Anawati, M., & Flynn, R. (2006). Factors favoring psychological resilience among fostered young people. *Children and Youth Services Review*, *28*(9), 1024–1038. doi:10.1016/j.childyouth.2005.10.006

Lehmann, L., Jimerson, S., & Gaasch, A. (2001a). *Mourning child grief support group curriculum: Early childhood edition.* Philadelphia, PA: Brunner-Routledge.

Lehmann, L., Jimerson, S., & Gaasch, A. (2001b). *Mourning child grief support group curriculum: Middle childhood edition.* New York, NY: Routledge.

Lehmann, L., Jimerson, S., & Gaasch, A. (2001c). *Teens together grief support group curriculum: Adolescence edition.* New York, NY: Routledge.

Lemon, K., Hines, A. M., & Merdinger, J. (2005). From foster care to young adulthood: The role of independent living programs in supporting successful transitions. *Children and Youth Services Review*, *27*(3), 251–270. doi:10.1016/j.childyouth.2004.09.005

Leone, P., & Weinberg, L. (2012). *Addressing the unmet educational needs of children and youth in the juvenile justice and child welfare systems.* Washington, DC: Georgetown University, Center for Juvenile Justice Reform.

Leslie, L. K., Gordon, J. N., Lambros, K., Premji, K., Peoples, J., & Gist, K. (2005). Addressing the developmental and mental health needs of young children in foster care. *Journal of Developmental and Behavioral Pediatrics*, *26*(2), 140–151. doi:10.1097/00004703-200504000-00011

Leslie, L. K., Hurlburt, M. S., Landsverk, J., Barth, R., & Slymen, D. J. (2004). Outpatient mental health services for children in foster care: A national perspective. *Child Abuse and Neglect*, *28*(6), 699–714. doi:10.1016/j.chiabu.2004.01.004

Leslie, L. K., Landsverk, J., Ezzet-Lofstrom, R., Tschann, J. M., Slymen, D. J., & Garland, A. F. (2000). Children in foster care: Factors influencing outpatient mental health service use. *Child Abuse and Neglect*, *24*(4), 465–476. doi:10.1016/S0145-2134(00)00116-2

Lester, P., Mogil, C., Saltzman, W., Woodward, K., Nash, W., Leskin, G., . . . Beardslee, W. (2011). Families overcoming under stress: Implementing family-centered prevention for military families facing wartime deployments and combat operational stress. *Military Medicine*, *176*(1), 19–25. Retrieved from http://publications.amsus.org/

Lester, P., Stein, J., Saltzman, W., Woodward, K., MacDermid, S., Milburn, N., . . . Beardslee, W. (2013). Psychological health of military children: Longitudinal evaluation of a family-centered prevention program to enhance family resilience. *Military Medicine*, *178*(8), 838–845. Retrieved from http://publications.amsus.org/

Letourneau, N. L., Stewart, M. J., & Barnfather, A. K. (2004). Adolescent mothers: Support needs, resources, and support-education interventions. *Journal of Adolescent Health, 35*(6), 509–525. doi:10.1016/j.jadohealth.2004.01.007

Levin, H. M., & Rouse, C. E. (2012, January 25). The true cost of high school dropouts. *The New York Times*. Retrieved from http://www.nytimes.com/2012/01/26/opinion/the-true-cost-of-high-school-dropouts.html?_r=2

Lightfoot, C., Cole, M., & Cole, S. (2009). *The development of children*. New York, NY: Worth Publishers.

Linehan M. (1993). *Skills training manual for treating borderline personality disorder*. New York, NY: Guilford Press.

Logsdon, C. M., Birkimer, J. C., Simpson, T., & Looney, S. (2003). Postpartum depression and social support in adolescents. *Journal of Obstetric, Gynecologic, and Neonatal Nursing, 34*(1), 46–54. doi:10.1177/0884217504272802

Lopez, C., & Bhat, C. (2007). Supporting students with incarcerated parents in schools: A group intervention. *Journal for Specialists in Group Work, 32*(2), 139–153. doi:10.1080/01933920701227125

Luttrell, W. (2003). *Pregnant bodies, fertile minds: Gender, race, and the schooling of pregnant teens*. New York, NY: Routledge.

MacLaren, C., & Freeman, A. (2006). Cognitive behavior therapy model and techniques. In T. Ronen & A. Freeman (Eds.), *Cognitive behavior therapy in clinical social work practice* (pp. 3–24). New York, NY: Springer.

Malley, M., & Tasker, F. (2007). "The difference that makes a difference": What matters to lesbians and gay men in psychotherapy. *Journal of Gay and Lesbian Psychotherapy, 11*(1), 93–109. doi:10.1300/J236v11n01_07

Mannarino, A. P., Cohen, J. A., & Deblinger, E. (2014). Trauma-focused cognitive-behavioral therapy. In S. Timmer & A. Urquiza (Eds.), *Evidence-based approaches for the treatment of maltreated children* (pp. 165–185). New York, NY: Springer.

Maputle, M. (2006). Becoming a mother: Teenage mothers' perspectives of first pregnancy. *Curationis, 29*(2), 87–95. Retrieved from www.curationis.org.za

Marecek, J. (1987). Counseling adolescents with problem pregnancies. *American Psychologist, 42*(1), 89–93. Retrieved from www.apa.org

Marshal, M. P., Dermody, S. S., Cheong, J., Burton, C. M., Friedman, M. S., Aranda, F., & Hughes, T. L. (2013). Trajectories of depressive symptoms and suicidality among heterosexual and sexual minority youth. *Journal of Youth and Adolescence, 42*, 1243–1256. doi:10.1007/s10964-013-9970-0

Marshal, M. P., Friedman, M. S., Stall, R., King, K. M., Miles, J., Gold, M. A., ... Morse, J. Q. (2008). Sexual orientation and adolescent substance use: A meta-analysis and methodological review. *Society for the Study of Addiction, 103*, 546–556. doi:10.1111/j.1360-0443.2008.02149.x

Masten, A. S. (2007). Resilience in developing systems: Progress and promise as the fourth wave rises. *Development and Psychopathology, 19*, 921–930. doi:10.1017/S0954579407000442

Masten, A. S. (2011). Resilience in children threatened by extreme adversity: Frameworks for research, practice, and translational synergy. *Development and Psychopathology, 23*(2), 493. doi:10.1017/S0954579411000198

Masten, A. S., Herbers, J. E., Cutuli, J. J., & Lafavor, T. L. (2008). Promoting competence and resilience in the school context. *Professional School Counseling, 12*(2), 76–84. Retrieved from www.jstor.org/journal/profschocoun

Masten, A. S., Sesma, A., Jr., Si-Asar, R., Lawrence, C., Miliotis, D., & Dionne, J. A. (1997). Educational risks for children experiencing homelessness. *Journal of School Psychology, 35*(1), 27–46. doi:10.1016/S0022-4405(96)00032-5

McCallumore, K. M., & Sparapani, E. F. (2010). The importance of the ninth grade on high school graduation rates and student success in high school. *Education, 130*(3), 447–456. Retrieved from http://www.projectinnovation.biz/education_2006.html

McClain, M. C., & Pfeiffer, S. (2012). Identification of gifted students in the United States today: A look at state definitions, policies, and practices. *Journal of Applied School Psychology, 28*(1), 59–88. doi:10.1080.15377903.2012.643757

McKay, A., & Barett, M. (2010). Trends in teen pregnancy rates from 1996–2006: A comparison of Canada, Sweden, U.S.A., and England/Wales. *Canadian Journal of Human Sexuality, 12*(1–2), 43–52. doi:10.1016/j.jadohealth.2014.09.007

McMillen, J. C., Scott, L. D., Zima, B. T., Ollie, M. T., Munson, M. R., & Spitznagel, E. (2004). Use of mental health services among older youths in foster care. *Psychiatric Services, 55* (7), 811–817. doi:10.1176/appi.ps.55.7.811

McRoy, R. G. (2014). Disproportionate representation of children and youth. In G. P. Mallon & P. M. Hess (Eds.), *Child welfare for the twenty-first century: A handbook of practices, policies, and programs* (2nd ed., pp. 680–690). Thousand Oaks, CA: Sage.

Meade, C. S., Kershaw, T. S., & Ickovics, J. R. (2008). The intergenerational cycle of teenage motherhood: An ecological approach. *Health Psychology, 27*(4), 419–429. doi:10.1037/0278-6133.27.4.419

Meadows-Oliver, M. (2006). Homeless adolescent mothers: A metasynthesis of their life experiences. *Journal of Pediatric Nursing, 21*(5), 340–349. doi:10.1016.j.pedn.2006.004

Merdinger, J. M., Hines, A. M., Osterling, K. L., & Wyatt, P. (2005). Pathways to college for former foster youth: Understanding factors that contribute to educational success. *Child Welfare: Journal of Policy, Practice, and Program, 84*(6), 867–896. Retrieved from www.cwla.org/child-welfare-journal/

Merrell, K. W. (2008). *Helping students overcome depression and anxiety: A practical guide* (2nd ed.). New York, NY: Guilford Press.

Merrell, K., Carizalez, D., Feuerborn, L., Gueldner, B., & Tran, A. (2007a). *Strong kids grades 3–5: A social and emotional learning curriculum*. Baltimore, MD: Paul H. Brookes.

Merrell, K., Carizalez, D., Feuerborn, L., Gueldner, B., & Tran, A. (2007b). *Strong kids grades 6-8: A social and emotional learning curriculum*. Baltimore, MD: Paul H. Brookes.

Merrell, K., Carizalez, D., Feuerborn, L., Gueldner, B., & Tran, A. (2007c). *Strong teens: A social and emotional learning curriculum*. Baltimore, MD: Paul H. Brookes.

Merrell, K., Parisi, D., & Whitcomb, S. (2007). *Strong start grades K–2: A social and emotional learning curriculum*. Baltimore, MD: Paul H. Brookes.

Messacar, D., & Oreopoulos, P. (2013). Staying in school: A proposal for raising high-school graduation rates. *Issues in Science and Technology, 29*(2), 55–61. Retrieved from www.issues.org

Milan, S., Ickovics, J. R., Kershaw, T., Lewis, J., Meade, C., & Ethier, K. (2004). Prevalence, course, and predictors of emotional distress in pregnant and parenting adolescents. *Journal of Consulting and Clinical Psychology, 27*(2), 328–340. doi:10.1037/0022-006X.72.2.328

Miller, K. (2006). The impact of parental incarceration on children: An emerging need for effective interventions. *Child and Adolescent Social Work, 23*(4), 472–486. doi:10.1007/s10560-006-0065-6

Miller, W. R., & Rollnick, S. (2002). *Motivational interviewing: Preparing people for change* (2nd ed.). New York, NY: Guilford Press.

Miller, W. R., & Rollnick, S. (2004). Talking oneself into change: Motivational interviewing, stages of change, and therapeutic process. *Journal of Cognitive Psychotherapy, 18*(4), 299–308. doi:0.1891/jcop.18.4.299.64003

Miller, W. R., & Rollnick, S. (2013). *Motivational interviewing: Helping people change* (3rd ed.). New York, NY: Guilford Press.

Miller, W. R., & Rose, G. S. (2009). Toward a theory of motivational interviewing. *American Psychologist, 64*(6), 527–537. doi:10.1037/a0016830

Minnick, D. J., & Shandler, L. (2011). Changing adolescent perceptions on teenage pregnancy. *Children and Schools, 33*(4), 241–248. doi:10.1093/cs/334.241

Minter, S. P. (2012). Supporting transgender children: New legal, social, and medical approaches. *Journal of Homosexuality, 59*, 422–433. doi:10.1080/00918369.2012.653311

Mitchell, R. C., Panzarello, A., Grynkiewicz, A., & Galupo, M. P. (2015). Sexual minority and heterosexual former foster youth: A comparison of abuse experiences and trauma-related beliefs. *Journal of Gay and Lesbian Social Services, 27*, 1–16. doi:10.1080/10538720.2015.988316

Möller, B., Schreier, H., Li, A., & Romer, G. (2009). Gender identity disorder in children and adolescents. *Current Problems in Pediatric and Adolescent Health Care, 39*(5), 117–143. doi:10.1016/j.cppeds.2009.02.001

Moon, S. M. (2009). Myth 15: High-ability students don't face problems and challenges. *Gifted Child Quarterly, 53*(4), 274–276. doi:10.1177/0016986209346943

Moon, S. M., & Hall, A. S. (1998). Family therapy with intellectually and creatively gifted children. *Journal of Marital and Family Therapy, 24*(1), 59–80. doi:10.1111/j.1752-0606.1998.tb01063.x

Moore, C. (2009). *The WhyTry program—Elementary teacher's manual*. Orem, UT: WhyTry.

Moore, J. (2013). *Research summary: Teaching and classroom strategies for homeless and highly mobile students*. Retrieved from http://center.serve.org/nche/downloads/res-summ-teach-class.pdf

Moore, T., & McArthur, M. (2011). "Good for kids": Children who have been homeless talk about school. *Australian Journal of Education, 55*(2), 147–160. doi:10.1177/000494411105500205

Moriarty, D. A., Sadler, L. S., & Reynolds, H. D. (2013). Tailoring clinical services to address the unique needs of adolescents from the pregnancy test to parenthood. *Pediatric Adolescent Health Care, 43*, 71–95. doi:10.1016/j.cppeds.2013.01.001

Morningstar, M. E., Kleinhammer-Tramill, P. J., & Lattin, D. L. (1999). Using successful models of student-centered transition planning and services for adolescents with disabilities. *Focus on Exceptional Children, 31*(9), 1–16. Retrieved from lovepublishing.com/journals.htm

Morsette, A., Swaney, G., Stolle, D., Schuldberg, D., van den Pol, R., & Young, M. (2009). Cognitive Behavioral Intervention for Trauma in Schools (CBITS): School-based treatment on a rural American Indian reservation. *Journal of Behavior Therapy and Experimental Psychiatry, 40*, 169–178. doi:10.1016/j.jbtep.2008.07.006

Mosher, C. M. (2001). The social implications of sexual identity formation and the coming-out process: A review of the theoretical and empirical literature. *Family Journal: Counseling and Therapy for Couples and Families, 9*(2), 164–173. doi:10.1177/1066480701092011

Mueller, T. G., Bassett, D. S., & Brewer, R. D. (2012). Planning for the future: A model for using principles of transition to guide the development and behavior intervention plans. *Intervention in School and Clinic, 48*(1), 38–46. doi:10.1177/1053451212443130

Mumola, C. (2000). *Bureau of Justice statistics bulletin: Incarcerated parents and their children*. Washington, DC: U.S. Department of Justice.

Murdock, T. B., & Bolch, M. B. (2005). Risk and protective factors for poor school adjustment in lesbian, gay and bisexual (LGB) high school youth: Variable and person-centered analyses. *Psychology in the Schools, 42*, 159–172. doi:10.1002/pits.20054

Murphy, J. J. (2008). *Solution-focused counseling in schools* (2nd ed.). Alexandria, VA: American Counseling Association.

Murphy, R. A., & Fairbank, J. A. (2013). Implementation and dissemination of military informed and evidence-based interventions for community dwelling military families. *Clinical Child and Family Psychology Review, 16*(4), 348–364. doi:10.1007/s10567-013-0149-8

Muskin, M. B. (2004). The need for comprehensive competency-based career guidance curriculum for teen mothers. *Educational Considerations, 31*(2), 41–45. Retrieved from https://coe-k-state.edu/educonsiderations/

Mustanski, B., & Liu, R. T. (2012). A longitudinal study of predictors of suicide attempts among lesbian, gay, bisexual, and transgender youth. *Archives of Sexual Behavior, 42*(3), 437–448. doi:10.1007/s10508-012-0013-9

National Association for Gifted Children. (2001). *Position paper: Appropriate education for gifted GLBT students*. Retrieved from http://nagc.org/index.aspx?id=390

National Association for Gifted Children. (2009a). *Position paper: Nurturing social and emotional development of gifted children*. Retrieved from http://nagc.org/index2.aspx?id=5092

National Association for Gifted Children. (2009b). *White paper: Twice-exceptionality*. Retrieved from http://www.nagc.org/sites/default/files/Position%20Statement/twice%20exceptional

National Association for Gifted Children. (2011). *Position statement: Identifying and serving culturally and linguistically diverse gifted students*. Retrieved from http://www.nagc.org/sites/default/files/Position%20Statement/Identifying%20and%20Serving%20Culturally%20and%20Linguistically.pdf

National Association for the Education of Homeless Children and Youth. (2009). *The most frequently asked questions on the education rights of children and youth in homeless situations*. Retrieved from http://www.naehcy.org/dl/naehcy_faq.pdf

National Association of School Psychologists. (2010). *Principles for professional ethics*. Bethesda, MD: Author. Retrieved from http://www.nasponline.org/standards/2010standards.aspx

National Association of School Psychologists. (2011). *Lesbian, gay, bisexual, transgender, and questioning (LGBTQ) youth (Position Statement)*. Bethesda, MD: Author. Retrieved from http://www.nasponline.org/about_nasp/positionpapers/LGBTQ_Youth.pdf

National Association of School Psychologists. (2014). *Safe schools for transgender and gender diverse students (Position Statement)*. Bethesda, MD: Author. Retrieved from http://www.tyes-colorado.org/documents/NASP_Transgender_PositionStatement.pdf

National Campaign to Prevent Teen Pregnancy. (2002). *Not just another single issue: Teen pregnancy prevention's link to other critical social issues*. Retrieved from http://www.teenpregnancy.org

National Campaign to Prevent Teen and Unplanned Pregnancy. (2013). *Counting it up: Key data*. Washington, DC: Author. Retrieved from https://thenationalcampaign.org/sites/default/files/resource-primary-download/counting-it-up-key-data-2013-update.pdf

National Center for Homeless Education. (2007). *Best practices in homeless education: Supporting homeless students with disabilities: Implementing IDEA*. Retrieved from http://center.serve.org/nche/downloads/briefs/idea_qa.pdf

National Center for Homeless Education. (2014). *Education for homeless children and youths programs: Data collection summary*. Retrieved from http://center.serve.org/nche/downloads/data-comp-0910-1112.pdf

National Child Traumatic Stress Network. (2005). *Facts on trauma and homeless children*. Retrieved from http://nctsnet.org/nctsn_assets/pdfs/promising_practices/Facts_on_Trauma_and_Homeless_Children.pdf

National Coalition for the Homeless. (2008). *Homeless youth*. Retrieved from http://www.nationalhomeless.org/factsheets/youth.pdf

National Coalition for the Homeless. (2009a). *LGBTQ homeless*. Retrieved from http://www.nationalhomeless.org/factsheets/lgbtq.pdf

National Coalition for the Homeless. (2009b). *Why are people homeless?* Retrieved from http://www.nationalhomeless.org/factsheets/Why.pdf

National Working Group on Foster Care and Education. (2014). *Fostering success in education: National factsheet on the educational outcomes of children in foster care*. Retrieved from National Resource Center for Permanency and Family Connections website: http://www.fostercareandeducation.org/DesktopModules/Bring2mind/DMX/Download.aspx?EntryId=1279&Command=Core_Download&method=inline&PortalId=0&TabId=124

Nebbitt, V. E., House, L. E., Thompson, S. J., & Pollio, D. E. (2007). Successful transitions of runaway/homeless youth from shelter care. *Journal of Child and Family Studies, 16*(4), 545–555. doi:10.1007/s10826-006-9105-2

Neihart, M. (2012). Anxiety, depression, and resilience. In T. L. Cross & J. R. Cross (Eds.), *Handbook for counselors serving students with gifts and talents* (pp. 615–629). Waco, TX: Prufrock Press.

Nesmith, A., & Ruthland, E. (2008). Children of incarcerated parents: Challenges and resiliency, in their own words. *Children and Youth Services Review, 30*, 1119–1130. doi:10.1016/j.childyouth.2008.02.006

Newton, R. R., Litrownik, A. J., & Landsverk, J. A. (2000). Children and youth in foster care: Disentangling the relationship between problem behaviors and number of placements. *Child Abuse and Neglect, 24*(10), 1363–1374. doi:10.1016/S0145-2134(00)00189-7

Nicpon, M. F., & Pfeiffer, S. I. (2011). High-ability students: New ways to conceptualize giftedness and provide psychological services in the schools. *Journal of Applied School Psychology, 27*, 293–305. doi:10.1080/15377903.2011.616579

Obradović, J., Long, J. D., Cutuli, J. J., Chan, C. K., Hinz, E., Heistad, D., & Masten, A. S. (2009). Academic achievement of homeless and highly mobile children in an urban school district: Longitudinal evidence on risk, growth, and resilience. *Development and Psychopathology, 21*(2), 493–518. doi:10.1017/S0954579409000273

Oetzel, K. B., & Scherer, D. G. (2003). Therapeutic engagement with adolescents in psychotherapy. *Psychotherapy: Theory, Research, Practice, Training, 40*(3), 215–225. doi:10.1037/0033-3204.40.3.215

Ollendick, T. H., King, N. J., & Chorpita, B. F. (2006). Empirically supported treatments for children and adolescents. In P. C. Kendall (Ed.), *Child and adolescent therapy: Cognitive-behavioral procedures* (3rd ed., pp. 492–520). New York, NY: Guilford Press.

Olszewski-Kubilius, P. (2002). Parenting practices that promote talent development, creativity and optimal adjustment. In M. Neihart, S. M. Reis, N. M. Robinson, & S. M. Moon (Eds.), *The social and emotional development of gifted children: What do we know?* (pp. 205–212). Waco, TX: Prufrock Press.

O'Malley, M., Voight, A., Renshaw, T. L., & Eklund, K. (2014). School climate, family structure, and academic achievement: A study of moderation effects. *School Psychology Quarterly, 30*(10), 142–157. doi:10.1037/spq0000076

Orr, A., & Komosa-Hawkins, K. (2013). Law, policy, and ethics: What school professionals need to know. In E. S. Fisher & K. Komosa-Hawkins (Eds.), *Creating safe and supportive learning environments: A guide for working with lesbian, gay, bisexual, transgender, and questioning youth and families* (pp. 156–174). New York, NY: Routledge.

Oswald, S., Heil, K., & Goldbeck, L. (2010). History of maltreatment and mental health problems in foster children: A review of the literature. *Journal of Pediatric Psychology, 35*(5), 462–472. doi:10.1093/jpepsy/jsp114

Ovaert, L. B., Cashel, M. L., & Sewell, K. W. (2003). Structured group therapy for posttraumatic stress disorder in incarcerated male juveniles. *American Journal of Orthopsychiatry, 73*(3), 294–301. doi:10.1037/0002-9432.73.3.294

Pakrosnis, R., & Cepukiene, V. (2012). Outcomes of solution-focused brief therapy for adolescents in foster care and health care settings. In C. Franklin, T. S. Trepper, W. J. Gingerich, & E. E. McCollum (Eds.), *Solution-focused brief therapy: A handbook on evidence-based practices* (pp. 299–326). New York, NY: Oxford University Press.

Park, J. M., Metraux, S., Culhane, D. P., & Mandell, D. S. (2012). Homelessness and children's use of mental health services: A population-based study. *Children and Youth Services Review, 34*(1), 261–265. doi:10.1016/j.childyouth.2011.10.022

Park, N. (2011). Military children and families: Strengths and challenges during peace and war. *American Psychologist, 66*(1), 65–72. doi:10.1037/a0021249

Pecora, P. J. (2012). Maximizing educational achievement of youth in foster care and alumni: Factors associated with success. *Children and Youth Services Review, 34*(6), 1121–1129. doi:10.1016/j.childyouth.2012.01.044

Pecora, P. J., White, C. R., Jackson, L. J., & Wiggins, T. (2009). Mental health of current and former recipients of foster care: A review of recent studies in the USA. *Child and Family Social Work, 14*, 132–146. doi:10.1111/j.1365-2206.2009.00618x

Perper, K., Peterson, K., & Manlove, J. (2010). Diploma attainment among teen mothers. Child Trends, Fact Sheet Publication No. 2010-01: Washington, DC.

Petch, P., & Rochlen, A. (2009). Children of incarcerated parents: Implications for school counselors. *Journal of School Counseling, 7*, 1–27. Retrieved from JSC.montana.edu

Peters, M., & Bain, S. K. (2011). Bullying and victimization rates among gifted and high-achieving students. *Journal for the Education of the Gifted, 34*(4), 624–643. doi:10.1177/016235321103400405

Peterson, J. S. (2009). Myth 17: Gifted and talented individuals do not have unique social and emotional needs. *Gifted Child Quarterly, 53*(4), 280–282. doi:10.1177/0016986209346946

Peterson, J. S., & Moon, S. M. (2008). Counseling of the gifted. In S. I. Pfeiffer (Ed.), *Handbook of giftedness in children* (pp. 247–270). New York, NY: Springer.

Peterson, J. S., & Ray, K. E. (2006). Bullying and the gifted: Victims, perpetrators, prevalence, and effects. *Gifted Child Quarterly, 50*(2), 148–168. doi:10.1177/001698620605000206

Peterson, J. S., & Rischar, H. (2000). Gifted and gay: A study of the adolescent experience. *Gifted Child Quarterly, 44*(3), 231–246. doi:10.1177/001698620004400404

Petrenko, C. M., Culhane, S. E., Garrido, E. F., & Taussig, H. N. (2011). Do youth in out-of-home care receive recommended mental health and educational services following screening evaluations? *Children and Youth Services Review, 33*(10), 1911–1918. doi:10.1016/j.childyouth.2011.05.015

Petrick, D. L., Jr. (2014). School drop outs: Poverty and consequences for society. *Insights to a Changing World, 2014*(4), 127–136. Retrieved from http://franklinpublishing.net

Pfeiffer, S. I. (2013). *Serving the gifted: Evidence-based clinical and psychoeducational practice.* New York, NY: Routledge.

Pietrowski, J. L. (2006). *Understanding the experience of teenage parents: An empirical examination of attitudes and expectations among education professionals* (Doctoral dissertation). Retrieved from http://commons.emich.edu/cgi/viewcontent.cgi?article=1028&context=theses

Pilowsky, D. J., & Wu, L. (2006). Psychiatric symptoms and substance use disorders in a nationally representative sample of American adolescents involved with foster care. *Journal of Adolescent Health, 38*(4), 351–358. doi:10.1016/j.jadohealth.2005.06.014

Pisano, M. (2014). Best practices in service to children in military families. In A. Thomas & J. Grimes (Eds.), *Best practices in school psychology* (pp. 181–191). Bethesda: MD: National Association of School Psychologists.

Poehlmann, J., Dallaire, D., Booker, L., & Shear, L. (2010). Children's contact with their incarcerated parents: Research findings and recommendations. *American Psychologist, 65*(6), 575–598. doi:10.1037/a0020279

Pope, M., Bunch, L. K., Szymanski, D. M., & Rankins, M. (2004). Counseling sexual minority students in the schools. In B. Erford (Ed.), *Handbook for professional school counseling* (pp. 221–235). Greensboro, NC: CAPS Press.

Poteat, V. P., Aragon, S. R., Espelage, D. L., & Koenig, B. W. (2009). Psychosocial concerns of sexual minority youth: Complexity and caution in group differences. *Journal of Consulting and Clinical Psychology, 1*, 196–201. doi:10.1037/a0014158

Price, J. M., & Brew, V. (1998). Peer relationships of foster children: Developmental and mental health service Implications. *Journal of Applied Developmental Psychology, 19*(2), 199–218. doi:10.1016/S0193-3973(99)80036-7

Prochaska, J. O., & DiClemente, C. C. (1982). Transtheoretical therapy: Toward a more integrative model of change. *Psychotherapy: Theory, Research and Practice, 19*(3), 276–288. doi:10.1037/h0088437

Purcell, D. W., Campos, P. E., & Perilla, J. L. (1996). Therapy with lesbians and gay men: A cognitive behavioral perspective. *Cognitive and Behavioral Practice, 3*, 391–415. doi:10.1016/S1077-7229(96)80025-3

Putnam-Hornstein, B., Needell, B., King, B., & Johnson-Motoyama, M. (2013). Racial and ethnic disparities: A population-based examination of risk factors for involvement with child protective services. *Child Abuse and Neglect, 37*, 33–46. doi:10.1016/j.chiabu.2012.08.005

Quest, A. D., Fullerton, A., Geenen, S., Powers, L., & the Research Consortium to Increase the Success of Youth in Foster Care. (2012). Voices of youth in foster care and special education regarding their educational experiences and transition to adulthood. *Children and Youth Services Review, 34*(9), 1604–1615. doi:10.1016/j.childyouth.2012.04.018

Quinlivan, J. A., & Condon, J. (2005). Anxiety and depression in fathers in teenage pregnancy. *Australian and New Zealand Journal of Psychiatry, 39*, 915–920. doi:10.111/j.1440-1614.2005.01664.x

Quint, J. C., Bos, H. M., & Polit, D. F. (1997). New Chance: Final report on a comprehensive program for young mothers in poverty and their children. New York, NY: Manpower Demonstration Research Corporation.

Rafferty, Y., Shinn, M., & Weitzman, B. C. (2004) Academic achievement among formerly homeless adolescents and their continuously housed peers. *Journal of School Psychology, 42*(3), 179–199. doi:10.1016/j.jsp.2004.02002

Raviv, T., Taussig, H. N., Culhane, S. E., & Garrido, E. F. (2010). Cumulative risk exposure and mental health symptoms among maltreated youth placed in out-of-home care. *Child Abuse and Neglect, 34*(10), 742–751. doi:10.1016/j.chiabu.2010.02.011

Reed-Victor, E., & Stronge J. H. (2002). Homeless students and resilience: Staff perspectives on individual and environmental factors. *Journal of Children and Poverty, (8)*2, 159–183. doi:10.1080/1079612022000005375

Reeves, T., Horne, S. G., Rostosky, S. S., Riggle, E. D. B., Baggett, L. R., & Aycock, R. A. (2010). Family members' support for GLBT issues: The role of family adaptability and cohesion. *Journal of GLBT Family Studies, 6*(1), 80–97. doi:10.1080/15504280903472857

Reichman, N., & McLanahan, S. (2001). Self-sufficiency programs and parenting interventions: Lessons from New Chance and the teenage parent demonstration. *Social Policy Report, 15*(2), 879–889. Retrieved from www.srcd.org

Reid, V., & Meadows-Oliver, M. (2007). Postpartum depression in adolescent mothers: An integrative review of the literature. *Journal of Pediatric Health Care, 21*(5), 289–298. doi:10/1016/j.pedhc.2006.05.010

Reis, S. M., & Renzulli, J. S. (2004). Current research on the social and emotional development of gifted and talented students: Good news and future possibilities. *Psychology in the Schools, 41*(1), 119–130. doi:10.1002/pits.10144

Reis, S. M., & Renzulli, J. S. (2009). Myth 1: The gifted and talented constitute one single homogeneous group and giftedness is a way of being that stays in the person over time and experiences. *Gifted Child Quarterly, 53*(4), 233–235. doi:10.1177/0016986209346824

Riggs, S., & Riggs, D. (2011). Risk and resilience in military families experiencing deployment: The role of the family attachment network. *Journal of Family Psychology, 25*(5), 675–687. doi:10.1037/a0025286

Rimm, S. (2002). Peer pressures and social acceptance of gifted students. In M. Neihart, S. M. Reis, N. M. Robinson, & S. M. Moon (Eds.), *The social and emotional development of gifted children: What do we know?* (pp. 13–18). Waco, TX: Prufrock Press.

Roberts, A. L., Rosario, M., Corliss, H. L., Koenen, K. C., & Austin, S. B. (2012). Childhood gender nonconformity: A risk indicator for childhood abuse and posttraumatic stress in youth. *Pediatrics, 129*(3), 410–416. doi:10.1542peds.2011-3696

Robertson, S. G., Pfieffer, S. I., & Taylor, N. (2011). Serving the gifted: A national survey of school psychologists. *Psychology in the Schools, 48*(8), 786–799. doi:10.1002/pits.20590

Robinson, J., Cox, G., Malone, A., Williamson, M., Baldwin, G., Fletcher, K., & O'Brien, M. (2013). A systemic review of school-based interventions aimed at preventing, treating, and responding to suicide-related behavior in young people. *Crisis, 34*(3), 164–182. doi:10.1027/0227-5910/a000168

Robinson, J. P., & Espelage, D. L. (2011). Inequities in education and psychological outcomes between LGBTQ and straight students in middle and high school. *Educational Researcher, 40*(7), 315–330. doi:10.3102/0013189X11422112

Robinson, N. M. (2002). Introduction. In M. Neihart, S. M. Reis, N. M. Robinson, & S. M. Moon (Eds.), *The social and emotional development of gifted children: What do we know?* (pp. xi–xxiv). Waco, TX: Prufrock Press.

Roderick, M., Kelley-Kemple, T., Johnson, D. W., & Beechum, N. O. (2014). *Preventable failure: Improvements in long-term outcomes when high schools focused on the ninth grade year.* Retrieved from http://ccsr.uchicago.edu/

Rolfsnes, E. S., & Idsoe, T. (2011). School-based intervention programs for PTSD symptoms: A review and meta-analysis. *Journal of Traumatic Stress, 24*(2), 155–165. doi:10.1002/jts

Ronen, T. (2006). Clinical social work and its commonalities with cognitive behavior therapy. In T. Ronen & A. Freeman (Eds.), *Cognitive behavior therapy in clinical social work practice* (pp. 3–24). New York, NY: Springer.

Rosario, M., Schrimshaw, E. W., & Hunter, J. (2004). Ethnic/racial differences in the coming out process of lesbian, gay, and bisexual youths: A comparison of sexual identity development over time. *Cultural Diversity and Ethnic Minority Psychology, 10*(3), 215–228. doi:10.1037/1099-9809.10.3.215

Rosario, M., Schrimshaw, E. W., & Hunter, J. (2008). Predicting different patterns of sexual identity development over time among lesbian, gay, and bisexual youths: A cluster analytic approach. *American Journal of Community Psychology, 42*(3-4), 266–282. doi:10.1007/s10464-008-9207-7

Rosario, M., Schrimshaw, E. W., & Hunter, J. (2012). Risk factors for homelessness among lesbian, gay, and bisexual youths: A developmental milestone approach. *Children and Youth Services Review, 34*, 186–192. doi:10.1016/j.childyouth.2011.09.016

Rosario, M., Schrimshaw, E. W., Hunter, J., & Braun, L. (2006). Sexual identity development among lesbian, gay, and bisexual youths: Consistency and change over time. *Journal of Sex Research, 43*(1), 46–58. doi:10.1080/00224490609552298

Rose, H. A., Rodgers, K. B., & Small, S. A. (2006). Sexual identity confusion and problem behaviors in adolescents: A risk and resilience approach. *Marriage and Family Review, 40*(2–3), 131–150. doi:10.1300/j002v40n02_07

Ross, A. M., & DeVoe, E. R. (2014). Engaging military parents in a home-based reintegration program: A consideration of strategies. *Health and Social Work, 39*(1), 47–54. doi:10.1039/hsw/hlu001

Rossen, E. (2011). Supporting students with incarcerated parents. *Principal Leadership, 11*, 12–16. doi:10.1080/01933920701227125

Rowell, L., & Hong, E. (2013). Academic motivation: Concepts, strategies, and counseling approaches. *Professional School Counseling, 16*(3), 158–171. Retrieved from http://www.schoolcounselor.org/

Rubak, S., Sandbæk, A., Lauritzen, T., & Christensen, B. (2005). Motivational interviewing: A systematic review and meta-analysis. *British Journal of General Practice, 55*(513), 305–312. Retrieved from pjgp.org

Rubenstein, L. D., Seigle, D., Reis, S. M., McCoach, D. B., & Burton, M. G. (2012). A complex quest: The development and research of underachievement interventions for gifted students. *Psychology in the Schools, 49*(7), 678–694. doi:10.1002/pits.21620

Rubin, D. M., O'Reilly, A., Luan, X., & Localio, A. R. (2007). The impact of placement stability on behavioral well-being for children in foster care. *Pediatrics, 119*(2), 336–344. doi:10.1542/peds.2006-1995.

Rudd, M. D. (2008). Suicide warning signs in clinical practice. *Current Psychiatry Reports, 10*, 87–90. Retrieved from link.springer.com/journal/11920

Rudd, M. D., Berman, A. L., Joiner, T. E., Nock, M. K., Silverman, M. M., Mandrusiak, M., . . . Witte, T. (2006). Warning signs for suicide: Theory, research and clinical applications. *Suicide and Life-Threatening Behavior, 36*(3), 255–262.

Rumberger, R., & Lim, S. (2008). Why students drop out of school: A review of 25 years of research. California Dropout Research Project. Retrieved from http://www.cdrp.ucsb.edu/pubs_reports.htm

Rush, C. M., & Akos, P. (2007). Supporting children and adolescents with deployed caregivers: A structured group approach for school counselors. *Journal for Specialists in Group Work, 32*(2), 113–125. doi:10.1080.01933920701227034

Russell, G. M., & Bohan, J. S. (2007). Liberating psychotherapy: Liberation psychology and psychotherapy with LGBT clients. *Journal of Gay and Lesbian Psychotherapy, 11*(3), 59–75. doi:10.1300/J236v11n03_04

Russell, S. T., Ryan, C., Toomey, R. B., Diaz, R. M., & Sanchez, J. (2011). Lesbian, gay, bisexual, and transgender adolescent school victimization: Implications for young adult health and adjustment. *Journal of School Health, 81*(5), 223–230. doi:10.1111/j.1746-1561.2011.00583.x

Russell, S. T., Toomey, R. B., Ryan, C., & Diaz, R. M. (2014). Being out at school: The implications for school victimization and young adult adjustment. *American Journal of Orthopsychiatry, 84*(6), 635–643. doi:10.1037/ort0000037

Rutter, P. A., & Behrendt, A. E. (2004). Adolescent suicide risk: Four psychosocial factors. *Adolescence, 39*, 295–301. Retrieved from www.journals.elsevier.com/journal-of-adolescence/

Ryan, C. (2001). Counseling lesbian, gay, and bisexual youths. In A. R. D'Augelli & C. J. Patterson (Eds.), *Lesbian, gay, and bisexual identities and youth: Psychological perspectives* (pp. 224–250). New York, NY: Oxford University Press.

Ryan, C. (2010). Engaging families to support lesbian, gay, bisexual, and transgender youth: The family acceptance project. *Prevention Researcher, 17*(4) 11–13. Retrieved from http://www.tpronline.org/article.cfm/Engaging_Families_to_Support_LGBT_Youth

Ryan, C., Huebner, D., Diaz, R. M., & Sanchez, J. (2009). Family rejection as a predictor of negative health outcomes in white and Latino lesbian, gay, and bisexual young adults. *Pediatrics, 123*(1), 346–351. doi:10.1111/j.1744-6171.2010.00246

Ryan, C., Russell, S., Huebner, D., Diaz, R., & Sanchez, J. (2010). Family acceptance in adolescence and the health of LGBT young adults. *Journal of Child and Adolescent Psychiatric Nursing, 23*(4), 205–213. doi:10.1111/j.1744-6171.2010.00246

Saewyc, E. (2005). Pregnancy among lesbian, gay and bisexual adolescents: Influences of stigma, sexual abuse, and sexual orientation. In A. M. Omoto & H. S. Kurtzman (Eds.), *Sexual orientation and mental health: Examining identity and development in lesbian, gay, and bisexual people* (pp. 95–116). Washington, DC: American Psychological Association.

Safren, S. A., Hollander, G., Hart, T. A., & Heimberg, R. G. (2001). Cognitive-behavioral therapy with lesbian, gay, and bisexual youth. *Cognitive Behavioral Practice, 8,* 215–223. doi:10.1016/S1077-7229(01)80056-0

Sander, J. B., & Fisher, A. L. (2014). Best practices in school psychologists' services for juvenile offenders. In P. Harrison & A. Thomas (Eds.), *Best practices in school psychology* (pp. 217–228). Bethesda, MD: National Association of School Psychologists.

Sapp, M., Farrell, W., & Durand, H. (1995). Cognitive-behavioral therapy: Applications for African-American middle school at-risk students. *Journal of International Psychology, 22*(2), 169–177. Retrieved from www.tandfonline.com/loi/pipj20

Sarri, R., & Phillips, A. (2004). Health and social services for pregnant and parenting high risk teens. *Children and Youth Services Review, 26*(6), 547–560. doi:10.1016/j.childyouth.2004.02.010

Sazie, E., Ponder, D., & Johnson, J. (2003). How to explain jails and prisons to children: A caregiver's guide. Oregon Department of Corrections, Children of Incarcerated Parents Project. Retrieved from http://www.f2f.ca.gov/res/pdf/How_To_Explain_Jails.pdf

Schantz, K. (2015). *Pregnancy risk among bisexual, lesbian, and gay youth: What does research tell us?* Act for Youth Center of Excellence Research Facts and Findings. Retrieved from http://www.actforyouth.net/resources/rf/rf_lgb-prg_0415.pdf

Schelbe, L. A. (2011). Policy analysis of Fostering Connections to Success and Increasing Adoptions Act of 2008. *Journal of Human Behavior in the Social Environment, 21*(5), 555–576. doi:10.1080/10911359.2011.580246

Schuler, P. A. (2000). Perfectionism and gifted adolescents. *Journal of Secondary Gifted Education, 11*(4), 183–196. doi:10.4219/jsge-2000-629

Schuler, P. (2002). Perfectionism in gifted children and adolescents. In M. Neihart, S. M. Reis, N. M. Robinson, & S. M. Moon (Eds.), *The social and emotional development of gifted children: What do we know?* (pp. 71–80). Waco, TX: Prufrock Press.

Schuyler Center for Analysis and Advocacy. (2008). *Teenage births: Outcomes for young parents and their children.* Albany, NY: Author. Retrieved from http://www.scaany.org/documents/teen_pregnancy_dec08.pdf

Schwartz, R. C., & Rogers, J. R. (2004). Suicide assessment and evaluation strategies: A primer for counselling psychologists. *Counselling Psychology Quarterly, 17*(1), 89–97. doi:10.1080/09515070410001665712

Scott, T. M., Nelson, C. M., & Liaupsin, C. J. (2002). Addressing the needs of at-risk and adjudicated youth through positive behavior support: Effective prevention practices. *Education and Treatment of Children (ETC), 25*(4), 532–551. Retrieved from http://www.jstor.org/stable/42899727

Seymour, C. (1998). Children with parents in prison: Child welfare policy, program, and practice issues. *Child Welfare, 77*(5), 460–493. Retrieved from http://www.cwla.org/child-welfare-journal/

Shanok, A. F., & Miller, L. (2007). Depression and treatment with inner city pregnant and parenting teens. *Archive of Women's Health, 10,* 199–210. doi:10.1007/s00737-007-0194-8

Shechtman, Z. (2007). *Group counseling and psychotherapy with children and adolescents: Theory, research, and practice.* Mahway, NJ: Lawrence Erlbaum.

Shechtman, Z., & Silektor, A. (2012). Social competencies and difficulties of gifted children compared to nongifted peers. *Roeper Review, 34*(1), 63–72. doi:10.1080/02783193.2012.627555

Shields, J. P., Whitaker, K., Glassman, J., Franks, H. M., & Howard, K. (2012). Impact of victimization on risk of suicide among lesbian, gay, and bisexual high school students in San Francisco. *Journal of Adolescent Health, 50*(4), 418–420. doi:10.1016/j.jadohealth.2011.07.009

Shillingford, M., Trice-Black, S., & Whitfield-Williams, M. (2013). Children with an incarcerated parent. Child-centered play therapy. In J. R. Curry & L. J. Fazio-Griffith (Eds.), *Integrating play techniques in comprehensive school counseling programs* (pp. 167–184). Charlotte, NC: Information Age.

Shin, S. H. (2005). Need for and actual use of mental health service by adolescents in the child welfare system. *Children and Youth Services Review, 27*(10), 1071–1083. doi:10.1016/j.childyouth.2004.12.027

Shuger, L. (2012). *Teen pregnancy and high school dropout: What communities can do to address these issues.* Washington, DC: National Campaign to Prevent Teen and Unplanned Pregnancy and America's Promise Alliance.

Sickmund, M., & Puzzanchera, C. (Eds.). 2014. *Juvenile offenders and victims: 2014 national report.* Pittsburgh, PA: National Center for Juvenile Justice. Retrieved from http://www.ojjdp.gov/ojstatbb/nr2014/downloads/NR2014.pdf

Siegle, D., McCoach, D. B., & Rubenstein, L. D. (2012). Understanding and addressing underachievement in gifted students. In T. L. Cross & J. R. Cross (Eds.), *Handbook for counselors serving students with gifts and talents* (pp. 511–528). Waco, TX: Prufrock Press.

Silverman, L. K. (2002). Asynchronous development. In M. Neihart, S. M. Reis, N. M. Robinson, & S. M. Moon (Eds.), *The social and emotional development of gifted children: What do we know?* (pp. 31–40). Waco, TX: Prufrock Press.

Simmonds, J. (n.d.). *Children in change: A group curriculum for kids ages 8–14 who are experiencing family change.* Minneapolis, MN: Family and Children's Service. Retrieved from http://www.thefamilypartnership.org/vertical/Sites/%7B180D3755-B455-4299-8D88-544431B73DE8%7D/uploads/%7BE278FB8B-6117-4BFD-BAA5-97832071236F%7D.PDF

Skagerberg, E., Parkinson, R., & Carmichael, P. (2013). Self-harming thoughts and behaviors in a group of children and adolescents with gender dysphoria. *International Journal of Transgenderism, 14*(2), 86–92. 10.1080/15532739.2013.817321

Sklare, G. B. (2014). *Brief counseling that works: A solution-focused therapy approach for school counselors and other mental health professionals.* Thousand Oaks, CA: Sage.

Slesnick, N., Meyers, R. J., Meade, M., & Segelken, D. H. (2000). Bleak and hopeless no more: Engagement of reluctant substance-abusing runaway youth and their families. *Journal of Substance Abuse Treatment, 19*(3), 215–222. doi:10.1016/S0740-5472(00)00100-8

Smith, A., & Thomson, M. (2014). Alternative education programmes: Synthesis and psychological perspectives. *Educational Psychology in Practice, 30*(2), 111–119. doi:10.1080/02667363.2014.891101

Smith, P. B., Buzi, R. S., & Weinman, M. L. (2002). Programs for young fathers: Essential components and evaluation issues. *North American Journal of Psychology, 4*(1), 81–92. Retrieved from najp.us

SmithBattle, L. (2013). Reducing the stigmatization of teen mothers. *American Journal of Maternal Child Nursing, 38*(4), 235–241. doi:10.1097/NMC.0b013e3182836bd4

SmithBattle, L., Freed, P., & McLaughlin, D. (2015). *Moms Growing Together (MGT): Piloting a mental health intervention for teen mothers*. American Public Health Association. Retrieved from https://apha.confex.com/apha/143am/webprogram/Paper322786.html

Smucker, K. S., Kauffman, J. M., & Ball, D. W. (1996). School-related problems of special education foster-care students with emotional or behavioral disorders: A comparison to other groups. *Journal of Emotional and Behavioral Disorders, 4*(1), 30–39. doi:10.1177/106342669600400104

Snapp, S. D., Watson, R. J., Russell, S. T., Diaz, R. M., & Ryan, C. (2015). Social support networks for LGBT young adults: Low cost strategies for positive adjustment. *Family Relations, 64*, 420–428. doi:10.1111/fare.12124

Southam-Gerow, M. A., & Kendall, P. C. (2002). Emotion regulation and understanding: Implications for child psychopathology and therapy. *Clinical Psychology Review, 22*(2), 189–222. doi:10.1016/S0272-7358(01)00087-3

Spencer, T. D., Detrich, R., & Slocum, T. A. (2012). Evidence-based practice: A framework for making effective decisions. *Education and Treatment of Children, 35*(2), 127–151. www.educationandtreatmentofchildren.net

Springer, D., Lynch, C., & Rubin, A. (2000). Effects of a solution-focused mutual aid group for Hispanic children of incarcerated parents. *Child and Adolescent Social Work Journal, 17*(6), 431–442. Retrieved from link.springer.com/journal/10560

Stark, P., & Noel, A. (2015). *Trends in high school dropout and completion rates in the United States: 1972–2012 (NCES 2015-015)*. U.S. Department of Education. Washington, DC: National Center for Education Statistics. Retrieved from http://nces.ed.goc/pubsearch

Stein, B. D., Jaycox, L. H., Kataoka, S. H., Wong, M., Tu, W., Eliot, M. N., & Fink, A. (2003). A mental health intervention for school children exposed to violence: A randomized controlled trial. *JAMA: Journal of the American Medical Association, 290*(5), 603–611. doi:10.1001/jama.290.5.603

Stein, L. R., Colby, S. M., Barnett, N. P., Monti, P. M., Golembeske, C., & Lebeau-Craven, R. (2006a). Effects of motivational interviewing for incarcerated adolescents on driving under the influence after release. *American Journal on Addictions, 15*(1), 50–57. Retrieved from www.tandfonline.com/loi/iaja20

Stein, L. R., Colby, S. M., Barnett, N. P., Monti, P. M., Golembeske, C., Lebeau-Craven, R., & Miranda, R. (2006b). Enhancing substance abuse treatment engagement in incarcerated adolescents. *Psychological Services, 3*(1), 25–34. doi:10.1037/1541-1559.3.1.0

Stein, L. R., Lebeau, R., Colby, U. M., Barnett, N. P., Golembeske, C., & Monti, P. M. (2011). Motivational interviewing for incarcerated adolescents: Effects of depressive symptoms on reducing alcohol and marijuana use after release. *Journal of Studies on Alcohol and Drugs, 72*(3), 497–506. doi:10.15288/jsad.2011.72.497

Stephan, S. H., Weist, M., Kataoka, S., Adelsheim, S., & Mills, C. (2007). Transformation of children's mental health services: The role of school mental health. *Psychiatric Services, 58*(10), 1330–1338. doi:10.1176.p.s.2007.58.10.1330

Stetser, M., & Stillwell, R. (2014). *Public high school four-year on-time graduation rates and event dropout rates: School years 2010–11 and 2011–12. First Look (NCES 2014-391)*. U.S. Department of Education. Washington, DC: National Center for Education Statistics. Retrieved from http://nces.ed.gov/pubresearch

Stewart, A. J., Steiman, M., Cauce, A. M., Cochran, B. N., & Whitbeck L. B. (2004). Victimization and posttraumatic stress disorder among homeless adolescents. *Journal of the American Academy of Child and Adolescent Psychiatry, 43*(3), 325–331. doi:10.1097/01.chi.0000106852.88132.c8

Stoltzfus, E. (2008). Child welfare: The fostering connections to success and increasing adoptions act of 2008. *CRS Report for Congress.* Retrieved from http://greenbook.waysandmeans.house.gov/sites/greenbook.waysandmeans.house.gov/files/2012/RL34704_gb.pdf

Stone, S. (2007). Child maltreatment, out-of-home placement and academic vulnerability: A fifteen-year review of evidence and future directions. *Children and Youth Services Review, 29*(2), 139–161. doi:10.1016/j.childyouth.2006.05.001

Stott, T. (2012). Placement instability and risky behaviors of youth aging out of foster care. *Child and Adolescent Social Work Journal, 29*(1), 61–83. doi:10.1007/s10560-011-0247-8

Strait, G., Smith, B., McQuillin, J., Swan, S., & Malone, P. (2012). A randomized trial of motivational interviewing to improve middle school students' academic performance. *Journal of Community Psychology, 40*(8), 1032–1039. Retrieved from www.wileyonlinelibrary.com/journal/jcop

Substance Abuse and Mental Health Services Administration (n.d.). *The Nurturing Parent Program.* Retrieved from www.samhsa.gov

Suh, S., & Suh, J. (2007). Risk factors and levels of risk for high school dropouts. *Professional School Counseling, 10*(3), 297–306. Retrieved from https://www.schoolcounselor.org

Suldo, S. M., Gormley, M. J., DuPaul, G. J., & Anderson-Butcher, D. (2014). The impact of school mental health on student and school-level academic outcomes: Current state of the research and future directions. *School Mental Health, 6,* 84–98. doi:10.1007/s12310-013-9116-2

Sulkowski, M. L., & Michael, K. (2014). Meeting the mental health needs of homeless students in schools: A multi-tiered system of support framework. *Children and Youth Services Review, 44,* 145–151. doi:10.1016/j.childyouth.2014.06.014

Swick, K. J., & Bailey, L. B. (2004). Communicating effectively with parents and families who are homeless. *Early Childhood Education Journal, 32*(3), 211–215. doi:10.1023/B:ECEJ.0000048975.59024.c4

Szymanski, D. M., & Gupta, A. (2009a). Examining the relationship between multiple internalized oppressions and African American lesbian, gay, bisexual, and questioning persons' self-esteem and psychological distress. *Journal of Counseling Psychology, 56*(1), 110–118. doi:10.1037/a0013317

Szymanski, D. M., & Gupta, A. (2009b). Examining the relationship between multiple oppressions and Asian American sexual minority persons' psychological distress. *Journal of Gay and Lesbian Social Services, 21,* 267–281. doi:10.1080/10538720902772212

Taussig, H. N. (2002). Risk behaviors in maltreated youth placed in foster care: A longitudinal study of protective and vulnerability factors. *Child Abuse and Neglect, 26*(11), 1179–1199. doi:10.1016/S0145-2134(02)00391-5

Teasdale, B., & Bradley-Engen, M. S. (2010). Adolescent same-sex attraction and mental health: The role of stress and support. *Journal of Homosexuality, 57,* 287–309. doi:10.1080/00918360903489127

Thomas, D. V., & Looney, S. W. (2004). Effectiveness of a comprehensive pyschoeducational intervention with pregnant and parenting adolescents: A pilot study.

Journal of Child and Adolescent Psychiatric Nursing, 17(2), 66–77. doi:10.1111/j.1744-7171.2004.00066.x

Thompson, R. G., & Auslander, W. F. (2007). Risk factors for alcohol and marijuana use among adolescents in foster care. *Journal for Substance Abuse Treatement, 32*, 61–69. doi:10.1016/j.jsat.2006.06.010

Thompson, S. J., Bender, K. A., Lewis, C. M., & Watkins, R. (2008). Runaway and pregnant: Risk factors associated with pregnancy in a national sample of runaway/homeless female adolescents. *Journal of Adolescent Health, 43*(2), 125–132. doi:10.1016/jadohealth.2007.12.015

Thompson, S. J., McManus, H., & Voss T. (2006). Posttraumatic stress disorder and substance abuse amoung youth who are homeless: Treatment issues and implications. *Brief Treatment and Crisis Intervention, 6*(3), 206–214. doi:10.1093/brief-treatnebt/mhl002

Thompson, S. J., & Sanchez, K. (2012). Solution-focused family therapy for troubled and runaway youths. In C. Franklin, T. Trepper, W. Gingerich, & E. McCollum (Eds.), *Solution-focused brief therapy: A handbook of evidence-based practices* (pp. 216–230). New York, NY: Oxford University Press.

Thrane, L. E., & Chen, X. (2012). Impact of running away on girls' pregnancy. *Journal of Adolescence, 35*, 443–449. doi:10.1016/j.adolescence.2011.017.011

Tobin, K., & Murphy, J. (2013). Addressing the challenges of child and family homelessness. *Journal of Applied Research on Children: Informing Policy for Children at Risk, 4*(1), 1–29. Retrieved from http://digitalcommons.library.tmc.edu/childrenatrisk/vol4/iss1/9

Toomey, R. B., & Russell, S. T. (2013). The role of sexual orientation in school-based victimization: A meta-analysis. *Youth and Society*, 1–26, first published on April 8, 2013. doi:10.1177/0044118X13483778

Toomey, R. B., Ryan, C., Diaz, R. M., Card, N. A., & Russell, S. T. (2013). Gender-nonconforming lesbian, gay, bisexual, and transgender youth: School victimization and young adult psychosocial adjustment. *Psychology of Sexual Orientation And Gender Diversity, 1*(S), 71–80. doi:10.1037/2329-0382.1.S.71

Townsend, E. (2007). Cognitive-behavioural interventions for young offenders. In Vostanis, P. (Ed.), *Mental health interventions for vulnerable children and young people* (pp. 110–120). London, England: Jessica Kingsley.

Trad, P. V. (1994). Teenage pregnancy: Seeking patterns that promote family harmony. *American Journal of Family Therapy, 22*(1), 42–56. doi:10.1080/01926189408251296

Trad, P. V. (1999). Assessing the patterns that prevent teenage pregnancy. *Adolescence, 34*(133), 221–240. Retrieved from journals.elsevier.com/journal-of-adolescence

Trout, A. L., Hagaman, J., Casey, K., Reid, R., & Epstein, M. H. (2008). The academic status of children and youth in out-of-home care: A review of the literature. *Children and Youth Services Review, 30*(9), 979–994. doi:10.1016/j.childyouth.2007.11.019

Trupin, E. W., Stewart, D. G., Beach, B., & Boesky, L. (2002). Effectiveness of dialectical behaviour therapy program for incarcerated female juvenile offenders. *Child and Adolescent Mental Health, 7*(3), 121–127. doi:10.1111(ISSN)1475-3588

Underwood, L. A., Phillips, A., von Dresner, K., & Knight, P. D. (2006). Critical factors in mental health programming for juveniles in corrections facilities. *International Journal of Behavioral Consultation and Therapy, 2*(1), 107–140. Retrieved from http://psycnet.apa.org/journals/bct/

United States Interagency Council on Homelessness. (2010). *Opening doors: Federal strategic plans to prevent and end homelessness.* Retrieved from http://usich.gov/PDF/OpeningDoors_2010_FSPPreventEndHomeless.pdf

University of California Los Angeles Mental Health in Schools Center. (1996). *Addressing barriers to learning*. Retrieved from http://smhp.psych.ucla.edu/pdfdocs/newsletter/fall96.pdf

U.S. Department of Defense. (2013). *2013 Demographics: Profile of the military community*. Retrieved from http://download.militaryonesource.mil/12038/MOS/Reports/2013-Demographics-Report.pdf

U.S. Department of Defense, Educational Opportunities Directorate. (n.d.). *Educator's guide to the military child during deployment*. Retrieved from https://www2.ed.gov/about/offices/list/os/homefront/homefront.pdf

U.S. Department of Education, Institute of Education Sciences, What Works Clearinghouse. (2015, May). *Check and Connect*. Retrieved from http://whatworks.ed.gov

U.S. Department of Health and Human Services: Administration for Children and Families. (2013a). *The AFCARS report: Preliminary FY 2012 estimates as of November 2013, 20*. Retrieved from http://www.acf.hhs.gov/sites/default/files/cb/afcarsreport20.pdf

U.S. Department of Health and Human Services: Administration for Children and Families. (2013b). *Recent demographic trends in foster care*. Retrieved from http://www.acf.hhs.gov/sites/default/files/cb/data_brief_foster_care_trends1.pdf

U.S. Department of Health and Human Services: Administration for Children and Families. (2014). *Trends in foster care and adoption: FFY 2002–FFY 2013*. Retrieved from http://www.acf.hhs.gov/sites/default/files/cb/trends_fostercare_adoption2013.pdf

Van Acker, R. & Mayer, M. J. (2009). Cognitive-behavioral interventions and the social context of the school: A stranger in a strange land. In M. J. Mayer, R. Van Acker, J. E. Lochman, & F. M. Gresham (Eds.), *Cognitive-behavioral interventions for emotional and behavioral disorders: School-based practice* (pp. 82–108). New York, NY: Guilford Press.

Van Velsor, P. (2004). Revisiting basic counseling skills with children. *Journal of Counseling and Development, 82*, 313–318. doi:10.1002/j.1556-6678.2004.tb00316.x

Varjas, K., Dew, B., Marshall, M., Graybill, E., Singh, A., Meyers, J., & Birckbichler, L. (2008). Bullying in schools toward sexual minority youth. *Journal of School Violence, 7*(2), 59–86. doi:10.1300/J202v07n02_05

Vaughn, M. G., Ollie, M. T., Mcmillen, J. C., Scott, L., & Munson, M. (2007). Substance use and abuse among older youth in foster care. *Addictive Behaviors, 32*, 1929–1935. doi:10.1016/j.addbeh.2006.12.012

Veysey, B. (2008). Mental health, substance abuse, and trauma. In N. Guerra & P. Boxer (Eds.), *Treating the juvenile offender* (pp. 210–238). New York, NY: Guilford Press.

Vogel, D. L., Wester, S. R., & Larson, L. M. (2007). Avoidance of counseling: Psychological factors that inhibit seeking help. *Journal of Counseling and Development, 85*, 410–422. doi:10.1002/j.1556-6678.2007.tb00609.x

Waller, M. A., Brown, B., & Whittle, B. (1999). Mentoring as a bridge to positive outcomes for teen mothers and their children. *Child and Adolescent Social Work Journal, 16*(6), 467–480. doi:10.1023/A:1022353422676

Walsh, S. M., & Donaldson, R. E. (2010). Invited commentary: National safe place: Meeting the immediate needs of runaway and homeless youth. *Journal of Youth and Adolescence, 39*(5), 437–445. doi:10.1007/s10964-010-9522-9

Wang, K. T., Fu, C. C., & Rice, K. G. (2012). Perfectionism in gifted students: Moderating effects of goal orientation and contingent self-worth. *School Psychology Quarterly, 27*(2), 96–108. doi:10.1037/90029215

Weiner, D. A., Schneider, A., & Lyons, J. S. (2009). Evidence-based treatments for trauma among culturally diverse foster care youth: Treatment retention and outcomes. *Children and Youth Services Review, 31*(11), 1199–1205. doi:10.1016/j.childyouth.2009.08.013

Weinman, M. L., Smith, P. B., & Buzi, R. S. (2002). Young fathers: An analysis of risk behaviors and service needs. *Child and Adolescent Social Work Journal, 19*(6), 437–453. doi:10.1023/A:1021193629472

Weist, M. D., Myers, C. P., Hastings, E., Ghuman, H., & Han, Y. L. (1999). Psychosocial functioning of youth receiving mental health services in the schools versus community mental health centers. *Community Mental Health Journal, 35*(1), 69–81. doi:10.1023/A:1018700126364

Whitman, J. S. (2013). Training school professionals to work with lesbian, gay, bisexual, transgender, and questioning students and parents. In E. S. Fisher & K. Komosa-Hawkins (Eds.), *Creating safe and supportive learning environments: A guide for working with lesbian, gay, bisexual, transgender, and questioning youth and families* (pp. 123–139). New York, NY: Routledge.

Wiemann, C. M., Vaughn, R. I., Berenson, A. B., & Volk, R. J. (2005). Are pregnant adolescents stigmatized by pregnancy? *Journal of Adolescent Health, 36*(4), 1–8. doi:10.1016/j.jadohealth.2004.06.006

Wilder, S. (2004). Educating youthful offenders in a youth development center. *Journal of Addictions and Offender Counseling, 24*(2), 82–91. doi:10.1002/j.2161-1874.2004.tb00184.x

Wilkinson, L., & Pearson, J. (2009). School culture and well-being of same-sex-attracted youth. *Gender and Society, 23*, 542–565. doi:10.1177/0891243209339913

Williams, B. (2013). Supporting middle school students whose parents are deployed: Challenges and strategies for schools. *Clearing House, 86*(4), 128–135. doi:10.1080/00098655.2013.782849

Williams, N. R., Lindsey, E. W., Kurtz, P. D., & Jarvis, S. (2001). From trauma to resiliency: Lessons from former runaway and homeless youth. *Journal of Youth Studies, 4*(2), 233–253. doi:10.1080/13676260123589

Willoughby, B. L. B., Malik, N. M., & Lindahl, K. M. (2006). Parental reactions to their sons' sexual orientation disclosures: The roles of family cohesion, adaptability, and parenting style. *Psychology of Men and Masculinity, 7*(1) 14–26. doi:10.1037/1524-9220.7.1.14

Wilson, S., Wilkum, K., Chernichky, S., MacDermid Wadsworth, S., & Broniarczyk. (2011). Passport toward successs: Description and evaluation of a program designed to help children and families reconnect after a military deployment. *Journal of Applied Communication Research, 39*(3), 223–249. doi:10.1080/00909882.2011.585399

Winborne, D. G., & Murray, G. J. (1992). Address unknown: An exploration of the educational and social attitudes of homeless adolescents. *High School Journal, 75*(3), 144–149. Retrieved from http://www.jstor.org/stable/40364838

Wong, M., Rosemond, M. E., Stein, B. D., Langley, A. K., Kataoka, S. H., & Nadeem, E. (2007). School-based intervention for adolescents exposed to violence. *Prevention Researcher, 14*(1), 17–20. Retrieved from www.eric.ed.gov/?id=EJ793244

Wood, R. J., Wood, A. R., & Mullins, D. T. (2008). Back to school: Recommendations to assist mentally ill, post-incarcerated youth return to school. *Journal of School Health, 78*(9), 514–517. Retrieved from http://onlinelibrary.wiley.com/journal/10.1111/%28ISSN%291746-1561

Wood. S. (2009). The socioemotional needs of gifted students in secondary schools. In F.A. Dixon (Ed.), *Programs and services for gifted secondary students: A guide to recommended practices* (pp. 21–53). Waco, TX: Prufrock Press.

Wood, S., & Gavin. M. K. (2009). Exploring issues and opportunities in gifted students' transitions to college and career. In F. A. Dixon (Ed.), *Programs and services for gifted secondary students: A guide to recommended practices* (pp. 55–66). Waco, TX: Prufrock Press.

Woodward, L., Fergusson, D. M., & Horwood, L. J. (2004). Risk factors and life processes associated with teenage pregnancy: Results of a prospective study from birth to 20 years. *Journal of Marriage and Family*, 63(4), 1170–1184. doi:10.1111/doi.1741-3737.2001.01170.x

Yaffe, R. M., & Hoade, L. F. (2000). *When a parent goes to jail: A comprehensive guide for counseling children of incarcerated parents.* Windsor, CA: Rayve Productions.

Young, T. L. (2013). Using motivational interviewing within the early stages of group development. *Journal for Specialists in Group Work*, 38(2), 169–181. doi:10.1080/01933922.2013.764369

Yu, J. (2010). Sex education beyond school: Implications for practice and research. *Sex Education*, 10(2), 187–199. Retrieved from www.tandfonline.com/adion/journalinformation?journalCode=cse20

Yu, M., North, C. S., LaVesser, P. D., Osborne, V. A., & Spitznagel, E. L. (2008). A comparison study of psychiatric and behavior disorders and cognitive ability among homeless and housed children. *Community Mental Health Journal*, 44(1), 1–10. doi:10.1007/s10597-007-9100-0

Zima, B. T., Bussing, R., Bystritsky, M., Widawsky, M. H., Belin, T. R., & Benjamin, B. (1999). Psychosocial stressors among sheltered homeless children: Relationship to behavior problems and depressive symptoms. *American Journal of Orthopsychiatry*, 69(1), 127–133. doi:10.1037/h0080389

Zima, B. T., Bussing, R., Forness, S. R., & Benjamin, B. (1997). Sheltered homeless children: Their eligibility and unmet need for special education evaluations. *American Journal of Public Health*, 87(2), 236–240. doi:10.2105/AJPH.87.2.236

Zima, B. T., Bussing, R., Freeman, S., Yang, X., Belin, T. R., & Forness, S. R. (2000). Behavior problems, academic skill delays and school failure among school-aged children in foster care: Their relationship to placement characteristics. *Journal of Child and Family Studies*, 9(1), 87–103. doi:10.1023/A:1009415800475

Zins, J. E., Bloodworth, M. R., Weissberg, R. P., & Walberg, H. J. (2007). The scientific base linking social and emotional learning to school success. *Journal of Educational and Psychological Consultation*, 17(2–3), 191–210. doi:10.1080/10474410701413145

Zlotnick, C., Tam, T. W., & Soman, L. A. (2012). Life course outcomes on mental and physical health: The impact of foster care on adulthood. *American Journal of Public Health*, 102(3), 534–540. doi:10.2105/AJPH.2011.300285

Zlotnick, C., Tam T., & Zerger, S. (2012). Common needs but divergent interventions for U.S. homeless and foster care children: Results from a systematic review. *Health and Social Care in the Community*, 20(5), 449–476. doi:10.1111/j.1365-2524.2011.01053.x

Zucker, K. J., Cohen-Kettenis, P. T., Drescher, J., Meyer-Bahlburg, H. F. L., Pfafflin, F., & Womack, W. M. (2013). Memo outlining evidence for change for gender identity disorder in the *DSM-5*. *Archives of Sexual Behavior*, 42, 901–914. doi:10.1007/s10508-013-0139-4

Zyromski, B. (2008). Utilizing cognitive behavioral interventions to positively impact academic achievement in middle school students. *Journal of School Counseling*, 6(15), 1–22. Retrieved from www.schoolcounselor.org

ABOUT THE AUTHORS

Emily S. Fisher, PhD, is an Associate Professor of school psychology at Loyola Marymount University. She teaches courses in counseling and mental health treatment, and she has published and presented on topics related to counseling and promoting positive development for at-risk students.

Kelly S. Kennedy, PhD, is an Associate Professor and Dean in the counseling and school psychology graduate training programs at Chapman University. Her interests include social justice, school-based mental health services, resilience, juvenile justice, and the international practice of school psychology.

INDEX

abortion, pregnant students considering, 93–95, 96
abstinence-only sex education, 91, 100–101
abuse, 24, 61, 87. *See also* physical abuse; sexual abuse; *specific student groups*
academic achievement. *See also* educational attainment
  of children of teen mothers, 87
  dropout risk and, 152, 153, 154
  of homeless students, 9–10, 11
  impact of CBITS on, 34
  of LGBT students, 68
  mental health and, 2
  of students in military families, 141
  of students with incarcerated parents, 124
  of teen fathers, 91
academic enabling skills, increasing, 160–163
academic skills, building, 160–163
academic success groups, 164
accompanied homeless students, 8, 10, 19, 20–21
ADHD (attention deficit hyperactivity disorder), 44
adjudicated juveniles, 38–39, 40
adoption, pregnant students considering, 93–95, 96
adulthood, transition to, 28, 35–37, 72, 91
adult–student relationships at school, 83, 112–113
advocacy, 61–62, 165
affective education programs, 116

affective regulation, 33
African American students, 23, 25, 39, 72, 107, 118, 152
aggression, 30–31, 44, 46, 124, 141
Aggression Replacement Training (ART), 57
Alaskan Native students, 23
alternative education, 42, 60, 165
American Indian/Pacific Islander students, 23, 34, 107, 152
anger
  counseling approaches for, 31
  in foster youth, 30–31
  in juvenile offenders, 44–45, 55, 57
  in LGBT youth, 74
  in students in military families, 141
  suicidality and, 81
anger control training, 57
"anthropologist in the classroom" strategy, 110
antibullying programs, 69, 82–83
anxiety
  counseling approaches for, 3, 31, 34, 55
  in foster youth, 24
  in homeless students, 10
  in juvenile offenders, 44
  in LGBTQ students, 72, 74
  in military families, 142
  in pregnant students, 91
  in students with incarcerated parents, 123
  trauma and PTSD related to, 24
ART (*Aggression Replacement Training*), 57
Asian American students, 25, 72, 152
asynchronous development, 105

attachment, 25–26, 122, 141
attention deficit hyperactivity disorder (ADHD), 44
attributional beliefs, 154
authority, distrust of, 122, 124, 125
autism spectrum disorder, 73

behavior, self-destructive, 52, 53
behavioral disorders
   in foster youth, 24, 25, 27, 28, 33
   in homeless students, 10, 11
   in juvenile offenders, 40, 43–44, 45
   trauma and PTSD related to, 24
behavioral rehearsal, 161, 162
behavioral risks for dropout, 153
behaviors, risky
   in foster youth, 92
   in homeless students, 92
   in LGBT students, 70, 72
   in pregnant and parenting teens, 91, 92
   in students with incarcerated parents, 122–123
   suicidality and, 81
beliefs, impact of, 98, 153–154
bibliotherapy, 126–127, 130
bisexuality, 65. *See also* LGBTQ students
bisexual youth, 66, 71
Black students. *See* African American students
bullying, 69, 82–83, 84, 106, 108

California Youth Authority (CYA), 46
career counseling and development, 108, 113–114
case formulation, for juvenile offenders, 49–50
CBITS (*Cognitive Behavior Intervention for Trauma in Schools*), 32, 34–35
CBT. *See* cognitive-behavioral therapy
CD (conduct disorder), 44, 52
change process, 156–157, 159
change talk, 54, 55, 158, 159
Check and Connect intervention, 165–166
Children in Change curriculum, 146
child welfare system, 28, 29, 31, 35, 36. *See also* foster youth
choice counseling, 93–95, 96

cisgenderism, defined, 65
classroom-based supports, 147
CLD (culturally and linguistically diverse) students, 107, 110–111, 116, 151–152
clients, in counseling relationship, 93
coaching, 57, 161–162
cognitive-based study skills, 161
cognitive-behavioral therapy (CBT)
   basic approach of, 3–4
   conditions addressed by, 3, 31–32, 34, 52
   for foster youth, 31–35
   for gifted students, 112
   goals and benefits of, 159–160, 162–163
   for homeless students, 18–19
   for juvenile offenders, 52, 57
   for LGBTQ students, 80–81
   for students at risk of dropout, 159–160, 162–163
   for students in military families, 144–145
   for students with incarcerated parents, 126
   techniques used in, 4, 31, 32–33, 162–163
   for trauma, 18–19, 32–33, 34–35
Cognitive Behavior Intervention for Trauma in Schools (CBITS), 32, 34–35
cognitive development, in pregnant teens, 90
cognitive processing techniques, 33
collaboration in counseling approaches
   for foster youth, 29–30, 33, 35
   for homeless students, 17, 21
   for juvenile offenders, 38, 50, 57, 58, 59, 60–61
   for pregnant students, 88
coming out, by LGBT students, 69, 70, 72, 78–80
communication and social skills, 19, 30–31, 57, 109–111
comorbid depression, 52
comorbidity of diagnoses and conditions, 46–47, 49–50
conduct disorder (CD), 44, 52
confidentiality, 49, 75–76
consent, 11–12, 12–13

contraception education, 101
conversion therapy, 76
Coping Cat, 126, 144
coping strategies, 109–111, 126, 143–144, 145, 146
counseling, school-based
    importance of, 8
    parenting practices supported by, 20
    scope of, 1–2, 48, 144
    use by homeless students, 14–15
Counseling Children and Adolescents Through Grief and Loss (Fiorini & Mullen), 145
counseling education, 48–49
counselor (term), 2
counselors, characteristics of, 13–15
culturally and linguistically diverse (CLD) students, 107, 110–111, 116, 151–152
CYA (California Youth Authority), 46

DBT (dialectical behavior therapy), 53–54
death or injury of parents, 32, 138, 145
decision-making frameworks, 94
delinquency, 40, 42–43, 52, 71, 124
deployment phases, military, 139–140
depression
    counseling approaches for, 3, 31, 34, 52
    in foster youth, 24
    in juvenile offenders, 50
    in LGBTQ students, 69, 70, 71, 72, 74
    in military families, 140–141, 142
    in pregnant and parenting students, 89, 92
    related to trauma and PTSD, 24
    in students with incarcerated parents, 123
depressive disorder, 44, 54, 55
desisters, defined, 43
developmental needs, 9, 24, 25–26
diagnosis, for juvenile offenders, 49–50
Diagnostic and Statistical Manual of Mental Disorders (DSM), 67
dialectical behavior therapy (DBT), 53–54
disabilities, students with, 11–12, 108, 152, 155
discrepancy, developing, 157
discrimination, 64, 68–69, 73, 74, 107

diversity
    among gifted students, 104, 106–108
    among LGBTQ students, 72, 78
    in curriculum, 132
    in sexual orientation and gender identity, 64–66, 84
domestic violence, 8, 10
dropout, students at risk of
    advocacy for, 165
    at-risk populations, 152
    Check and Connect intervention for, 165–166
    consequences faced by, 151–152
    individual risks, 153–155
    resources for, 166–167
    skill *vs.* performance deficit in, 155
dropout prevention, counseling approaches for
    challenges and importance of, 151–152
    group counseling, 163–165
    increasing academic enabling skills, 160–163
    increasing motivation, 156–160
    for pregnant or parenting students, 97–98
DSM *(Diagnostic and Statistical Manual of Mental Disorders),* 67

ecological factors in high school completion, 153, 154
ED (emotional disturbance), 26–27, 28, 46
educational attainment. *See also* academic achievement; dropout
    of foster youth, 26–27, 36
    high school graduation, 151–152, 166
    of juvenile offenders, 45–46
    of LGBTQ students, 64, 68
    of pregnant and parenting students, 87, 88–89, 97–98
    preschool participation linked to, 153
elementary students, 114, 130, 153
ELL (English Language Learners), 152
emotional abuse, 24
emotional disturbance (ED), 26–27, 28, 46
emotional regulation, 20, 21
Empowering Children of Incarcerated Parents (Burgess, et. al), 130

empowerment, sense of, 29–30, 99
English Language Learners (ELL), 152
Equal Access Act (1984), 83
ethics, 75–76, 93–95
ethnic diversity, 72, 107
evidence-based practice, 2–3
exception questions, 53
executive functioning, 20
expulsion from school, 26
externalizing behaviors, 43–44, 45, 124, 140
extracurricular activities, 42, 59, 60, 132, 137, 143

families, homeless, 8, 20
families, military, 135, 136, 140–143, 146, 147, 148–149
families, two-parent, 153
Families OverComing Under Stress (FOCUS), 148–149
family involvement in schooling, 19–21, 107
family relationships, dysfunctional, 8, 9, 10, 19, 20, 26, 31
family support, 31, 36, 70, 71
fathers, incarcerated, 118, 120
fathers, teen, 90, 91–92
feelings thermometer technique, 144
financial strain, 121–122, 142
flagging the minefield, 126
FOCUS (*Families OverComing Under Stress*), 148–149
Fostering Connections Act (2008), 28–29, 35
foster youth
 aging out of system, 28, 29, 31, 35, 36
 developmental needs of, 24
 educational attainment of, 26–27, 36
 mental health needs of, 24–25, 29
 other special populations intersecting with, 9, 28, 72, 73, 92, 120–121
 placement of, 27
 policy initiatives for, 28, 35
 resources for, 37
 situations leading to, 23, 24
 social support for, 23–24, 26, 29, 30–31, 36
 special education for, 26–27
 substance use and abuse in, 24, 28
 transition to adulthood, 28, 29, 35–37
foster youth, counseling approaches for
 cognitive-behavioral therapy for trauma, 31–35
 empowerment and self-determination, 29–30
 social support, 23–24, 26, 29, 30–31, 36
 solution-focused brief therapy, 30

Gay, Lesbian and Straight Education Network (GLSEN), 68
"gay lifestyle," 65
gayness, defined, 65. *See also* LGBTQ students
gay-straight alliances (GSAs), 68, 69, 83, 84
gender diversity, defined, 65
gender dysphoria, 67, 73. *See also* transgenderism
gender expression, defined, 65
gender identity, 64, 65–66, 67, 79. *See also* transgender youth
gender identity disorder, 67
gender queer, defined, 65
gender variance, defined, 65
"gifted and talented" students, 103
gifted students
 counseling approaches for, 109–115
 defined, 103
 diversity among, 104, 106–108
 resources for, 117
 social and emotional development of, 104–106
Girl Scouts Beyond Bars, 127, 132
Global War on Terror (GWOT), 135, 139
GLSEN (Gay, Lesbian and Straight Education Network), 68
goal setting, 17, 95, 98, 163, 164, 165
graduation rates, 151–152, 166
grief, 124, 138, 145
group counseling
 for gifted students, 114–115
 for juvenile offenders, 54–55, 56–57
 for pregnant and parenting students, 97, 99
 for students at risk of dropout, 163–165

for students in military families, 143, 144, 145–146
for students with incarcerated parents, 129–130
group homes. *See* residential facilities
GSAs (gay-straight alliances), 68, 69, 83, 84
GWOT (Global War on Terror), 135, 139

health needs, general
  comorbidity of diagnoses and conditions, 46–47, 49–50
  of foster youth, 24, 27
  of homeless students, 9, 11
  of students aging out of foster care, 28
  of teen mothers, 88
heterosexism, 72, 77
heterosexuality, defined, 65
high school graduation, 151–152, 166
Hispanic students, 107, 118, 152
homeless students
  academic achievement of, 9–10, 11
  accompanied, 8, 10, 19, 20–21
  developmental, academic, and health needs of, 8, 9–10, 11
  educational support for, 10–11
  foster youth and, 9, 28
  with incarcerated parents, 119, 120
  with juvenile offenses, 7
  LGBTQ, 9, 10, 72–73
  policy initiatives for, 10–11, 12
  population estimates, 7
  resources for, 22
  situations leading to homelessness, 8–9
  special education assessment for, 11–12
  stigma and invisibility experienced by, 11, 14
  substance use and abuse in, 10, 18
  teen pregnancy in, 91
  unaccompanied, 8, 10, 12–13, 14–15, 19–20
homeless students, counseling approaches for
  cognitive-behavioral therapy, 18–19
  collaboration, 21
  consent issues, 12–13
  counselor characteristics, 13–15
  family involvement, 19–21

mandated reporting, 13, 14–15
promoting resilience, 15–18
solution-focused brief therapy, 17–18
Structured Psychotherapy for Adolescents Responding to Chronic Stress, 18–19
homophobia, internalized, 72, 77, 80–81
homosexuality, 67. *See also* LGBTQ students

identity development, 90, 104, 107, 110–111
independent living skills, 36
Individuals with Disabilities Education Act (IDEA), 12
inner strength, 15
internalizing behaviors, 43, 44, 45, 123, 140, 143
interventions, tailoring, 50–51
isolation, social
  in gifted students, 106, 108
  in LGBTQ students, 81
  in pregnant and parenting students, 89
  in students in military families, 134, 142, 146
  in students with incarcerated parents, 121, 129, 132

Juvenile Justice and Delinquency Prevention Act (1974), 41
juvenile justice system, 39, 40–42, 73
juvenile offenders
  advocacy for, 61–62
  comorbid diagnoses and conditions in, 46–47, 49–50
  crimes committed by, 38, 39
  demographics of, 39
  educational achievement of, 45–46
  educational settings for, 41–42, 46, 59–62
  internalized and externalized disorders in, 43–44, 45
  learning disabilities in, 45–46
  mental health needs of, 40, 43, 45, 59, 61
  other special populations intersecting with, 7, 39, 73, 124
  placement of, 40

juvenile offenders (*Cont.*)
  population estimates, 38–39
  recidivism in, 41, 44, 49, 50
  resources for, 62–63
  skill deficits of, 47, 52
  special education services for, 46, 59, 62
  substance abuse in, 45
  trajectories of, 42–43
  transition and re-entry preparation, 57–60
  trauma experienced by, 44–45
juvenile offenders, counseling approaches for
  addressing trauma, 55
  aggression replacement training, 57
  case formulation and diagnosis, 49–50
  cognitive-behavioral therapy, 52
  collaboration in, 38, 50, 57, 58, 59, 60–61
  counseling competence, 48–49
  dialectical behavior therapy, 53–54
  ethical considerations, 49
  group counseling, 56–57
  motivational interviewing, 54–55
  multisystemic therapy, 56
  relationship building, 51–52
  solution-focused brief therapy, 52–53
  treatment planning and tailoring interventions, 47–48, 50–51

kinship care, 27, 120, 130–131

labels, changing, 97. *See also* social stigma
language diversity, 107. *See also* culturally and linguistically diverse students
Latino students, 23, 25, 70, 107
learning disabilities, 45–46, 51, 155
lesbianism, defined, 65
LGBTQ students
  academic achievement of, 68
  counseling approaches for, 64
  disclosure by, 69–70
  diversity among, 72–73
  mental health problems in, 9, 10, 11
  other special populations intersecting with, 10, 72, 73, 108
  policy initiatives affecting, 67, 83
  resources, 85–86
  school climate improvements, 69, 82–84
  sociopolitical context surrounding, 67
  special education services for, 73
  victimization of, 10, 64, 67, 68–71, 72, 108
LGBTQ students, counseling approaches for
  ethical considerations, 75–76
  identity development and disclosure support, 78–80
  LGBTQ-affirmative mindset, 74, 77–81
  suicide prevention and intervention, 81–82
  transgender-specific considerations, 74–75, 77–78

mandated counseling, 49, 52–53, 56
mandated reporting, 12–13, 14–15
McKinney-Vento Homeless Assistance Act, 10–11, 12
medication, 59
mental health needs and outcomes
  of children of incarcerated parents, 120
  of foster youth, 24–25, 27
  of gifted students, 109
  of homeless students, 9, 10, 11
  of incarcerated parents, 119–120
  of juvenile offenders, 40, 43, 45, 59
  of LGBTQ students, 64, 70–72
  of returning military members, 142
  screening for, 61
mental health services, 25, 29
mentoring programs, 131, 165–166
metacognitive-based study skills, 161, 162
MI. *See* motivational interviewing
migratory students, 8
Military Children's Interstate Compact, 137
military families, 135, 136, 140–143, 147, 148–149. *See also* students in military families
miracle question, 17–18, 96, 163
mobility, 9–10, 11, 12, 17, 137
modeling, 161
mood disorders, 10, 24, 44
moral reasoning, 57

Index

mothers, incarcerated, 118, 120
mothers, teen, 88–89, 90–91, 96–97. *See also* pregnant or parenting students
motivation
   academic achievement related to, 160
   counseling approaches promoting, 156, 157–160
   factors influencing, 153–154, 160
   in gifted students, 112–113
   graduation rates related to, 152, 153–155
motivational interviewing (MI)
   basic principles of, 54, 157–158
   goals and benefits of, 54, 157–159, 158
   in group counseling, 164
   for juvenile offenders, 54–55
   for students at risk of dropout, 157–159, 164
   techniques used in, 54, 55, 157, 158–159
Mourning Child Grief Support Group Curriculum series, 145
multipotentiality, 113
multisystemic therapy (MST), 56
Multisystemic Therapy for Antisocial Behavior in Children and Adolescents (Henggeler, et. al), 56
My Daddy Is in Jail (Bender), 127

National Association of School Psychologists (NASP), 75, 93
National Coalition for the Homeless, 8, 72
National Guard families, 136, 146, 148
neglect, parental, 8, 24, 25, 44, 61
New Chance program, 98
ninth-grade year, 166
No Child Left Behind Act (2001), 10–11
nonrelative family care, 27, 120, 130–131
Nurturing Parenting Program (NPP), 98–99

open-ended questioning, 29, 94, 95, 158, 164
oppositional defiant disorder (ODD), 44, 45
organizational-based study skills, 161

parent/caregiver involvement, 32, 34, 140, 148
parent–child relationships
   for foster youth, 26
   for homeless students, 10
   for LGBTQ youth, 70, 71, 72
   in military families, 141
   neglect, 8, 24, 25, 44, 61
   for students with incarcerated parents, 122, 124, 129, 132
parenting practices and psychoeducation, 20–21, 56, 88, 98–99, 115–116
parents, deployed, 138, 140, 142, 145
parents, students as. *See* pregnant or parenting students
peer relationship development, 25–26, 30
perfectionism, 105–106, 111–112
performance deficits, 155
persisters, defined, 43
personality disorder, borderline, 53
physical abuse
   of foster youth, 24, 25
   of homeless students, 8, 10
   of LGB youth, 70
   mandated reporting of, 13
   of students with incarcerated parents, 119, 120
physical development, in pregnant teens, 90
play therapy techniques, 126
postpartum depression, 89
post-traumatic stress disorder (PTSD)
   counseling approaches for, 19, 31–32, 34, 52, 53, 55
   in foster youth, 24
   in homeless students, 10, 11
   in juvenile offenders, 53, 55
   in returning military members, 142
poverty, 8, 9, 87, 88, 120, 121–122. *See also* socioeconomic status
precontemplation stage of change process, 156–157
predeployment phase, 139
pregnancy prevention programs, 87, 99–101
pregnant or parenting students
   depression in, 89
   educational attainment of, 88–89
   engagement in risky sexual practices, 92
   factors affecting, 89–91

pregnant or parenting students (*Cont.*)
   health of, 88
   intersection with other special populations, 28, 92
   negative consequences faced by, 87, 88–89
   rates of, 87
   resources, 101–102
   social isolation experienced by, 89
   social support for, 87, 89–90, 94, 96–97
   socioeconomic status of, 88–89
pregnant or parenting students, counseling approaches for
   building social support, 87, 96–97
   dropout prevention, 97–98
   legal and ethical issues, 93–95
   parenting psychoeducation, 88, 98–99
   policies affecting, 93
   social prototypes, 89–90
   solution-focused brief therapy, 95–96
   Taking Charge intervention, 99
   vocational counseling, 88, 98
preschool participation, 153
Principles for Professional Ethics (NASP), 93
problem solving
   in cognitive-behavioral therapy, 4
   in foster youth, 30, 31
   in gifted students, 110, 111, 113
   in homeless youth, 15, 17
   in juvenile offenders, 52
   in pregnant or parenting students, 99, 100
   in students in military families, 144, 146, 149
   in students with incarcerated parents, 126
procedural study skills, 161
psychiatric disorders, 10, 11. *See also* mental health needs; *specific conditions*
psychoeducation
   in aggression replacement training, 57
   in cognitive-behavioral therapy, 4, 31, 32
   in *Cognitive Behavior Intervention for Trauma in Schools*, 34
   in counseling LGBTQ students, 79, 80
   parenting, 88, 96, 98–99, 115–116
   for students at risk of dropout, 162, 164
   for students in military families, 143, 145, 146, 148, 149
   in treatment planning for incarcerated youth, 50
psychological development, in pregnant teens, 91
psychotic disorders, 33, 45
PTSD. *See* post-traumatic stress disorder

queerness, defined, 65
questioning, defined, 65
questioning youth, 71

racial diversity, 72
racism, 72, 111
recidivism, 41, 44, 49, 50, 58
redirection, 57
re-entry, preparation for, 57–60, 129
re-entry phase of deployment, 140, 142
reflecting, 158
reframing, 18, 33, 57
rehearsal-based study skills, 160–161
reinforcement, 161, 162
reintegration phase of deployment, 140, 142
relationship building, 51–52
relationship development, peer, 25–26, 30
relationship questions, 160, 163
relaxation techniques, 32–33, 110
religion, 69, 70
reparative therapy, 76
repetition-based study skills, 160–161
Reserve families, 136, 146, 148
residential facilities
   foster care placement in, 27
   for juvenile offenders, 38, 40, 41–42, 57–60, 62
resilience
   counseling approaches promoting, 15–18
   defined, 2, 15
   educational programs for, 97
   factors in, 2, 17, 26, 30
   in foster youth, 24, 26, 30
   in gifted students, 107, 109–111

Index 215

in homeless students, 15–18, 20, 21
in LGBTQ students, 70
in pregnant and parenting teens, 95, 98–99
in students at risk of dropout, 164–165
in students in military families, 134, 142
in students with incarcerated parents, 124
resistance to counseling, 156, 157–158
response to intervention approach, 61
reunification phase of deployment, 140, 142
rights, legal, 29, 46, 62, 67, 125–126
role plays, 52, 57, 60, 80, 128, 129
runaway youth, 8, 20, 72. *See also* homeless students

scaling questions, 18, 53, 163
school climate and stability, 27, 69, 82–83, 131–132
school completion. *See* educational attainment
school engagement, 153, 154, 165
school expulsions, 26
school staff, 83, 147
school suspensions, 26
school teams, 59
school transfers, 58–59
screening, universal, 61–62
self-destructive behavior, 52, 53, 141
self-determination, 29–30, 35–36
self-disclosure, 51–52
self-efficacy
  counseling approaches promoting, 17, 30, 54, 158
  motivation and, 154
  in pregnant and parenting students, 89, 98
  resilience and, 2, 17, 30
self-esteem
  of LGBTQ students, 69, 70, 71, 83
  perfectionism and, 106
  in pregnant and parenting students, 98
  resilience and, 15
self-harm, 141
self-reliance, 15

SEL (social and emotional learning) programs, 116
SES. *See* socioeconomic status
sex education, 73, 84, 87, 91, 99–101
sexual abuse
  counseling approaches for, 32
  of foster youth, 24, 25
  of homeless students, 8, 10
  of LGBTQ youth, 70, 72
  of students with incarcerated parents, 119, 120
sexual development, in pregnant teens, 91
sexual identity, 65–66, 71, 79. *See also* LGBTQ students
sexuality, societal views on, 100
sexual orientation, 64, 65, 71, 76, 104, 107. *See also* LGBTQ students
"sexual preference," 65
SFBT. *See* solution-focused brief therapy
silence, patience with, 51
skill building
  academic skills, 160–163
  coping skills, 109–111, 126, 143–144, 145, 146
  coping strategies, 109–111, 126, 143–144, 145, 146
  independent living skills, 36
  for juvenile offenders, 47
  social skills, 19, 30–31, 57, 109–111
  for students in military families, 143, 144–145
  in trauma-focused CBT, 32–33
skills/acquisition deficits, 155
SLDs (specific learning disabilities), 46
SNAP technique, 144
social and emotional learning (SEL) programs, 116
social isolation. *See* isolation, social
social prototypes, 89–90, 91–92
social skills, building, 19, 30–31, 57, 109–111
social stigma
  about homelessness, 11, 14
  about incarceration, 118–119, 121, 122, 129, 130, 131
  about teen pregnancy, 91, 97

social support
  for foster youth, 23–24, 26, 29, 30–31, 36
  for gifted students, 112–113
  for LGBT students, 70, 71
  for pregnant and parenting teens, 87, 89–90, 94, 96–97
  for students with incarcerated parents, 126
socioeconomic status (SES)
  acceptance of LGBT youth and, 70
  of children of teen mothers, 87, 88
  of foster youth, 23
  giftedness and, 107
  graduation rates related to, 152, 153, 154
  of homeless students, 8, 9, 10
  of pregnant and parenting students, 88–89, 90, 91
  of students with incarcerated parents, 120, 121–122
Socratic questioning, 33
solution-focused brief therapy (SFBT)
  basic approach of, 4–5, 53
  for foster youth, 30
  for gifted students, 113
  goals and benefits of, 17–18, 30, 160, 163
  for homeless students, 17–18
  for juvenile offenders, 51, 52–53
  for pregnant and parenting students, 95–96
  for students at risk of dropout, 160, 163
  for students with incarcerated parents, 126, 130
solution-focused brief therapy (SFBT), techniques used in
  definitive phrasing, 53
  exception questions, 53
  flagging the minefield, 126
  goal setting, 17, 95, 163
  miracle question, 17–18, 96, 163
  problem talk avoided in, 51
  reframing, 18
  relationship-building strategies, 51
  relationship questions, 160, 163
  scaling questions, 18, 53, 163
  silence, 51

SPARCS (*Structured Psychotherapy for Adolescents Responding to Chronic Stress*), 18–19, 32
special education services
  assessment of homeless students for, 11–12
  for foster youth, 26–27
  for juvenile offenders, 46, 59, 62
  for LGBTQ students, 73
special populations, overlap among, 1, 5–6
specific learning disabilities (SLDs), 46
stabilization, 32–33
status offenses, 38
straightness, defined, 65
strength-based approaches. *See also* solution-focused brief therapy
  for gifted students, 109
  for homeless students, 17–18, 20–21
  for juvenile offenders, 53
  for pregnant and parenting students, 92–93, 95, 96
  for students in military families, 143, 144
strength box technique, 144
stress reduction techniques, 110
Strong Kids series, 126, 144
Structured Psychotherapy for Adolescents Responding to Chronic Stress (SPARCS), 18–19, 32
"student education passport," 59
students in military families
  connecting with available resources, 148
  counseling approaches for, 143–146
  educational challenges for, 136, 147
  effect of deployment on, 134–135, 140–142
  effect of moving and relocation on, 137
  effect of parental loss or injury on, 138, 145
  Families OverComing Under Stress, 148–149
  population estimates, 134, 136
  resilience of, 134, 142
  resources for, 149–150
  school-wide support for, 147–148

students of color. See also *specific groups*
  in foster care, 23
  giftedness in, 107
  graduation rates, 152
  with incarcerated parents, 118
  in juvenile justice system, 39, 44
  teen pregnancy in, 89
  use of mental health services by, 25
students with incarcerated parents
  attachment and relationship factors, 122–123
  comprehensive programs for, 132
  counseling approaches for, 125–129
  demographics of, 118–119
  improving school climate for, 131–132
  loss experienced by, 119, 122–123, 124
  mentoring of, 131
  population estimates, 118
  preexisting risk factors for, 119–120, 123
  resources for, 132–133
  risks associated with, 120–121, 123–124
  social stigma faced by, 121
  support for custodial parents or guardians of, 130–131
study skills, promoting, 160–161, 162
substance use and abuse
  counseling approaches for, 54–55
  in families with incarcerated parents, 119, 120
  in foster youth, 24, 28
  in homeless students and their families, 10, 18
  in juvenile offenders, 45, 54, 61
  in LGBTQ students, 70, 71, 74
  in military families, 141, 142
  screening for, 61
suicidality
  counseling approaches and, 33, 52
  in foster youth, 24
  in homeless youth, 10, 72
  in juvenile offenders, 44, 52
  in LGBT students, 70, 71, 72, 81–82
  prevention and intervention, 81–82
  in returning military members, 142
summarizing, 158, 159

support groups, 145
suspensions, school, 26
sustain talk, 54, 55

Taking Charge (TC) intervention, 99
teacher training, regarding military youth, 147
teen fathers, 90, 91–92
teen mothers, 88–89, 90–91, 96–97. See also pregnant or parenting students
TF-CBT (trauma-focused cognitive-behavioral therapy), 18–19, 32–33
therapeutic foster care, 27
transgenderism, defined, 65
transgender youth. See also LGBTQ students
  counseling approaches for, 77–78, 79–80
  discrimination experienced by, 68
  gender identity development in, 66
  medical treatment for, 74–75
  mental health outcomes for, 71–72
  school supports for, 69
  sexual abuse of, 70
  sexual orientation of, 66
  suicide risk for, 71
transition planning, 28, 35–37, 57–60, 72, 91
transphobia, 77, 80–81
trauma, 24, 44–45, 55, 56. See also emotional abuse; physical abuse; post-traumatic stress disorder; sexual abuse; violence, exposure to
trauma-focused therapies, 18–19, 31–35
trauma narrative and processing, 33
treatment foster care, 27
treatment planning, 50–51
trust, building, 14–16, 125, 129, 164
"twice exceptional" students, 108

unaccompanied homeless students, 8, 10, 12–13, 14–15, 19–20
underachievement, 105, 107, 112–113
unemployment, 88, 91
universal screening, 61–62

violence, community, 19, 25
violence, domestic, 8, 10, 32, 142
violence, exposure to. *See also* physical abuse; sexual abuse; trauma
   in children with incarcerated parents, 120
   counseling approaches for, 34
   in homeless students, 9, 10
   in juvenile offenders, 44, 61
   in military families, 142
   screening for, 61
vocational counseling, 98

When a Parent Goes to Jail (Yaffe & Hoade), 126–127
White students, 23, 89, 107, 152
Why Did You Die? (Fiorini & Mullen), 145
WhyTry program, 97, 164